Paying for Welfare

Paying for Welfare
The 1990s

Howard Glennerster

London School of Economics

HARVESTER
WHEATSHEAF

NEW YORK LONDON TORONTO SYDNEY TOKYO SINGAPORE

First published 1992 by
Harvester Wheatsheaf
Campus 400, Maylands Avenue
Hemel Hempstead
Hertfordshire, HP2 7EZ
A division of
Simon & Schuster International Group

Typeset in 10/12pt Times by
Photoprint, Torquay, Devon

Printed and bound in Great Britain by
Biddles Ltd, Guildford and King's Lynn

British Library Cataloguing in Publication Data

A catalogue record for this book is available from the British Library

ISBN 0-7450-0997-2 (hbk)
ISBN 0-7450-0998-0 (pbk)

2 3 4 5 96 95 94 93

CONTENTS

List of tables vii
List of figures ix
List of abbreviations xi
Preface xiii

Part I Welfare and the state: theories and concepts 1

1 Mixed modes of finance 3
2 The theoretical basis for the state funding of services 15
3 A market for welfare? 31

Part II The controlling institutions 47

4 Setting the limits at the centre 49
5 Containing the locals 72
6 Setting the limits locally 94

Part III The sources of funds 105

7 Taxes 107
8 Fees and charges 128
9 Charity and giving 141

Part IV Financing the services 157

10 Paying for health services 159
11 Paying for personal social services 184

12 Paying for education 199
13 Paying for housing 225
14 Paying for social security 245

Part V The future: into the 1990s 267

15 Can we afford the welfare state? 269

Bibliography 285
Index 312

TABLES

Table 2.1	European social protection expenditure as a percentage of GDP at market prices 1981, 1985, 1988	15
Table 4.1	The PES planning timetable	62
Table 7.1	Sources of tax revenue in the United Kingdom 1948–91	114
Table 7.2	Taxes as a percentage of gross income by income group in the United Kingdom 1988	124
Table 7.3	Taxes and social security contributions as a percentage of GNP at factor cost in various countries 1971, 1981, 1988	126
Table 8.1	Revenue from charges as a percentage of total current income in the United Kingdom	129
Table 9.1	Voluntary fund-raising and other activities of households in Britain in 1987	145
Table 10.1	Total expenditure on health care, public and private, as a percentage of GDP in OECD countries 1989	165
Table 10.2	Payments to general practitioners per annum in the United Kingdom 1991	174
Table 12.1	Public expenditure on education as a percentage of GDP in the United Kingdom 1950–90	204
Table 12.2	International comparisons in education spending as a percentage of GDP 1987 or nearest year	204

Table 12.3	Private school current expenditure in England and Wales (£ million) 1951/2–1985/6	211
Table 14.1	Social security benefits internationally as a percentage of GDP 1960–89	253
Table 14.2	Total social security benefit expenditure in Britain 1990–1	254
Table 14.3	National insurance fund 1989/90	255
Table 14.4	Employers' contributions for workers in SERPS 1991/2	257
Table 15.1	Number of pensioners in various countries relative to numbers in 1980	274
Table 15.2	Real pay increases in the public sector in the United Kingdom 1981/2 to 1990/1	278
Table 15.3	Attitudes to the state in different countries 1988	282
Table 15.4	Those wanting more state spending on various services in different countries 1988	283
Table 15.5	Attitudes to raising taxes in Britain 1983–90	283

FIGURES

Figure 1.1	The finance–provision distinction	6
Figure 1.2	Welfare finance in a simple economy	8
Figure 1.3	Welfare finance by cash redistribution	9
Figure 1.4	Welfare finance: mixed methods	10
Figure 2.1	A political economy view	27
Figure 4.1	NHS expenditure in cash, real and volume terms	61
Figure 4.2	The cost of social services as a percentage of GDP in the United Kingdom 1900–90	64
Figure 4.3	Public spending on welfare as a percentage of GDP in the United Kingdom 1973–90	65
Figure 4.4	Public spending on welfare in the United Kingdom in £ billion (1990–1 prices) 1973–90	66
Figure 5.1	Central resource levers	78
Figure 7.1	The effect of direct tax and benefit changes in Great Britain since 1978–9	123
Figure 9.1	The uses of corporate contributions: percentage share of total contributions by top companies by purpose of gift in the United Kingdom 1990	148
Figure 10.1	Estimated gross current expenditure per head by age in hospital and community health services in the United Kingdom 1988–9	166
Figure 10.2	Allocating the Health Service budget in England 1990/1	170

Figure 11.1	Personal social services local authority net current expenditure by client group in England 1988–91	190
Figure 11.2	Elderly people in residential accommodation in the United Kingdom 1981–8	198
Figure 12.1	The distribution of the state education budget: current expenditure in England 1990–1	205
Figure 12.2	The operation of LMS	208
Figure 12.3	The sources of funds for higher education in the United Kingdom in the 1990s	214
Figure 13.1	Public expenditure on housing in Britain 1976/7–1989/90	232
Figure 15.1	The political market for social services	271
Figure 15.2	The dependent population in the United Kingdom 1941–2001	274

ABBREVIATIONS

ACG	Annual capital guideline
AEF	Aggregate external finance
AIDS	Acquired Immune Deficiency Syndrome
BCA	Basic credit approval
BMA	British Medical Association
BUPA	British United Provident Association
CIPFA	Chartered Institute of Public Finance and Accountancy
CPRS	Central Policy Review Staff
CTC	City technology college
DES	Department of Education and Science
DHSS	Department of Health and Social Security (replaced by DoH and DSS)
DoE	Department of the Environment
DoH	Department of Health
DSS	Department of Social Security
EEC	European Economic Community
FIS	*Either* the financial information system operated by the Treasury *or* family income supplement
GDP	Gross domestic product (the value of goods and services produced on the economy)
GLC	Greater London Council
GNI	General Needs Index (for housing purposes)
GNP	Gross national product (as gross domestic product but with the addition of net property income from abroad)
GRE	Grant related expenditure figures which helped

	determine local authorities' entitlement to rate support grant
HAG	Housing association grant
HMI	Her Majesty's Inspectors of Schools
HMO	Health maintenance organisation
HRA	Housing revenue account
IAF	Industry Act forecasts
ILEA	Inner London Education Authority
LEA	Local education authority
LMS	Local management of schools
MSC	Manpower Services Commission
NHS	National Health Service
NNDR	National non-domestic rate
OECD	Organisation for Economic Co-operation and Development
PAR	Programme analysis and review
PARR	Health service formula for allocations in N. Ireland
PAYE	Pay As You Earn (tax collection)
PES	Public expenditure survey is the annual round of negotiations between the Treasury and spending departments
PESC	Public Expenditure Survey Committee
PPA	Private patients' association
PSB	Potential schools budget
RAWP	Resource Allocation Working Party (on NHS funding in England)
RSG	Rate Support Grant (later Revenue Support Grant)
RTIA	Receipts taken into account
SCA	Supplementary credit approval
SCRAW	Scottish resource allocation formula for health services
SERPS	State earnings-related pension scheme
SMR	Standardised mortality ratio or death rate
UFC	Universities Funding Council
UGC	University Grants Committee
VAT	Value added tax
WPA	Western Provident Association
WRVS	Women's Royal Voluntary Service (previously WVS)

PREFACE

In 1984, having lectured for many years to undergraduates at the London School of Economics on the finance of the social services, I became increasingly frustrated by the fact that there was no single directly relevant text book. The only answer seemed to be to write one. There are, of course, useful basic texts on public finance for economics students, but they are very thin on the institutional background – how money actually reaches schools and hospitals and housing associations. This is not an economics text book but it is designed to be complementary to basic public finance texts.

At the same time as I was writing the first edition my colleague, Dr Barr in the economics department at the LSE, also decided to write up his more theoretical lectures on *The Economics of the Welfare State*. We conceived these as complementary texts for our students, and hoped they might be for others too!

Seven years later we were both writing our second editions. It is difficult to credit just how much has changed in those years. In writing the first edition I thought for some time whether to include anything on a rather ancient form of tax known as the poll tax. In the end I decided to give it thirteen lines and say that it had been discussed by Mrs Thatcher's government in 1981 and rejected. Since then the 'community charge' has come and all but gone. I have recorded the changes of the 1980s and tried to set out alternative strategies for the 1990s.

The book begins with a fuller theoretical treatment than in the first edition of the economic case for and against state and private finance of services that are central to human existence in advanced societies. It goes on to discuss the pros and cons of introducing competition or quasi markets into the provision of such services, a principle that had underpinned many of the Conservative reforms in the late 1980s.

The book is aimed at undergraduates in political science, social policy and economics, and at those on professional training courses who will need to know how the services in which they work are financed – how their salaries at the end of the month get paid, to put it crudely. This should apply to teachers, social workers, housing managers, doctors and nurses. The book is also aimed at the more general public who have become more interested and concerned with the quality of their social services as a result of the changes and cuts of the 1980s and because of institutional changes like the local management of schools. These have made parents more directly aware of the problems of financing the higher-quality services they are demanding.

I am grateful to Nic Barr, John Hills and all the members of the Welfare State Programme at the LSE with whom I have worked over the past few years. They were a continual source of help and expertise. I am grateful also to the ESRC who have supported that research team (grant reference X206 32 2001).

Geraldine Drew and Coral Llewellyn coped with my disk problems, and with my handwriting too, in their quiet and competent way. Above all, there is all I owe to Ann, who agreed to forego a summer and autumn of weekends to make it all possible and helped with all the corrections.

London School of Economics, December 1991

PART I

Welfare and the state: theories and concepts

CHAPTER 1

MIXED MODES OF FINANCE

This book is deliberately entitled *Paying for Welfare* and not *Paying for the Welfare State*. That title would have begged the fundamental questions. Need welfare be provided by the state? Does something that is *financed* by the state have to be *provided* by the state? Does 'the state' necessarily imply a central governmental agency? The answer to each of these questions is 'no'. This first chapter describes the wide variety of ways in which welfare services can be financed. We begin with some definitions and concepts that will be used throughout the book.

Definitions

What do we mean by welfare? To the American on the sidewalk it means cash handouts to hoodlums. To the professional economist it is a collective term for happiness, utility or that which individuals desire. The word itself dates from the seventeenth century at least, and means the same as 'fare well' – to remain in good health and sufficiency (*Shorter Oxford English Dictionary*). That does point us to the essence of its modern meaning. The proclaimed objective of welfare provision in most societies is to ensure a basic standard of living for their citizens. This will usually entail a minimum income and access to food, shelter, education, health care and support if they are sick or disabled. It leaves open how that objective is to be achieved and what the motives are – humane or sinister.

Probably the most important achievement in the thirty years after the Second World War was that of nearly full employment. The labour market ensured the welfare of most of the population for most of their working lives. Thus work is part of welfare, not its antithesis (Sinfield, 1983). The firm can ensure that its employees fare well when they are temporarily sick, compensate them when they have an accident at work and ensure that they continue to fare well in their retirement. Many firms in this country have done so for part of their work force for many years and are now obliged to make pension provision and to pay sickness benefits for a minimum period. In Japan, occupational welfare of this kind in the largest firms is more extensive. In Europe, industry-wide pension schemes are more common. Then, of course, individuals can buy their own insurance against calamity – to try to secure their own family's wellbeing. Charitable organisations, friends, family and neighbours can all help in adversity, but the state in most countries steps in to secure a minimum income and access to basic services. In short, the maintenance of people's welfare lies in the power of many agencies and individuals *including* local, regional and national organs of government.

Cash or kind?

Ensuring a minimum standard of living can also be achieved in a variety of ways. A firm, charity or government can give a dependent person or poor family cash, and leave them to buy what they need, or it can give the family goods or service free. We can give disabled people a cash allowance to pay for their transport or a small car to get about in. We can give the family or elderly person next door a donation of cash or go in and do the shopping. Provision for people's welfare can be in cash or in kind or in service done.

Finance or provision?

Another crucial distinction runs throughout all discussions on the finance of the social services – the distinction between *finance* and *provision*. A typical lay person's error is to assume that if a service like education or residential care is provided by a public agency it must also be financed out of public funds, by taxation, or conversely that if a service is provided by a private agency it must be financed privately, by fees. These are in fact only two of a wide range of possible options. For example, a local authority old people's home charges fees. Some of these fees are paid by individuals themselves, some are paid out of pensions the old people receive from central government. The sources of funds are mixed – public and private. Government or firms can issue quasi cash – luncheon vouchers or school vouchers, say – which enable one to buy a particular service in a particular market. The service is thus financed by one agency but provided by another.

Since this important distinction will reappear throughout the succeeding chapters, it is worth spending time now being clear about it. Much public discussion of the 'privatisation' issue is hopelessly confused on this matter. Figure 1.1 sets out the logical possibilities in their simplest form. First, there is the question of what kind of agency provides the service. The column headings in the figure indicate this. A service can be provided by public sector bodies. These may be central government or a local agent of central government, like a district health authority, or services may be run by a locally elected council. In the 1980s, legislation passed by Thatcher's government introduced a number of hybrid organisations that are neither directly central nor local government bodies but independent trusts financed by central government – hospital trusts and opted-out schools are examples.

Then again, a service can be *privately provided* by a non-statutory agency. This may be by a private profit-making company, a non-profit agency or a self-help group, or by one individual for another. Various profit-making hospitals, language schools and nursing homes for old people come into the first group. Dr Barnardo's homes, the Family Service Units and church schools count as non-profit agencies; playgroups or informal groups of AIDS sufferers as self-help groups. Help for relatives, spouses or neighbours counts as provision by private households.

Second, we must turn to the question of who finances the service. The rows in Figure 1.1 distinguish this. Welfare agencies can be financed out of public funds, or privately, or a mixture of the two. National Health Service hospitals largely fall into the top left-hand category. They are financed by central government

	Provision: Public sector bodies – Central government	Provision: Public sector bodies – Public trusts	Provision: Public sector bodies – Local government	Provision: Private organisations – Profit	Provision: Private organisations – Non-profit	Provision: Private–informal
Types of institution	e.g. NHS hospitals	e.g. NHS hospital trusts, grant-maintained schools	e.g. LEA schools, old people's homes, council houses	e.g. Language schools, clinics, nursing homes	e.g. church schools, universities, housing associations, Barnardo homes	Families, neighbours, households, self-help groups
Finance: Public	Grants to health authorities from the Exchequer	Grants from central government, purchases by local government	Grants from central government, council tax	Social security payments to meet nursing home fees, LEA purchase of boarding-school places	Government grants to housing associations, universities, church schools, and places brought for children by LEAs	Social security payments to carers of disabled people, payment by local authorities to foster parents
Finance: Private	Income from private pay-beds, prescription charges	Fees paid by private users, households or companies	Fees paid to colleges of further education, charges by old people's homes	Fees paid by households	Rents to housing associations	Income lost in giving up work to care for a family member

Figure 1.1 The finance–provision distinction

through money given to district health authorities. However, some money comes from private individuals who pay for private care in private pay-beds in these hospitals. Some hospitals have small private funds and most receive voluntary help from people in the local community. Local schools are paid for out of a mixture of local revenue – the new council tax or the old rates *and* by central government grants. Local further education colleges, however, provide training courses and charge for the courses. The fees may be paid by the individual or the firm, perhaps. Both count as private sources of income.

The pure case of private welfare provision financed entirely privately is less easy to find than one might imagine. Language schools are an example. Private schools have pupils paid for out of public funds and receive indirect state aid in the form of tax relief. Private nursing homes have patients financed out of social security benefit. For an extended discussion see Papadakis and Taylor-Gooby (1987).

Universities are private bodies largely funded from central government but with elements of private fee paying and private research funding. We find a whole range of 'voluntary' or non-government agencies providing social care services – case work, counselling, care of the elderly and handicapped – that are heavily dependent on public funds. Individuals who perform caring duties may receive help from social security benefits if the person being cared for is disabled. Foster parents are paid by the local social services department.

Thus in practice most provision of health and education is in the hands of a public authority with mixed sources of funding. Large parts of the social caring services are privately provided and publicly funded. Moreover, the largest part of social spending takes the form of cash given to individuals in social security benefits that they spend on privately produced goods and services. We already have a mixed economy of welfare. In later chapters of the book we shall unravel this complex situation of finance. It is enough to note that there is no one dominant mode of financing welfare in the United Kingdom.

'To privatise', it may be noted, ugly as the phrase is, must logically mean to move any service from a box in the top left-hand corner of Figure 1.1 either downwards, introducing an element of private funding, or to the right, to introduce an element of private provision within a publicly financed service like the NHS, or diagonally down to the right, to hive off services to a private body. These distinctions are too frequently confused. The case for and against each, as we shall see, is rather different. (For a discussion on these lines see Klein, 1984.)

The flow of funds

We now present a formal model that is capable of describing the finance of any system of welfare in any economy. In the very simplest economy of all, a pure market economy, incomes are generated by households or workers, and by enterprises or capital. The first kind of income we call wages, the second profit. Incomes are spent on the outputs of other enterprises or on services provided by individuals. Welfare providers are either private profit-making firms, charitable non-profit-making bodies or households. They are paid by other households purchasing services for a fee, by firms doing so for their employees and by charitable gifts. No government transfers take place. This simple economy can be illustrated in a flow of funds diagram. (See Figure 1.2.)

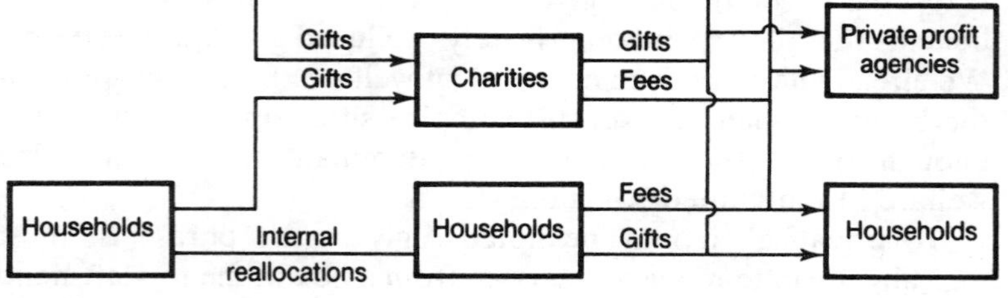

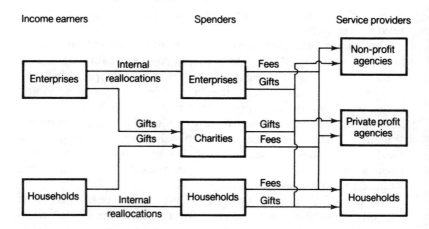

Figure 1.2 Welfare finance in a simple economy

Government may decide that it cannot leave all society's casualties to the mercy of private charity, employers and family, for reasons we shall discuss in Chapter 2. It can take the minimum step of intervention, impose taxes and give the proceeds away in cash or even quasi cash such as vouchers, which tie the money to a particular kind of purchase. In this case the flow of funds model can be elaborated (see Figure 1.3). Taxes flow to the Treasury to be allocated back to needy households in either cash or quasi cash. Households then spend their enhanced income on housing, schooling or food, provided by private institutions. Households are the sole or main final spenders.

Many would like to see the world in terms as simple as this. It is not possible. What has grown up in all industrial and post-industrial societies is a highly complex pattern of welfare finance. We sketch the main outlines in Figure 1.4. It looks complicated but we shall take it slowly, describing each part in turn. It forms the basis for the analysis that follows in the rest of the book and is therefore important to grasp here. It derives from an earlier study (Peacock *et al.*, 1968).

As in the simpler versions of the world, we begin on the left-hand side with the incomes that are generated in any economy – by households or workers and by enterprises or firms. We end with

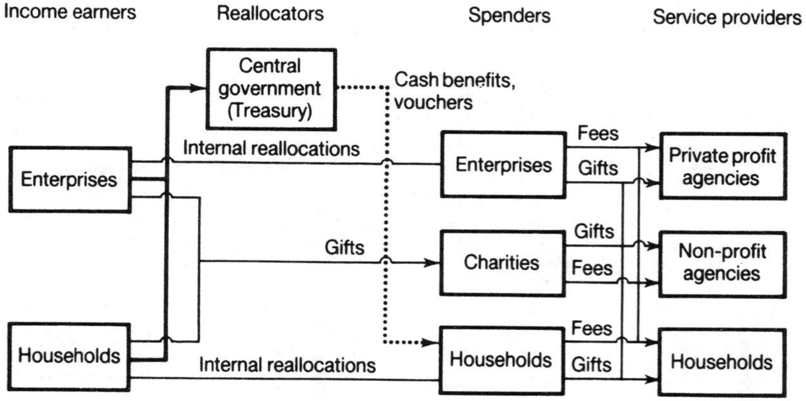

Figure 1.3 Welfare finance by cash redistribution

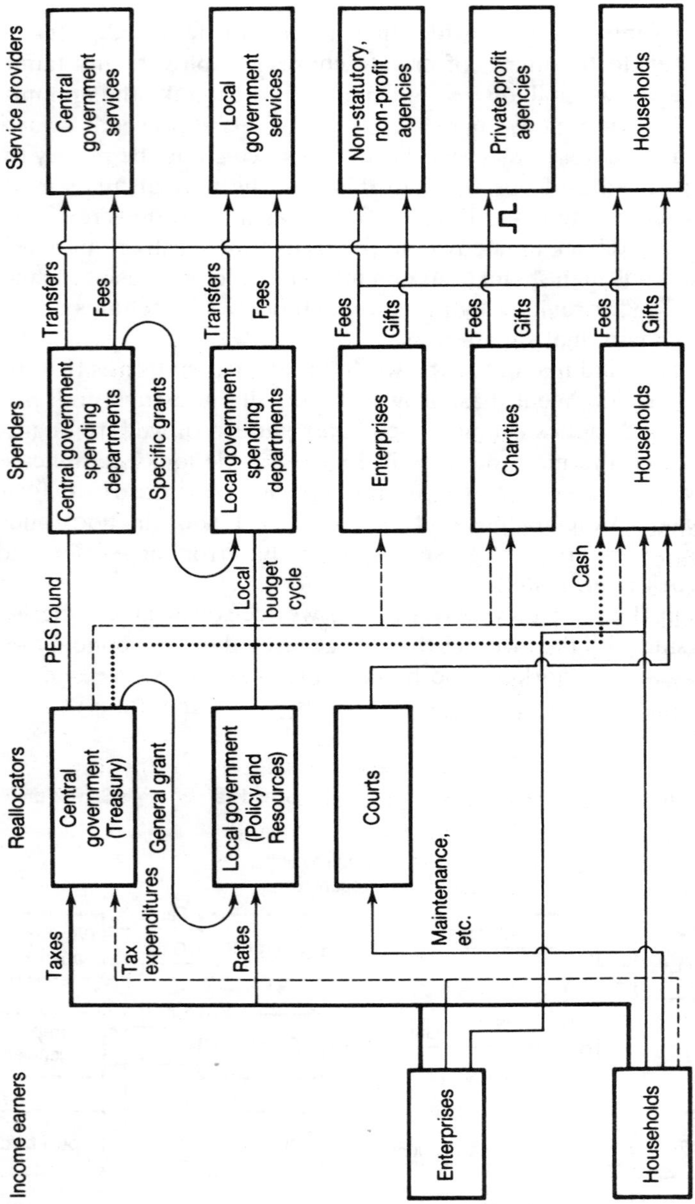

Figure 1.4 Welfare finance: mixed methods

the users of funds – welfare service providers including central and local government institutions like schools or homes. Remnants of the simple world of a purely private welfare economy still exist alongside these statutory providers. In some fields they dominate. What government in its various forms does is to introduce an intermediary – a reallocative system of finance, beyond the household. Central or local government raises revenue from households and firms through taxation. It then either returns the money to households in the form of cash benefits, or allocates money to its own spending departments. However, the government agency that raises taxation, above all central government, is not necessarily the body that administers services. Central government does not own schools or old people's homes. These institutions may be owned by local authorities, private bodies or voluntary organisations – the boxes on the extreme right of the diagram. Central government thus collects taxes and then rechannels much of the proceeds to local councils, which in turn 'allocate' funds to 'service providers' such as schools or old people's homes to perform their functions. Services can be provided by bodies owned and run by central or local government, or by private charitable agencies (which we call non-statutory, non-profit), or by profit-making enterprises, or by other households (as with foster parents or child minders), or within the family itself. The alternatives are set out on the right-hand side of the diagram, with central government providers at the top of the column, ordinary private households at the bottom and intermediate stages of collectivisation in the middle.

Let us begin at the bottom of Figure 1.4, familiar from the earlier diagrams. The horizontal line across the diagram, which ends in fees paid for services, describes the processes by which households earn income, reallocate income between partners, and spend it on various services. This line represents the ideal of a purely individualist society. Relatively unrecognised until recently was the reallocation that takes place within family units. There is now an emerging literature on the way families redistribute their money among different members (Becker, 1976; Pahl, 1989; Piachaud, 1982; Rimmer, 1982; Brannan and Wilson, 1987). As yet we know very little, except that the original distribution of income between men and women is highly unequal, to men's advantage, and that women nevertheless do most spending on items like food and clothing. It is also the case that women do much of the *caring* for dependants including the elderly in the family, a point to which we shall return.

We must now complicate the story by introducing the state not merely as a provider of service but as a collector of taxes and a reallocator of incomes (Figure 1.4, top two boxes, second column). It is important to emphasise that government in its local and national forms is not the only reallocative agency at work. The courts more or less effectively try to force some earners – ex-husbands – to pay other households to sustain their welfare. Hence we have included the courts in our welfare system. The Finer Committee (1974) on single-parent families remains the best source of analysis and discussion of this allocative system.

Not shown in the diagram is regulation. Government may insist, as we shall see later, that households contribute to private personal or occupational pension schemes to sustain their own wellbeing in old age. This is equivalent to a tax. It is enforced spending on a particular purpose but is merely a law requiring action by an individual. There are complex redistributive processes that go on between households as a result of this 'pooling' of risks. Though the outcome of such regulations does not appear in any government accounts, they have a similar economic effect to taxation. I shall discuss this more fully later on.

I have left the most important flows until last. The largest source of income for most welfare agencies is taxation. This takes many forms and it is levied by central government and by local government. For reasons of diagrammatic simplicity I exclude government borrowing as a separate flow, treating it as delayed taxation. In 1990 over a quarter of all UK incomes were taxed or borrowed to pay for social security benefits, education, health care, housing and social care. This is represented by the thick black line in Figure 1.4. This flow of revenue into the coffers of the central Treasury and local councils is then allocated between spending departments and services by a process described in Chapters 4–6. The public expenditure survey (PES) round will determine how much each department will get each year.

Tax and spending allocations are reasonably open and accountable. The remaining channel of resources is more obscure. It is called, by economists, *tax expenditure*. When government decides to reduce the tax liability of one household that is earning the same as another because, for example, one is buying a house or bringing up children, that has precisely the same effect as if government taxed both equally and gave the favoured household cash benefit – a housing allowance or a child benefit. American economists invented the title 'tax expenditure' to indicate that tax allowances had an effect similar to that of direct expenditure. These sums do appear in many countries' formal budgets and are illustrated by the dashed line in the diagram.

The next major flows in Figure 1.4 are from one level of government to another. Central government in Britain raises over 90 per cent of all taxes but *local* government is responsible for about a quarter of all public expenditure. That is made possible by big transfers of resources between central and local government. It can be done by simply giving a general grant as a supplement to local revenue to be spent on any purpose. Such a transfer is illustrated by the snake-like flow from central government (Treasury) to local government (Policy and Resources Committee). Another alternative is to route the money for specific purposes to specific authorities. Hence the second snake linking a central spending department – education, for example – to a local authority *education* department in the form of a specific education grant.

Once the local authorities receive their money, they may provide services themselves – in local authority children's homes, for example. Hence the 'transfer' of money to the box called 'local government services' – a children's home in this case. Alternatively the local authority can pay for children to attend a voluntary or private home – hence the flows labelled 'fees', linking local authorities to private providers. (I shall discuss fees and charging in Chapter 8, and gifts in cash and kind as sources of finance in Chapter 9.)

The purpose of elaborating this flow of funds approach has been partly to provide a framework for succeeding chapters, but it also emphasises the wide range of theoretical possibilities that is open to us in paying for welfare. Provision by state-run institutions financed out of taxation is only one of a very large number of options. In succeeding chapters we shall describe what happens in Britain today and show how that system has evolved, but we shall also direct the reader to some of the main alternative forms of finance that are under discussion and occur in other countries.

Further reading

Papadakis, E. and Taylor-Gooby, P. (1987) *The Private Provision of Public Welfare: State, market and community*, Hemel Hempstead: Harvester Wheatsheaf.

Parker, G. (1990) *With Due Care and Attention: A review of research on informal care*, 2nd edn, London: Family Policy Studies Centre.

CHAPTER 2

THE THEORETICAL BASIS FOR THE STATE FUNDING OF SERVICES

Despite the fact that the market allocates most goods, services and incomes in western industrial societies, and increasingly in eastern Europe too, governments have continued to raise large sums in taxes to sustain social welfare spending. Table 2.1 illustrates the point. The European Economic Community defines social protec-

Table 2.1 European social protection expenditure as a percentage of GDP at market prices 1981, 1985, 1988

Country	1981	1985	1988*
Belgium	–	29.0	28.7
Denmark	29.3	27.8	28.5
West Germany	29.5	28.1	28.1
Spain	–	18.0	17.7
France	27.2	28.8	28.3
Ireland	–	24.0	22.6
Italy	24.7	22.5	22.9
Luxembourg	–	25.4	26.6
Netherlands	31.7	31.1	30.7
Portugal	–	16.1	17.0
United Kingdom	23.5	24.5	23.6
Norway	–	–	26.4
Sweden	–	33.3	35.2
Finland	–	24.6	25.9

* Or nearest year.

Source: EEC, Eurostatistics (1991), *Basic Statistics of the Community 1990*, Luxembourg.

tion expenditure as covering health, old age support, family benefits and other social care. The category excludes housing and education, unlike this book. The share of all incomes that is taxed in some way to pay for social protection as defined in Europe mostly varies between a quarter and a third. In the United States and Japan the figure is nearer a fifth. These figures did not change greatly in the 1980s, the decade in which right-wing governments held political sway in many countries. Even in the United Kingdom the share of total incomes taxed for this purpose stabilised after 1976; it did not fall significantly overall (Hills, 1990).

How are we to explain this persistent scale of state spending on welfare? Different schools of economic thought have different answers to that question. They can be broadly grouped under four headings: traditional economic theories about market failure, a more recent emphasis on information failure in some kinds of market, Marxist economists' concern with the larger role of welfare spending in sustaining capitalist economies, and economists of the public choice school on the radical right who emphasise *government* failure.

Market failure

Political philosophers have their own justifications for social provision, for redistributing resources to poor people or opposing such action. Economists have a more hard-nosed approach. Whatever the equity of the case, they say, are there any economic efficiency grounds for the state intervening? Are there efficiency limits to the market's role?

Traditional economic thought has always accepted that markets do not work perfectly in all circumstances. Adam Smith (1776) recognised this and modern economists have a standard set of circumstances in which they agree market exchange fails to produce the most efficient outcome. The famous American economist Kenneth Arrow (1963) summed up his explanation for non-market social institutions thus: 'I propose here the view that, when the market fails to achieve an optimal state, society will, to some extent at least, recognise the gap, and non market social institutions will arise in attempting to bridge it' (p. 947). Some of the most common types of market failure are discussed below, although economics students will want to consult the further reading at the end of the chapter if they do not already know it.

Social or public goods

The most widely accepted limitation of market exchange derives from the inherent nature of some services or activities. For a market to exist, a particular object which is bought by me has to be thereby unavailable to someone else who wants to buy it. If my neighbour will benefit equally from my having a hose pipe in the garden he is likely to leave the buying to me. I may make the same calculation and no-one buys. The logical thing to do is to club together and buy it between us – a miniature social good. Social goods have two particular properties. One is that of *non-excludability*. A product will not be produced in quantities that maximise the efficient gain to society if people can benefit whether they pay or not. Clean air is a standard example, as is general policing of an area. You could not charge for the service. Another characteristic is non-rivalry. The essence of non-rivalry is that my consumption, e.g. of road space, does not reduce the amount available to other people. If I drive along an uncrowded road it is not costing any extra for me to do so: I am not using resources at the expense of others. There should, therefore, be no charge on that road. When the road becomes crowded the conclusion would be different. Non-excludability from benefit is one reason for defining a social good, non-rivalry another.

Economists often limit their examples of such cases to defence, police or environmental issues. Measures of public health, sanitation and the spread of infectious disease were recognised by the Victorians as vital social goods. The common education of all children in a nation, if viewed as a good thing, would be another example.

The existence of a social good suggests some kind of public action may be necessary. It does not tell us exactly what. Laws to require sanitation in your house may be enough. In other cases a state service, for example police, may be needed. Unfortunately, knowing that a service can only be provided collectively does not tell us how much to spend on it. Because no market bargains can be struck or exchange take place, there is no unambiguously right level of spending, at least in terms of traditional economic theory. All we can hope for is an open and informed electoral process.

Externalities

The number of pure public or social goods is small (see Foster *et al.*, 1980, for a discussion of this in relation to local government services). There is another set of situations in which economists recognise market failure. Activities may be undertaken or products bought in the market at a price that may not reflect the whole benefit or costs to the society.

If the benefits are private to the purchaser, a price paid in a free market will lead to an efficient allocation of resources on grounds any first-year economics text will explain. However, my car may affect your and the wider public's welfare in a number of ways. The lead in the exhaust fumes may harm your health, the gases may affect the ozone layer and the good of future generations. Driving a car down a crowded street may cause delays to others driving the same way. These are all negative externalities or social costs. Only if they are reflected in the price or in some charge upon me will my actions in the market-place represent a truly efficient allocation of resources – efficient, that is, for the whole community. If a congestion tax is levied on me as a car driver in a city centre, I shall only drive in if the gain to me in convenience is greater than the cost of the congestion I have caused. In the same way I may not take into account the benefits to the wider society of my child being able to communicate with others. I may not invest enough in her education from society's point of view.

So some market decisions may produce too much activity (car fumes) and others too little (education). Insanitary housing may be all a poor person can buy from a landlord, but the public health hazard is a cost to neighbours. As a parent who sees his daughter's future confined to motherhood, I might see no point in educating her to be other than a mother. Society as a whole, as well as the child, would be the loser. Secondary education is a necessary requirement for a democratic society and for individual self-fulfilment, but there is no reason why parents should wish to buy that amount of education or be able to.

Once more, collective action of some kind is called for. Externalities often justify regulation, or subsidy or taxation, rarely state provision. Education is the one possible exception because the externality derives from a common educational experience.

Monopoly and imperfect competition

Completely efficient allocations of resources only occur where there is perfect competition. These conditions rarely, if ever, exist and much public policy is concerned to limit monopoly power and introduce as much competition as is politically feasible. In many areas a local secondary school or a district general hospital will enjoy a *geographical monopoly*. This is not just because the state has made it so but because economies of scale require a big institution. A smaller one would not be able to enter the market and compete the larger out of existence. The travel costs and impracticability of going to the next school or hospital are such as to give the institution the same kind of power as a commercial monopoly.

This may argue for close state regulation of standards in such schools, along the lines followed by the regulators of private monopolies like British Telecom, or, given the nature of education and health, a case may be made for local political control. This economic theory does not help us here. It does suggest an unregulated market will not produce the most efficient outcome.

Charity or income externalities

We have seen that my activities, such as driving with lead in my petrol, may affect you. My low income or starving family may also affect your happiness. You may be greatly disturbed by the fact the market has not resulted in my family having enough to live on. Your utility, or happiness, may be a function not just of your income but of mine too. The classic statement of this theorem was by Hochman and Rodgers (1969). In a two-person world you can solve this by giving me part of your income. There are problems, however. I may feel resentful of such personal charity. My utility is not enhanced; it may even be worsened by the shame. If your real concern is with my utility you will not have benefited either. One way round this may be for individuals to use the agency of the state to impersonalise the giving and seek to remove the stigma by creating a set of rights to benefit.

More fundamentally, in a non-two-person world where poverty is generally disliked, others will benefit from your generosity and may be tempted to leave it all to you. They will ride free on your charity. Alternatively they might all agree to contribute, sharing the burden. It can be argued that what concerns people is an overall level of income distribution and that the state is the only agency capable of taking action to achieve this.

There is a converse problem, which greatly concerned the Victorians and has its modern counterpart. It is that by your charity you may make a beggar of me: I may never work again, my family's morals may be corrupted and I may trade on your susceptibilities. The Victorians concluded that some collective regulation of charitable giving was called for; if not, society would descend into beggary. In its modern form the argument would be that a collective decision has to be made about the appropriate trade-off between poverty relief and the disincentive effects of giving income support.

The difficulties of charitable giving are not at an end. You may want to see me and my family with enough to eat, but would be upset if I spent the cash you gave me on beer or drugs. You may want to tie the support you give to particular purposes. Private charities can do this by giving clothes or food, but the indignity may rise in line with the specificity of the gift. The state may be able to give tied benefits, like food stamps, but people will probably find ways to trade them.

These kinds of justification for state activity on grounds of market failure have been recognised by economists for many years. They do not, however, add up to an overwhelming case for widespread social service provisions of the kind that exist in most countries. Most services like schools, hospitals and pensions are clearly not public or social goods in the narrow economic sense. Large private markets exist for all these activities, even more in the case of housing. There are public good elements in many services like education, however, and certainly externalities.

More recent advances in economic theory have elaborated further deficiencies in markets that arise from information failures. This literature has been summarised by Barr (1992, 1993) and the following section draws on his work.

Information failure

Markets require perfect information to work perfectly. The less perfect the knowledge, the less well the market works. This is true generally and may be countered by attempts to improve consumer knowledge, for example. There is, however, a class of problems that are more deep seated and difficult to remedy by simple consumer protection measures.

Consumer knowledge limits

Consumers of health care lack information that would enable them to make rational choices for themselves in at least four ways:

1. It is unclear to the immediate consumer what service he or she requires, if any. Are you really ill or imagining it? If there is something wrong, what is it? What treatment is called for? The patient's capacity to judge the doctor's advice on this is limited in the extreme. If there were something wrong with your car, you might take it to several garages to get second and third opinions; and to some extent this happens in health care, especially in more consumer-conscious systems like the United States. In practice the importance of trust and a sense of continuity between doctor and patient, the whole social setting and the anxiety that surrounds illness mean that consumer loyalty is high and important. In urgent cases such shopping around is in any case impossible.

   Similar problems arise with the choice of school. The need for continuity in a child's education precludes continual changes of school to get the best buy. The problems posed by the mentally infirm or disabled are greater still.
2. Even when it has been decided what service is needed, the consumer may face great difficulty measuring the quality and comparing it with what might have been received elsewhere. So many of the circumstances are personal. How well my child does depends on individual capacities and family situation; how well the school is doing, taking these factors into account, is a highly complex exercise to determine, as we shall see in the next chapter. Where a producer is making a standard product

that can be tested comparisons are possible. What characterises most social services is their highly personal nature, and this makes simple, widely available measures of quality difficult to produce.

3. Quality is not the only thing consumers need to know about in the market-place; they will need accurate pricing information too. They will need to know whether paying a little bit more for such an operation is going to increase their chances of survival, and if so by how much. It is not just that such information is difficult to give because of the high degree of uncertainty attaching to the individual case; it is also costly to acquire. A full medical examination and cost information and prediction, undertaken more than once by different hospitals, will be necessary. The transaction costs, as economists call this, of getting the information necessary to act as a rational consumer are high.
4. Consumers may need to know about the probability of events occurring far into the future, and of a kind they would rather not think about, such as becoming infirm in advanced old age. Few people insure for the very high costs of long-term care in old age, even in the United States (Rivlin and Wiener, 1988).

Individual consumers thus face a more difficult prospect operating in these kinds of market than the everyday high street shop. The reasons all have to do with limited and uncertain information.

Provider information

Service providers in a market also face difficulties. They may know less than their customer, yet need perfect or good information about their potential patient or client to be able to quote a competitive price.

Adverse selection

An individual with a poor health record has every incentive to hide the fact from a private health insurer. The insurer needs to know what the probabilities are of that individual being a costly patient. If he or she is costly the insurer will ask a higher premium or price for the health insurance cover. A health maintenance organisation

(HMO) that promises to provide care for a flat-rate payment per year will want the same information in order to adjust its annual charge. The patient will have every incentive to lie or modify the truth. In response insurance companies try to find out as much as they can about applicants in order to isolate high-risk individuals and either charge them a higher premium or exclude them altogether. If any one company does not, its competitor will.

A company that fails to exclude high-cost patients will have to charge higher premiums to everyone, and that will put it at a disadvantage in competing for the custom of the most sought after – the low-risk patient. If the company is more attractive to the high-risk patient a downward spiral will set in, whereby it loses healthy patients and acquires less healthy ones, becoming less and less competitive (Rothschild and Stiglitz, 1976; Atkinson, 1989; Laffont, 1989). As one head of marketing for an American health insurer put it to me a few years ago, 'Let's face it competition in health care is all about making sure you don't have ill people on your books.'

These problems of 'cream skimming' have forced non-profit health insurers in the United States, like Blue Cross and Blue Shield, to adapt their policies. They have forced many HMOs out of business as private profit-making concerns compete with them, not on the basis of providing more efficient services (E-competition), but by selecting out or creaming off the low-risk individuals (S-competition). If the gain to a firm from S-competition is greater than that from competing on efficiency, it will of course choose the former. This does not, in theory, destroy the case for competition in health care, for it may be possible to identify risk factors and government may compensate firms who take on high-risk groups, but there is no easy way to do this (van de Ven and van de Vliet, 1990). By the same token health providers – GPs, for example – may try to avoid taking on patients who are costly in time, even in a non-cash-market situation, and that is difficult to stop, but it is more serious when the patient carries a price tag too.

The formal economic literature on adverse selection is largely confined to health services and insurance, but precisely the same problem arises in other welfare services. Indeed, it may be the one common factor that runs through all forms of social provision. Old people's homes and residential care for children from broken homes exhibit exactly the same response to similar incentives. More dependent people will not be taken on unless a higher price can be paid: those not yet dependent but with a higher risk of becoming so will be excluded. Schools face similar incentives. Given a flat fee for educating a child, a rational school will take the most educable child if it wishes to maximise its exam ratings or competitive edge in the market-place (Glennerster, 1991). It will cream off those from homes or with previous school performance scores that suggest it can get good results with minimum input. For more discussion of this point, see the next chapter.

Moral hazard

Drawing again on examples from insurance, economists point to the poor information insurance firms have about the insured's behaviour and the impact that being insured will have on that behaviour (Pauly, 1974). If I am insured against theft I may be less careful about locking up my house; *in extremis*, as a hard-up landlord I may indulge in deliberate arson. This does not make market insurance impossible, but it makes it more expensive. This is not a problem confined to private insurance. If I know that either the state or my family will look after me if I become elderly and infirm, I may be less willing to pay for insurance to support myself. If I have sickness insurance, state or private, I may be prepared to take more time off work or take fewer preventive measures. If there were insurance against marriage breakdown, would there be more breakdowns? Some would argue that social security provision has encouraged the breakdown of marriage.

The effects are largest in what economists call third-party insurance systems. My car is insured against accident, so when I have an accident and my car is damaged I am happy to go along with whatever the garage charges, so long as the insurance company will pay. This drives up costs. Precisely this situation obtains in health care insurance in many countries, thus driving up health prices. The response has been for insurance companies to insist on patients paying part of the price of their treatment – coinsurance – and on very close regulation of treatment given. Attempts have also been made to increase the competition between health providers. Private markets in health tend to generate very high prices, which competition has been unable to check at all effectively.

Certainty and uncertainty
A chronically sick person, for example, will find it difficult to get insured because of the certainty of very high-cost care. At the other extreme, when there is no basis for predicting outcomes, insurance markets will not work either. As Barr (1991) points out, the impossibility of predicting future levels of inflation over a retired person's life makes it almost impossible for private insurance companies to offer fully inflation-proofed pension schemes without some kind of government support.

Taken together these information failures go a long way to explain why social institutions have evolved that try to mitigate their consequences. Their salience clearly varies from one service to another. What they do is to provide a framework to which we shall return in discussing each service later in the book. Before that we review some less conventional economic theories that give a different reason for the existence and growth of social welfare.

A political economy view

Traditional economic analysis concentrates on particular failures in what is otherwise seen as a natural and efficient system of exchange – the market. For Marxist writers, and others besides, the whole system of market exchange is flawed. The role the welfare state plays is to rescue, albeit temporarily, capitalist market systems from collapse. This may not be a fashionable view in the early 1990s, especially in the light of the failure of non-market command systems in eastern Europe. But it is equally impossible to point to pure capitalist modes of exchange coexisting with democratic governments which possess no form of state income support or other welfare provision. During the 1980s the United Kingdom was forced through a major economic restructuring designed to make it more competitive. Whatever the judgements about its success, it would not have been possible if over three million people had been made unemployed with no form of support at all. Much the same lesson is being learnt in the eastern European nations. If they want to move to a free labour market system, they must have some way of giving income to those thrown out of work in the period of adjustment.

Many Marxists had ignored the welfare system. Some did see it as a partial victory for the working class, but others saw it as a sop that bought off the labour movement from seeking real change. (For a self-critical review of Marxists' work on welfare see Lee and Raban, 1988.) It was not until the 1970s that a coherent political economy view emerged, stimulated especially by the work of O'Connor (1973) in the United States and Gough (1979) in the United Kingdom. These authors maintained that welfare spending by the state was both essential for the functioning of a capitalist economy *and* bound to grow inexorably to the point where a capitalist economy would be unable to finance the scale of spending required. There was, in short, a basic contradiction built into the western economic system, and welfare spending was at its heart.

The essence of the first leg of the argument is set out in Figure 2.1. There are two broad categories of public expenditure: *social capital* and *social expenses*. The first category has a direct economic pay-off. It helps to sustain the economic infrastructure and thus sustains private capital. It has an *accumulation function*. This kind of activity can be further subdivided. There is the creation of new capital or investment by the state which can be of two kinds again: physical capital – roads, railways, airports, power generation – and human capital – investment in education, in training, in health to produce a healthy labour force, support for families to enable them to reproduce a new labour force. O'Connor (1973) distinguished that kind of state spending from consumption expenditure on the urban structure. Money for recreation, parks, and other public goods, concerts and services that the suburban middle class enjoy is largely denied to the inner-city classes. Then there are what he called social expenses, which are a drag on productive output but are necessary to keep the whole capitalist edifice in place. These mitigate the grossest inequalities. They take starving children from the streets, and old people from desperate penury. Without that the political legitimacy of the state would be undermined. The defence forces, the police and the secret service are the hard hand of legitimation.

There was nothing new about this analysis except its emphasis on the cost of such activities. The actual categories and their boundaries were disputed, for example by Gough (1979). What was new was O'Connor's theoretical analysis, which suggested that the levels of spending needed to sustain the capitalist system would

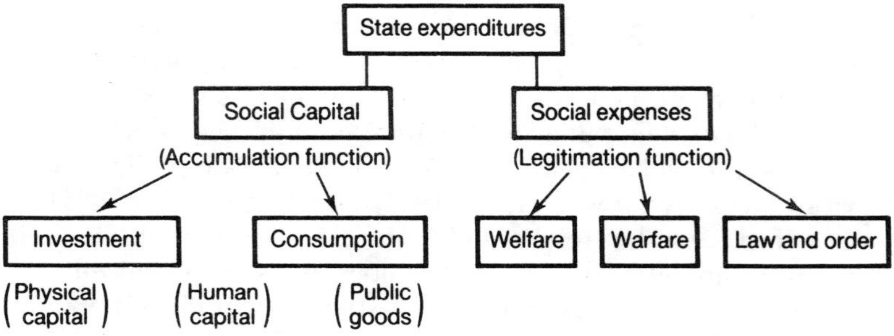

Figure 2.1 A political economy view (Source: Judge, 1982b)

grow steadily. The rate of profit was declining and would need more and more injections of state support, he argued. Unemployment would grow and cost steadily more, and the costs of services would be pushed up by workers in the state sector following the wage increases won by trade union activity in the private sector. Drawing on the analogy of the then nearly bankrupt New York City, he forecast that the whole state apparatus would not be able to raise the taxes to support this growing burden of public expenditure. The working class were being asked to pay increasing amounts in taxation and were able to resist both politically and by passing on the tax increases in wage demands. Here O'Connor agreed with the New Right. He, unlike them, believed that any attempt to rein back the level of state spending would, in the end, undermine the accumulation of capital and legitimacy of the state.

Written during a period of rapidly rising spending and taxation as well as economic crisis, this analysis had wide appeal. The middle-way response was that the growth in public spending was neither inevitable nor irreversible. It was possible to sustain a necessary level of welfare spending within a mixed economy and to control that spending effectively. The means for doing so are outlined in Chapter 4. In the 1970s and 1980s a very different set of ideas evolved on the radical right (see Glennerster and Midgley, 1991). These can be grouped under the heading *public choice theory*.

A public choice view

Mueller (1989) defines public choice as 'the economic study of non market decision making'. That is a very large and all encompassing category. Here we concentrate on that part of the work which is concerned to explain public expenditure growth, beginning with a seminal work by Niskanen (1971), though he was building on previous work by Downs (1957, 1967) and Tullock (1965). This approach places the responsibility for the growth of welfare spending on imperfections in the democratic process and on the nature of the incentives that exist within government bureaucracies.

Pressure groups wanting to get government to create a new service will have something to gain of a significant kind, while the general taxpayer will only see a small marginal loss and not spend the time organising to oppose more spending. Such purposes may be legitimate, as with pure public goods, or illegitimate, as with some scheme designed to get a congressman re-elected. An agency may begin with a legitimate purpose – planting trees to provide pit props for the mines in the First World War, for example – and then continue, as the Forestry Commission has, with no legitimate function. Once a welfare programme is in place those who run it have a direct interest in not merely keeping it going but expanding the size of the activity. Any public bureaucrat has the following possible gains from his or her job: 'salary, perquisites of the office, public reputation, power, patronage, output of the bureau, ease of making changes and ease of running the bureau' (Niskanen, 1971). With the exception of the last two, Niskanen claims all these possible personal gains are directly and positively linked to the size of the agency budget. Hence it is not surprising to find heads of services, like directors of social service departments, always arguing for more money. What is more, they are likely to have the best or only information about the social problem they are responsible for meeting, and can exaggerate its size and their impact. They are in a powerful position to persuade legislators or councillors to spend more. They have no pecuniary advantage in the efficient running of the organisation; thus public organisations tend to be both large and inefficient.

This kind of reasoning underpinned much Conservative opinion in the 1980s. More recently the assumptions and reasoning have come under powerful counter-attack (Dunleavy, 1991). The interests and motivations of those who work in public services are not so simply reduced to a pecuniary base. Nor is it clear that senior bureaucrats are necessarily closely tied to spending more money. Their careers may be advanced by gaining a reputation for tough management. The political climate will be critical.

Above all, the explanation, good as it may be for helping to understand one kind of demand for more spending, ignores the institutional and political constraints on spending that exist. It is important to realise that its authors draw largely on experience of the United States, where the spending lobbies are more powerful and where Congress has a freedom to spend that the House of Commons does not (see Glennerster, 1975). We describe the considerable powers of the Treasury in the United Kingdom in Chapter 4.

The lack of incentives for efficiency that exist in welfare services especially are not so easily dismissed. There are four main difficulties:

1. There is no easy way to measure the output of social service agencies. It is therefore difficult to know whether the public is getting good value for money. The price may be too high.
2. There is rarely a competitor with whom users or legislators can compare the quality of the service they are getting.
3. Because there is no ready alternative provider of the service, the users or clients cannot 'exit' easily. They cannot transfer their custom and therefore their cash. This puts the providers in the comfortable position of knowing that whatever happens the users will have to put up with their services, and this is unhealthy.
4. Because the service is free, consumers are less demanding than if they are paying. This puts them in a dependent position, tending to be grateful for the service received.

It is these kinds of consideration that lead some to advocate the extension of competition to social services. The case for the state financing social provision may well hold, these authors argue (Le Grand and Robinson, 1984). That does not mean that the state has to give a monopoly to a particular agency to provide that service.

In the next chapter we explore more fully this case and the proposed answer, quasi market competition.

Further reading

Barr, N.A. (1992), 'Economic theory and the welfare state: a survey and interpretation', *Journal of Economic Literature*, forthcoming.

Barr, N.A. (1993), *The Economics of the Welfare State*, 2nd edition, London: Weidenfeld.

Dunleavy, P. (1991), *Democracy, Bureaucracy and Public Choice*, Hemel Hempstead: Harvester Wheatsheaf. A critique of the public choice view.

Mueller, D.C. (1989), *Public Choice II*, Cambridge: Cambridge University Press. For those with an economics background.

Musgrave, R.A. and Musgrave, P.B. (1989), *Public Finance in Theory and Practice*, London and Tokyo: McGraw-Hill. See especially chapters on social goods.

O'Connor, J. (1973), *The Fiscal Crisis of the State*, New York: St Martins Press. A Marxist political economy view.

CHAPTER 3

A MARKET FOR WELFARE?

Old assumptions

The accepted way of thinking about the delivery of welfare services in the United Kingdom, from the 1940s through to the 1970s, was to assume that state intervention implied that services should be both financed *and* provided by some agency of the state. That might be central or local government or some body directly responsible to the central state, like a new town development corporation.

It had not always been so. In education, the state's involvement had begun, in the nineteenth century, with grants to private church schools. This aid was extended to private secondary grammar schools in the twentieth century. There was a widely held view in the nineteenth century that the state should not be in the business of providing schooling. If involved at all it should confine its role to aiding the private voluntary sector. The development of state schools was a slow one. (See Chapter 12.) In the area of housing for the poor, similarly, it was not local councils but housing associations that had been the first to respond. Even when it came, state support for housing had begun with subsidies made available to both private builders and local authorities. (See Chapter 13.) Much of the care and support of elderly and disabled people had begun as a form of charity that gained public support and then became a statutory service – family case work is a good example.

Reasons for the fusion of finance and provision

There were a number of technical reasons for the decline in state support for private agencies:

1. *Weak financial accountability*. It proved very difficult to stop private builders making excessive profits out of state subsidies. Tough Treasury and audit controls were easier to apply if the agent was a statutory authority.
2. *Difficulties in quality control*. Schools were an example of this. To receive a grant schools had to come up to minimum standards set by school inspectors. (See Chapter 12.) Simply to rely on personal judgements by individual inspectors was not deemed sufficient. Schools had to put their children through a set of fairly crude tests, and children had to pass them, before the school could be paid a grant for that child. Teachers and the inspectorate itself objected that this was a constraining and stultifying process which led to too much time being spent on exam practice. Achieving the close quality control needed to dispense cash to independent agencies was difficult to do effectively.
3. *Universality*. Pressure grew for services to be equally and universally available, pressure that reached its peak during and after the Second World War. It seemed that the easiest way to achieve this was to do it through the agency of a single provider charged with the responsibility of providing a universal service with equal access. This motivation lay behind the National Health Service and the nationwide social security system.
4. *Equity*. Public organisations must be seen to be dealing fairly with all those who use the service. Like cases must be treated alike. The tight rules that result may be difficult to administer at one remove in a private or independent organisation. Social security benefits are a good example.
5. *Unitary government*. All social services were in the end the responsibility of the appropriate Minister or Secretary of State in Westminster. He or she was held politically responsible. As politicians they wanted mistakes minimised and political credit maximised. Especially in a period of expansion, that was most readily achieved by concentrating control and delivery in the

hands of a statutory body over which the minister had ultimate charge.

6. *Political climate*. These partly technical, partly political factors were reinforced by a general climate of ideas which held public provision *per se* to be a good thing, an end in itself. This was not a view universally held, of course, but among those who favoured greater social equity, social provision was the almost instinctive solution.

The 1940s saw the end to social insurance provided by voluntary societies and trade unions. It saw the rapid growth of housing provided by local authorities because there were no other agencies large enough to undertake the rapid and massive housing programme needed after the war. Voluntary hospitals disappeared, seen as a root cause of unequal provision of health care and facing severe financial difficulties.

The organisational consequences

Once a structure has emerged in which central government has ultimate responsibility and in which equity and universality are political goals, bureaucracy and hierarchical control are likely outcomes. Neither term should be considered in a pejorative way, for the following reasons:

1. Consistency requires rules commonly observed. That is what bureaucracy, in its strict sense, provides.
2. Accountability upwards to a political master means a chain of command downwards.
3. The dangers of non-compliance by local agencies to political goals and standards require tight supervision and inspection.

In an account of the US system of public schooling, Chubb and Moe (1990) describe the impact of such factors in a very different, decentralised system.

Parallels in the private sector

In many ways these kinds of factor parallel, but are distinct from, the kinds of factor that lead to the growing centralisation or hierarchical structure of private firms (Williamson, 1975). Firms may resort to manufacturing components or owning a subsidiary rather than buying from another producer for a number of reasons:

1. *Complex contracts*. It may be difficult to draw up a contract that covers all the possible contingencies and to enforce the contract. The transaction costs, or the costs of negotiation, legal and administrative, may be high. The firm may wish to have the kind of flexible control that can be achieved within an organisation as distinct from putting everything on paper in advance in a contract with another organisation.
2. *Limited knowledge*. One organisation may find it difficult to make a contract with another very different one just because it lacks the expertise. To think up a contract to cover all possible eventualities may be too difficult for any expert.
3. *Uncertainty*. The service or product may be one for which future demands are highly uncertain. The contractor may want a very high price for giving the company an assured supply in those circumstances.

The costs of bureaucracy

There were efficiency costs associated with hierarchical organisation in both the public and the private sectors, as follows:

1. In the private sector large enterprises found it difficult to adapt to the economic uncertainties of the 1970s and 1980s. Restructuring large corporations with established ways proved difficult. It was thought that contracts with small but dispensable suppliers might be more flexible. Corporate decentralisation came to be fashionable (Kanter, 1984).
2. Information technology could enable senior management to monitor local branches and independent suppliers more effectively without powerful intervening hierarchies.

Similar problems and possibilities began to affect social service organisations.

3. The ambition to control organisations from the centre outran

the centre's capacity to generate sensible information to plan and monitor institutions. How many university students did the country need? What was the output of different universities? Government made itself look very foolish in trying to answer these kinds of question (Barnes and Barr, 1988).

4. As the steady expansion of funds available to the welfare services ceased, efficiency in the use of those funds became more important.
5. Consumers became increasingly accustomed to wide choice in private markets. Their expectations of public services grew, even if the resources devoted to them by the political process did not.
6. The political climate changed with the economic crisis of the mid-1970s. Equity and universality came lower down the political list of priorities. Private sector models came to be taken as the norm.

In this situation stress came to be laid on the weaknesses of the traditional model of delivering social services in the United Kingdom. Once again, much of the important literature was American.

Limitations to the traditional model

No incentives for efficiency

Economists distinguish two kinds of efficiency. *Allocative* efficiency exists in a situation where resources are distributed throughout the economy in ways that reflect the best possible fit between what consumers want and what can be produced. This concept is to be distinguished from *productive* efficiency – are the firms producing the goods or services doing so in the most efficient way? Critics argued that public and social services fell down in both respects. We begin with allocative efficiency.

Allocative efficiency and choice

Because parents or patients or clients mostly had no choice of school or hospital, they had no way of expressing their preferences for one kind of service or another. In the market-place it was in the interests of shops and firms to experiment in offering diverse products: the one that got the right mix got the most custom. This could not happen in a monopolist public service. Social service providers had no way of knowing what it was that consumers really wanted. Traditional supporters of the public service model responded by pointing out that the users of services had the vote and that political parties had an interest in finding out what users wanted. Economists claimed that representative power over the day-to-day running of services was minimal. The case was powerfully put in an influential book by an American economist, Hirschman (1970), called *Exit, Voice and Loyalty*.

Exit, Voice and Loyalty

Hirschman's book is often cited by those who seem to have read no more than the title, but the book merits more attention. Hirschman begins by asking why it is that inefficient organisations exist at all if the market really works as it is meant to. He claims that there are two kinds of sanction or power that consumers have over organisations to get them to respond to what they want.

One is by taking their custom elsewhere, to a firm that is providing what they want or doing it more efficiently. That is what traditional economic theory suggests will happen. In fact, there are considerable limits to people's capacity to exit. It may be costly to change provider, to build up links and personal networks. Hirschman cites schooling as a case where the child may suffer from a move and certainly from frequent moves. Consumers of personal services, like a family doctor, may have loyalty and trust that are important elements in the professional relationship. Thus 'exit' is limited by the nature of the service, not just by whether it is publicly or privately provided. There are inherent limits to competition. Nevertheless, exit is the most powerful sanction.

The alternative that users of public services have is 'voice'. This also has severe limitations. Voice is costly. It means attending parent teacher meetings, standing for election, campaigning. It is conditional on influence and bargaining power. That may be poorly distributed among the users. Those with high status or power in the outside social structure will be able to exert more leverage through voice. Hirschman ends by advocating a mixture of exit and voice in public services. Voice, through democratic institutions, has to be made more effective, and one way to do that is to introduce an element of exit. Consumers have to be able to change doctors, schools, landlords, to bring their dissatisfaction to bear.

Productive efficiency and markets

Another American economist, Leibenstein (1966), distinguished allocative efficiency from what he called X-inefficiency. By this he meant the tendency of firms to produce the kind of products people wanted, but in a more costly, less efficient way than they would in a really competitive climate. Working practices might be slack or management poor. Instead of monopolies working efficiently and their owners drawing supernormal profit, the surplus was being consumed, as it were, by those working in the organisation. They were not forced to be as sharp, innovative and hard working as they would be in a competitive environment.

It was possible to apply that analysis to the public sector. Public services are virtual monopolies. As public sector bodies they could not earn supernormal profits but the employees could make life easy for themselves:

1. Staff could adopt procedures that were comfortable for them but inconvenient for the public. Just as banks could close at 3 o'clock in the afternoon and at weekends, so could schools.
2. The rules which governed procedures were designed to prevent abuse of funds or political embarrassment. That often meant 'Do not do anything new.'
3. Those in positions of authority could abuse that power. The hospital consultant might spend his or her time in a private clinic or on the golf course and leave junior colleagues to do the job.
4. Social services, in particular, made the assumption that the professionals who worked in them regulated their own standards and were motivated by altruism or notions of professional duty to their clients or patients. This had the convenient side-effect of expecting them to work for low pay. Economists and social policy analysts argued that this view was unrealistic (Lees, 1966; Downs, 1967; Wilding, 1982). While

some bureaucrats and professionals were altruistic, self-interest, individual gain and the quiet life were equally important motives. Organisations that ignored this were likely to be inefficient.

Markets as the answer

In a competitive private market, the argument ran, these dangers were minimised because, if they became too great, customers would go elsewhere and the firm would close. This tended to ignore the limits to competition in the private sector and compare the perfect model of a private market with the real and imperfect world of the public sector, but the essential case was a powerful one. The solution was to introduce into the public sector the same competitive rigour that, in theory, applied in the private sector. That meant putting out to competitive tender the functions that were traditionally undertaken by public services (Savas, 1977, 1982).

The equity case

Although the case for markets put by the right in politics had concentrated on choice and productive efficiency arguments, there was a line of reasoning developed by what might be called the New Market Left which concentrated on equity or distributional issues.

The foundation for this view began with the observation that the welfare state had in many ways benefited the middle class more than it had the working class (Abel-Smith, 1958; Townsend and Bosanquet, 1972; Le Grand, 1982; Goodin and Le Grand, 1987). While cash benefits were highly redistributive, going largely to the poor, services in kind were different, Le Grand (1982) argued. The points he made were as follows:

1. Gaining access to services in kind could be costly, in time and earnings foregone. It could involve waiting for doctors, seeking a second opinion, persuading your GP to arrange for a bed in a London teaching hospital and not your local hospital, seeing head teachers or local authority education department officials

to persuade them to take your child at the best school. The poor could afford the time less than the rich.

2. Such activities required confidence and high status. These attributes also tended to make such groups more successful in bringing pressure to bear on governments to expand or defend those services that served the middle class most. The successful defence of free university education from the proposal to charge fees on a means-tested basis in the mid-1980s was an example that fitted the theory.

The same kinds of inequality of influence worked in favour of those services where the middle class were the main service providers – health care, for example. The collective protests by the Royal Colleges against cuts in the NHS in 1988 were taken a good deal more seriously than complaints by local authority manual workers or council house managers. The public expenditure cuts of the 1980s might therefore be expected to affect least those services that were supplied to the middle class by the middle class (Le Grand and Winter, 1987).

One policy conclusion from this analysis was to shift more state activity to cash benefits which could be targeted on the poor. Where services in kind were necessary they could be financed by tied cash payments – vouchers. These could be set at higher levels for the poor: children from low-income families, for example. This would mean that schools would take more notice of poor parents. They would attract more resources to their school if they attracted more poor children. To do that they would have to do a good job with deprived children. This was the kind of distinctive case the New Market Left made out for a market in welfare over and above the efficiency case the New Right were making.

Different kinds of market

Cash in a private market

The most extreme variant of bringing the market to welfare was to say that all state services should be abolished and their cash equivalent given to individuals. Simply to give cash, however, might lead to parents spending the money on themselves and not educating the child.

Vouchers

One way to minimise these difficulties, advocated by Milton Friedman (1962), was to add to individuals' purchasing power in ways that tied the assistance to the purchase of a particular service. This could be done, as described in Chapter 1, by issuing a voucher to an individual or family for them to spend on a defined service, rather like a luncheon voucher. Examples are as follows:

1. Parents could be given a voucher with a face value equivalent to the average cost of educating a child in a state school, and this could be used to purchase schooling for the child.
2. A young person could be given a training voucher, take it to an employer and require some form of training on the job. This was introduced in 1990. (See Chapter 12.)
3. The family of a mentally disabled child could be given a voucher to pay for care or training, and they would be free to spend it with any agency or mix of agencies they chose (Bosanquet, 1984). (See Chapter 11.)
4. Parents of children under 5 could be given a voucher to spend on whatever form of child care seemed most appropriate (Hewitt, 1989).
5. Though vouchers proper have not been introduced into British schools, the changes introduced in the 1988 Educational Reform Act go a long way towards introducing a *de facto* voucher scheme, under which pupils have, in theory, open access to all the state schools in the area. The school gets a grant for a child when he or she joins the school. The details of the new Act are described in Chapter 12.

Vouchers or voucher-like systems thus proliferated in the 1980s.

Tax or other refunds for specified expenditure

Another way of achieving the same effect is for government to promise to give a tax refund to individuals who spend money on an approved social purpose. Housing and pension contributions are well-established examples. Tax benefits were extended to encourage personal pensions in the 1980s. (See Chapter 14.) Examples are as follows:

1. Under the 1990 Finance Act private health insurance for the over 60s attracted tax relief. (See Chapter 10.)
2. Those who paid fees at a private nursing home could recover the cost from the social security system. This type of arrangement spread rapidly after 1983. (See Chapter 11.)
3. Housing benefit is another variant. (See Chapter 13.)

Quasi or internal markets

Where the inequality of market knowledge between purchaser and provider was not too great, moderate market reformers were prepared to advocate these kinds of change. Where that inequality was great, as in the case of health care, different solutions were advanced.

The basis of the 'reforms' to the National Health Service embodied in the 1990 National Health Service and Community Care Act was to pull apart the purchaser and provider role in the NHS. It was accepted that the central Exchequer should continue to finance health care for anyone who wanted to use the NHS. District health authorities would be charged with the responsibility of ensuring that the populations in their areas had available a high standard of care free at the point of use. However, instead of seeking to provide all the services themselves, the districts would be free to buy services from hospitals in other districts, or from newly independent hospital trusts, or from the private sector. The influential American advocate of this reform, Alan Enthoven (1985), argued that districts could 'use the possibility of buying outside as bargaining leverage to get better performance from their own providers.'

Some general practitioners would also have certain limited powers to purchase services from whichever hospital they chose. (For details of these changes see Chapter 10.) Districts and fundholding general practitioners would be the patients' informed purchasers of service. It was not a full market solution, and was criticised as such by disappointed and more radical reformers in the Institute for Economic Affairs (Green, 1990).

The same principle was applied to social services departments in the same Act. They were to become purchasing agencies for community care services in their areas. District health authorities and social services departments would make contracts with their own or other units to provide a specific service at a given price.

A fundamental change

The social policy legislation introduced by the Conservative government between 1988 and 1990 thus embodied a fundamental change in the social administration paradigm that had dominated thinking for a generation. It marked a complete break with the social administration principles of the 1940s–80s. The fusion of finance and control were to be replaced by competition and a contract culture. The role of local authorities was substantially down-graded. They were to become contractors, not providers. Government was to encourage those services that they did provide to contract out of local authority control. Other powers were delegated down to schools or housing estates. This left central government more powerful in relation to local authorities (Glennerster *et al.*, 1991).

The market had come to welfare and its origins were not entirely those of the right in politics. The changes looked as if they could be long-lasting.

Limits to quasi markets

Just as there are limits to markets and market failures of the kind we discussed in the last chapter, so there are possible limits to quasi markets. The importance of these limits varies in the case of each service and they are discussed in more detail in the service chapters later in the book. Here some general issues are highlighted.

For any market to perform certain conditions have to be satisfied. That is as true of quasi markets as real ones.

Multiple providers

If providers are to feel that if they do not do a good job they will lose the contract next year, there have to be other providers able to step in. There has to be genuine competition between, ideally, numerous organisations; all, for example, seeking to provide health care to a district. In many instances, some would say most, this is not a realistic picture outside the largest population centres, and often not even there. Because of what were seen to be the economies of scale associated with grouping functions in a large district general hospital, district health authorities concentrated services in units that serve large catchment areas. There may be, at the moment, no effective competitors for many procedures or for emergency care. Similar problems may arise in the case of secondary schools or voluntary care agencies.

The condition of multiple alternative providers may not apply.

Free entry

If there are few existing competitors, markets need there to be new entrants able to enter the market readily, set up business, give something new and more efficient and attract custom. The Treasury has kept tight control on new capital expenditure for hospitals, schools and caring services. Even hospital trusts will find it difficult to get Treasury approval for speculative ventures designed to put other public providers out of business. Private investors are likely to be wary of putting up money to compete where existing public agencies have a head start, unless there is clear evidence of additional demand that the state wants to meet. A tight budgetary climate is not conducive to that.

Conditions of free entry may not apply.

An even playing field

For competition to be fair, district health authorities or local education authorities would have to be indifferent to the fate of schools that they ran in competition with a private unit or a school in another area. This seems unlikely, because the local authority would bear the brunt of criticism if a local facility it owns is closed. The Conservative government's response may be to turn all schools and hospitals over to independent trusts, but as it stands the purchasing bodies are in an ambiguous position. Nor is it easy to see that government can readily walk away from the political fall-out from a hospital closing, for example.

A well-informed purchase

Consumers, even collective ones, need good information on service outcomes and quality. This does not exist in most areas of social policy. Though the need for it by purchasers may generate more, this will be costly. The same applies to price information. In the NHS this has been almost totally absent. The new contracts will require good accounting cost data, and that is extremely costly to get.

A free market for labour

One of the characteristics of health, education and social work is that they are provided by professional groups that restrict entry to their professions. These professionals also negotiate salaries as a group. This tends to mean that they have monopoly power in negotiating rewards for their services. We can see the most costly results in the United States, where doctors' incomes are high relative to those in this country.

In the United Kingdom, one outcome of the centralised system of service provision has been that the government has the ability to take a tough line, facing the professions with a single buyer of their services – a *monopsonist* position. Where sellers of services are free to make their own bargains with professions, and set their own salary levels, the state's monopsony power will go and the result may be an escalation in pay in those services concerned (Barr, Glennerster and Le Grand, 1989; Mayston, 1990).

Making contracts stick

In the private world of contracting, simple contracts can be repeated with little cost – buying a house, for example (though it may not seem that way!). We saw in the first part of the chapter that one of the original reasons why firms came to integrate their activities was the cost, complexity and risks of contracting. The same problems of uncertainty and complexity drove public organisations to do the job themselves. These factors have not gone away. To meet them will mean either very complex contracts which will be costly or very simple, broad-brush, block contracts, which may do no more than regularise in contractual language what happens now (Bartlett, 1991).

Nor is that all. It is far from clear what the government means when it talks of contracts between one statutory authority and another. They do not carry the same force as contracts between private bodies and are not contracts in the strict sense at all. What they are in law is still in some doubt (Jacob, 1991).

Cream skimming

Competition between public and private providers of services will create the same kinds of problems as in traditional markets. Cream skimming is the most obvious. If a hospital or a general practitioner is paid a price in a competitive situation to do a task, such as treat *X* patients, they will be able to offer a lower bid and get the contract if they manage to have more healthy patients. Competition to exclude the unhealthy could be as potent as it is in a private insurance market – the incentives are the same. It may be possible to create counter-incentives, paying providers to take less well patients, but it will be administratively difficult.

Factors of different weights

The general advantages markets may bring and the limits and costs they can entail vary from one type of service to another. Later chapters explore how far markets have been introduced into each and what they may mean in the long term.

Further reading

Bartlett, W. (1991), 'Quasi-markets and contracts: a markets and hierarchies perspective on NHS reform', *Public Money* , **11**, no. 3, pp. 53–61.

Culyer, A.J. (1990), *The Internal Market : An acceptable means to a desirable end*, Discussion Paper no. 67, Centre for Health Economics, York: York University

Demone, H.W. and Gibelman, M. (1989) (eds.), *Services for Sale: Purchasing health and human services*, New Brunswick and London: Rutgers University Press.

Le Grand, J., Glennerster, H. and Maynard, A. (1991), 'Quasi markets and social policy', *Economic Journal*, **101**, no. 408, pp. 1256–88.

Le Grand, J. (1989a), 'Markets, welfare, and equality', in J. Le Grand and S. Estrin, *Market Socialism*, Oxford: Clarendon Press.

Savas, E.S., (1982), *Privatising the Public Sector: How to shrink government*, Chatham, NJ: Chatham House.

PART II

The controlling institutions

CHAPTER 4

SETTING THE LIMITS AT THE CENTRE

There are three separate but interacting processes which determine how much we pay for welfare from the public purse. First, discussed in this chapter, is the procedure by which central government decides upon the total level of public expenditure it believes should be financed out of taxation. This not only determines what central government will spend itself, but also influences what other public agencies, including local authorities, will spend. Second, there is allocation of central funds to local authorities and the interaction between central government and local councils which provide services. Third, there is the budget process within those local authorities.

Before tracing the developments of public spending control at the centre, it is worth briefly setting out the contrasting ways in which other academics have sought to analyse it in order to make my own theoretical framework explicit.

Alternative views of spending control

The *pluralist* tradition is probably dominant in political science writing on budgeting. It is best exemplified in Wildavsky's work (Wildavsky, 1975, 1979; Heclo and Wildavsky, 1981). It sees public expenditure and taxing decisions as the outcome of competition between interest groups. Some represent users and providers of services. They exert leverage where their pressures can be most effective. In the United States, Congressional Committees are important. In the United Kingdom, users and providers focus their attention on the spending departments in Whitehall. Parliament itself is relatively passive. Other economic interests wish to restrain public spending. These are articulated, in particular, through finance and economic affairs departments – in the United Kingdom, the Treasury. In Whitehall the contest between the spenders and the controllers is largely played out behind closed doors (Heclo and Wildavsky, 1981). These writers scorn attempts to make budgeting into a 'rational' process. Budgets shift forwards or backwards by small 'increments' reflecting the balance of interests.

The *managerialist tradition* has produced numerous attempts at budgetary reform designed to encourage a more technical appraisal of spending choices, in order to produce longer-term spending plans and management systems that link the goals of departments to outcomes or success (Novick, 1965; Schick, 1966; Goldman, 1973; Cmnd 9058, 1983; Likierman, 1988; OECD, 1987a). It sees government as faced with the same task of managing and controlling spending as any large business. The techniques used by business can therefore be adapted to government.

The *Marxist tradition* emphasises the dominance of capital in the economy of western nations. Government spending and taxing strategies are therefore subservient to economic interests, but the state is also trying to contain pressures from the working class for more services and benefits. It is this conflict that is reflected in the Whitehall spending battle. Parts of the economy need more spending in order to sustain profits, but all need to be taxed less. These contradictions explain the recurrent expenditure crises. The control of public spending therefore becomes central to the sustenance of the capitalist system (Gough, 1979). Faced with unpopular cuts, the government increased central control while leaving much of the responsibility for making the cuts to local government, thus fragmenting opposition (Flynn, 1988).

In what follows, we adopt what might be called a modified pluralist approach (Hall *et al.*, 1975; Glennerster, 1975, 1979). The process of expenditure control can be seen as a competitive game between spending departments and the Treasury, but as the economic crisis has grown worse, the rules have shifted increasingly in the Treasury's favour and the centre's power to contain local spending has grown. The nature of the economic system and the conflicts within it influence the changing rules of the game. Decentralisation has been both a means of controlling public sector growth and a way to make public services more politically attractive, responsive and effective. (For an international perspective see Bennett, 1990.)

The institutions of control

In the seventeenth and eighteenth centuries it was the crown's desire to spend, and Parliament's desire to limit the tax burden, which led to regular conflicts between the king and Parliament. The House of Lords lost its powers of financial scrutiny in the 1911 Parliament Act, but the House of Commons continued to be jealous of its power to scrutinise ministers' proposals for expenditure. In theory that role persists. A government department can only spend money specifically approved by the House of Commons. The government's taxing agents, the Inland Revenue or Customs and Excise officials, levy taxes only with the House of Commons' approval. Local authorities may levy taxes only with Parliament's approval. The House of Commons Public Accounts Committee and its 'spies' (officials of the National Audit Office) make sure that money is not spent on purposes and in amounts that Parliament has not authorised. They also seek to ensure that it is spent with due 'economy, efficiency and effectiveness'. The Audit Commission performs the same functions as far as local authorities and the National Health Service are concerned, in England and Wales. It has a Scottish equivalent: the Commission for Local Authority Accounts.

In practice, however, as party discipline grew, the institutional battle over the level of spending and taxing took place more and more *within* the government machine. In the end the choices rest with the Cabinet and lie at the heart of modern politics. The Cabinet has as members ministers who are running major departments, wanting to see the service for which they are responsible improved, but aware that collectively their joint demands could ruin their party's chances in the next election. Too large an increase in personal taxation could lose them votes and deny them further ministerial office. The Chancellor, the Financial Secretary to the Treasury, and the Prime Minister have the task of pointing out the financial realities of life to their colleagues. The detailed battles go on between Her Majesty's Treasury, whose constitutional role is to contain spending, and the spending departments that are responsible for the individual services and aware of the demands they are under and of the nature of the rising costs to which they are subject.

To a large extent the spending authorisations that emerge are the result of the interplay between the Treasury and the 'spending' ministries. The complex rules of this game that have grown, been discarded and developed in another form are all part of a continuous struggle between the spenders and the controllers. The Treasury will develop a system of control that temporarily contains the pressures: the spending departments will adapt. They may actually turn the new rules to their advantage. The Treasury responds with another, more effective weapon. The present system of bargaining and control is therefore best understood by tracing its origins and developments. From Gladstone's period as Chancellor in the middle of the last century onwards, a set of rules or constitutional conventions evolved that gave the Treasury its central position as guardian of the public purse, as follows:

1. No individual MP can make a proposal to spend public money or raise taxes. Under standing orders of the House of Commons no proposal to spend money can be tabled for discussion unless it is countersigned by a Treasury minister. This is in contrast to the case in the United States for example, where individual Congressmen can initiate spending proposals.
2. No proposal involving additional spending can be discussed by ministers in Cabinet or Cabinet subcommittee unless it is accompanied by a Treasury paper on the cost consequences.
3. No spending proposals may be developed by a department from the earliest stages without consultation with the Treasury.
4. No department can spend money without Treasury approval.

The Treasury has staff to keep a continual watch over each department's spending. It is their business to know the strengths and weaknesses of each department's case. They are the individuals who must be given early warning if a new spending proposal is in the pipe-line. Their opposite numbers in the spending departments are the principal finance officers. They act as go-betweens, representing their department's best case but also educating their own administrators and professional staff in the realities of a confined budget. As Heclo and Wildavsky (1981) emphasise in their account of the 'Whitehall village', there must be a strong element of trust. Each must respect the other's role and be as open as possible – not with the public but with each other.

Even given good behaviour between ladies and gentlemen, spending departments have evolved some relatively effective tactics and strategies in pressing their cause with the Treasury or Cabinet (Glennerster, 1975), as follows:

1. Use the 'thin edge of the wedge' – press a proposal that has small short-term financial consequences but bigger long-term ones.
2. Appoint a committee of specialists to report on an aspect of a service. Its members, all interested in improving the service, are likely to produce an impressive case for expansion. The Ministry of Education and its successor, the Department of Education and Science, did this with great effect in the 1950s and 1960s.
3. Use a crisis or scandal constructively. Damaging revelations about conditions in mental subnormality hospitals were used by the minister, Richard Crossman, to gain funds to improve conditions in mental hospitals in the late 1960s.
4. Work with pressure groups in your field. The poverty lobby may be critical, but they may also be helpful in creating a constituency for your department's proposals.

If the climate of opinion is sympathetic and the Cabinet favourable, these tactics and strategies may be successful. At the end of the 1950s, the Treasury and its ministers came to believe that they were losing too many of the battles. The Chancellor and his team resigned. The House of Commons Select Committee on the Estimates (1958) argued that the whole system of Treasury control was breaking down and advocated a committee of inquiry. The result was an internal committee with an external chairman – Lord Plowden. His report (Cmnd 1432, 1961) resulted in major reforms in the system of Treasury control, many of which remain in place today, though substantially modified in the intervening years. The report's diagnosis, as well as its proposals, are important for understanding the procedures that followed.

Plowden's diagnosis and remedy

The system of setting limits to public spending had broken down because of the following:

1. The old climate of political opinion that was broadly hostile to the public sector had changed. The Treasury was swimming against the tide.
2. Proposals for new projects tended to 'bubble up' to Cabinet one at a time. Each on its own seemed admirable and only a small addition to the government's total expenditure. No total view of the consequences of all the commitments emerged until it was too late.
3. Policies were embarked upon with little notion of the long-term consequences on spending.
4. The overall effect was that total spending and hence taxation tended to rise faster than the Cabinet really wanted in the long term. This led to sudden and wasteful cuts in spending and cancellation of capital programmes.

To put this right, Plowden proposed a new system of control that would force the Cabinet collectively to set limits to its ambitions, as follows:

1. There should be regular surveys of the long-term expenditure implications of current and proposed policies. The aim would be 'to ensure that the long-term rate of expansion in public expenditure was properly aligned with prospective resources'. Cabinet was to be asked to look at the probable growth in the economy, and the amount of tax revenue it wished to generate, and *then* decide what in total it could afford to spend. Within that total ministers would bid for funds, but that total to which they had collectively agreed should not be breached. We can call this the *control function* of the new system. It was to extend beyond controlling central government's direct spending and

was to embrace the capital spending of nationalised industries and local authority spending too.

2. The second goal was 'to achieve greater stability in public spending decisions'. The limits to spending would be set out with a long-term perspective. Spending departments would be told how much they could spend in real terms in the next four years. This was a kind of *quid pro quo* for the spending departments. They could expect to receive a given level of real resources and plan accordingly for the medium term. We can call this the *planning function* of the new system.
3. The Treasury was 'to improve the tools for making choices'. At the time this was barely spelt out, but as the 1960s progressed, the Treasury began to introduce from America a range of new budgeting and cost benefit techniques that can be seen as the means of implementing this objective. It could be called the *efficiency function* of the new system.

It has become fashionable to argue that the post-Plowden, long-term planning of public spending proved a disaster and actually helped to increase the growth of public spending, though in the early 1970s an American observer thought the system one of the most sophisticated and successful in the world (Wildavsky, 1975).

It was, in fact, the rapid inflation of the early 1970s that gave the system its bad reputation. It had been designed in a period of relative economic stability and was not fitted for such tumultuous times. The economic crisis of 1976 and the advent of Mrs Thatcher's Conservative government in 1979 was to change all that.

The changing rules of the game – Plowden's legacy

During the early 1960s government departments were asked to produce fairly crude estimates of their spending four years ahead in constant prices. A new expenditure division in the Treasury was created to co-ordinate and develop these forecasts. Total claims from spending departments were set against expected growth targets in the economy to check their feasibility. A new minister, the Chief Secretary to the Treasury, was appointed, and a new system was created to oversee the whole exercise. Called the

Public Expenditure Survey, it gave its name to the whole process – PES.

By the time of the economic crisis of 1967 it was clear the system had failed to prevent an even more rapid rise in public spending than before 1961. The plans had been based on over-optimistic assumptions of the potential growth of the economy and hence of revenue. From 1968 onwards, the growth targets became somewhat lower but continued to be too optimistic. The estimates from each department became more detailed and were spelt out for each of the future years. The results of the whole exercise were published in an annual White Paper and have been published every year since. In 1970 the Heath government sought to fit in the third piece of the Plowden jigsaw – the efficiency function.

In a White Paper issued shortly after it came to office, the new Conservative administration reviewed the development of the PES system to date and argued that there should be regular in-depth reviews of spending programmes, on both a departmental and an interdepartmental basis. What emerged was a system that also became known by its initials, PAR – programme analysis and review. To help administer it, there was a body called the Central Policy Review Staff (CPRS) which reviewed policies interdepartmentally. It was a small group attached to the Cabinet Office, comprising mainly younger civil servants, academics and other outsiders seconded for brief periods. Some important issues were explored, from race relations and pre-school policy to issues of population change and the family, and the CPRS sought to establish a formal regular examination by Cabinet of social policy issues. It was called the Joint Framework for Social Policy (CPRS, 1975; Klein, 1988). It was not to last for long. Thatcher's administration eventually wound up both the PAR system and CPRS. (For an account and evaluation of the work of the CPRS by two people involved see Blackstone and Plowden, 1988.)

Individual departments also developed a series of service planning systems. The aim was to ensure that local authorities developed plans that were consistent with the government's spending target (Glennerster, 1981b).

By the mid-1970s, therefore, the major elements of the Plowden reforms were in place and had developed in sophistication; yet they failed, at that point, to prevent the fastest ever growth in public spending outside war-time. The reason lay in the large economic changes that were affecting the world economy, the government's own responses and the particular nature of the new machinery of control. In a turbulent economy, the planning and control functions turned out to be mutually incompatible. Departments' spending plans, which were bargained over and eventually published in the annual public expenditure White Papers, were expressed in constant prices or 'volume terms'. They excluded the effect of any general rise in prices or any rises specific to that service. Thus, if education were promised a rise in its allocation at 2 per cent a year, this would mean a real increase in its capacity to employ teachers or build schools of 2 per cent a year. Having fixed these 'volume' targets at the beginning of its period of office, a government would seek to hold to them even if the economy expanded faster or more slowly than expected, or if prices or wages rose. In these circumstances it was necessary for central government to pass supplementary estimates asking Parliament to vote more money to the Health Service or to local authorities. Public spending came to take a larger share of the nation's resources even though each service was keeping to its real volume target. It gave a degree of certainty to public sector managers in the short run, but when the tax costs began to mount governments resumed their sudden cuts – just the situation Plowden had hoped to avoid. The planning function, as the Treasury saw it, had been performed too well to the detriment of its control function. Growing criticism was once more reflected in a report by a House of Commons committee, this time the General Subcommittee of the Expenditure Committee (HC 718, 1975–6), and the economic crisis of 1976 brought another set of important changes.

The 1976 adaptions

The changes which the Treasury introduced in this period reasserted the primacy of the control function (Wright, 1980; Else and Marshall, 1981). The first and most important change was the general introduction of *cash limits*. This was a figure of actual spending that a department was not to overshoot in the coming year whatever happened to prices or the wages and salaries of its employees in the interim. In translating the original constant price figure for the department that had appeared in the public expenditure White Paper into the new cash limit figure, the Treasury estimated the likely price and wage increases for the year ahead. However, if these pay norms were breached or prices rose more than expected, the level of service was to be cut back to meet the cash limit. In 1976–7 this is precisely what happened. Prices rose more than expected, departments even so kept well inside their new limits, and the result was a cut in real spending of 2.5 per cent. This was a much larger cut than the government had planned, larger indeed than the announced cuts that had caused so much controversy in 1976.

Not all departments' spending could be cash limited. Some items of expenditure like supplementary benefit or sickness benefit are demand-led commitments. The DSS has a statutory duty to pay benefits of a given level approved by Parliament regardless of the level of sickness or unemployment that may arise in any one year. Altogether about 40 per cent of public spending was directly cash limited. Local authority spending *per se* is not included but grants to local authorities and their total capital spending are. Thus, directly and indirectly, over half of public spending was covered by cash limits.

The second innovation that flowed from the 1976 crisis was complementary to the first – a new *financial information system* (FIS). This is a regular return of departmental spending which gives the Treasury early warning of the possibility that a department may overshoot its cash limit.

The third innovation was to *limit the length of the planning cycle* – to reduce the period over which government published spending targets, at least in any detail. That period now covers the year ahead and two succeeding years in broader outline.

The present system of control: cash planning

When the Conservatives returned to power in 1979 they further revised the PES system. From 1982 the two separate sets of targets used by the Labour government – volume and cash limit – were abolished. From then on the figures used in the White Paper to set targets for future spending were set in 'cash terms'. That is, they were the actual amount of money that health authorities, for example, would get regardless of actual price or pay movements in the interim. The cash target includes a modest estimate for future pay and inflation, but this is usually too low. Moreover, instead of these cash limits being set one year ahead they are now to cover the *whole* planning period; that is, three years ahead. The Treasury set out what it saw as the advantages in the following way:

1. Ministers discuss the cash that will actually be spent, and therefore what will have to be financed by taxation or borrowing, instead of talking about 'funny money' – numbers which could be misleadingly different from the resultant cash spent.
2. Expenditure figures can be related more readily to the revenue projection, so that 'finance [can] determine expenditure and not expenditure finance'.
3. Changes in public sector costs are brought into the discussion. The previous constant price system did not bring out the effect of, for example, the rapid relative rise in public service pay in 1979–80 resulting from the Clegg Commission and other comparability awards.
4. Previously, the 'volume' plans – that is, plans in constant prices – were regarded by spending managers as entitlements, carried forward from year to year regardless of what was happening to costs. This meant that programme managers had little incentive to adapt their expenditures in response to increasing relative costs, except in the short term in response to the annual cash limits.
5. The decisions in the annual survey, as they relate to the year ahead, can be translated directly into the cash limits and estimates presented to Parliament, without revaluation from one price basis to another (HM Treasury, 1981).

By 1990–1 about 46 per cent of planned public expenditure was covered by cash limits. The system of cash planning introduced in 1982 remained fundamentally unchanged for the next decade, but see below.

Spending departments suffered a concomitant set of disadvantages. For the system to work at all smoothly from their point of view, the estimates of inflation built into the Treasury's cash target for their department must be accurate. If the Treasury underestimates the level of inflation, as it has every incentive to do, departments will be forced to cut their spending further in real terms to keep within the limits. No spending department can be sure what the figures in the White Paper will mean for its capacity to pay school teachers or run hospitals. The spending targets in the White Paper thus turn out to be unhelpful for long-term planning purposes. Once more the rules of the game had swung the Treasury's way.

Not only is it impossible now to tell what the figures for the *future* will actually mean for the service, but even the informed observer or MP cannot tell what *has* been happening. Past detailed service expenditure figures merely show the actual cash sums paid, uncorrected for price changes. A summary table in one of the appendices to the White Paper does show past overall spending department by department, deflated by an average price index – the GDP deflator. The Treasury call this 'real terms' spending. This shows how far general price inflation has eroded the level of spending shown in the detailed cash figures. It does *not* show how far price increases specific to the service have affected the service's capacity to sustain the *volume* of services provided.

The difference between cash, real and volume terms is illustrated in Figure 4.1. The top line shows the increase in the cash sums spent on the NHS. The much slower rise in the middle graph line shows what happens if you deflate this first figure by the general rise in prices in the economy. The lowest line shows what happens if you deflate by the rise in NHS salaries and prices.

The control cycle

Prior to 1993 the cycle began each spring (see Table 4.1). At the beginning of the year the Treasury set out the basis upon which departments were to roll forward and revise the last round of spending plans. The spending departments sent in their revisions, which were examined, pared down in discussions and presented to ministers in June and July. At the same time ministers received the Treasury's best guess about the country's economic prospects. Looking at the total expenditure and the economic projections, ministers decided broadly and in a preliminary way what limits had to be set for spending in the next financial year (then about nine months away). During the summer and into September and

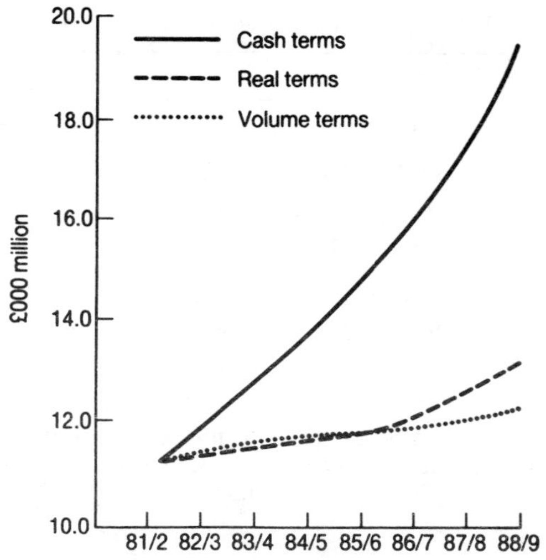

Figure 4.1 NHS expenditure in cash, real and volume terms (Source: Mayston, 1990)

October officials from spending departments and the Treasury, with ministers when the going got tough, tried to limit their spending within the overall cash target. These negotiations are called 'bilaterals'. Then the ministers were faced with the Treasury's 'autumn forecast'. With this and a preliminary draft of the expenditure plans, ministers had to go on arguing until they reach an agreed compromise. Finally, ministers who could not agree were sent before a 'Star Chamber' of non-spending ministers or ministers who have 'settled'. The result – an outline of public spending limits for the next financial year – was published by the Chancellor, together with the economic forecast, as an 'Autumn Statement'.

Departments could then begin work on putting detailed estimates to Parliament. The Department of the Environment could set the total grant for local authorities, and announce it. NHS treasurers or finance officers could be told how much they were likely to get. Prior to 1991 the details were published in a single Public Expenditure White Paper, albeit in different sections. Since then individual departments have each published their own spending plans for the next three years, approved by the Treasury.

Table 4.1 The PES planning timetable, prior to 1993

Month	Event
January	Postmortem on previous survey
February	—
March	Treasury issues guidelines for survey
April	Baselines agreed
May	Departments submit material on output, performance and value for money
June	Bids submitted by department Treasury analyses bids
July	Chief Secretary's proposals to Cabinet for overall survey totals Cabinet decides totals
August	—
September	Bilaterals start
October	Star Chamber meets to determine difficult cases Cabinet decisions on departmental totals
November	Autumn Statement
December	Departments submit estimates to Parliament NHS and local government hear about grant implications
January	Departmental public expenditure plans published
March	Budget

About the middle of March came the Budget with proposals to raise the taxes needed to finance this spending. From 1993 the budget will be moved back to December and combined with the expenditure plans (see below). The spending control cycle will remain largely unchanged.

Adaptations to cash planning 1982–92

Though the fundamentals of cash planning remained, the Treasury had to adapt and refine its strategy through the 1980s in response to the pressure it was under to remain ahead of the game (Thain and Wright, 1990).

Public sector pay and the unpredictability of pay settlements have always posed a major threat to public expenditure control. Pay constitutes two-thirds of all current expenditure. The move to cash planning meant that even if health service or teachers' unions succeeded in reaching a pay settlement, there was no likelihood it would be funded in full, except by the NHS or local authorities making cuts in their non-salary budgets or employing fewer staff. For the first five years of cash planning the Treasury put a 'pay factor' in its cash target. Public sector negotiators knew the consequences if they went over that limit, though in practice the Treasury might relent a little with groups like nurses and fund part of the extra settlement. The 'pay factor' was always set unrealistically low as an opening gambit by the Treasury to keep pay expectations down and to put a further squeeze on public services. Then, after five years, the Treasury tightened the rules again. It set separate cash limits for each central government department for pay and allied costs. It thus prevented settlements over the norm which could be financed by savings elsewhere.

The Contingency Reserve has always existed as a cushion to meet unexpected demands for spending without breaking the overall planning target for public spending set in the White Papers. In the early years this had always been kept small, but in the 1980s the Treasury increased it from the traditional 2 per cent of planned public spending in the 1976–9 period to over 6 per cent in 1990–1. This squeezed individual planned targets even more and came to be used to finance items like pay or local authority overspend. Central government knew this would happen but did not want to admit to it in its plans.

Local authorities have presented the Treasury with a particular problem from the outset. Though having no statutory power to control local authority spending in total, the Plowden reforms included local authority spending as part of public expenditure. It was, therefore, in theory, subject to PES overall limits. We describe in detail in the next chapter the consequent growing controls on local spending. However, from the 1990 White Paper (Cm 1021, 1990) the Treasury gave up including in the total of planned public expenditure that part of local authority expenditure which is locally financed through local taxes and charges. The logic – that the Treasury could not be expected to control something that was for local councils' electorates to decide –

finally sank in, not least because the Treasury had so regularly failed to keep them to their limits.

This was not before *other* constraints on local revenue raising and spending had been put in place (see Chapter 5). It is important to realise, however, that the planning totals in the Public Expenditure White Paper from 1990 onwards *exclude* an element of local spending which they used to include. Central government grants to local authorities are part of the published totals.

Cuts and controls – did they succeed?

Cuts in services

It was the Labour government of 1976 that first broke the trend of public spending taking a regularly higher share of total national income. The tight hold was maintained by Thatcher's government. As in previous economic crises, capital expenditure was hit hardest, but on a scale not experienced before – cut to a half or to a third of previous levels in some cases. Local authority housing expenditure suffered most. On current spending education was essentially stabilised in real volume terms for over a decade, and the rates of growth in health and personal social services slowed down or ceased for some periods. It was social security expenditure that increased, un-cash limited and driven by unemployment. The break with the past is most clearly seen in Figure 4.2.

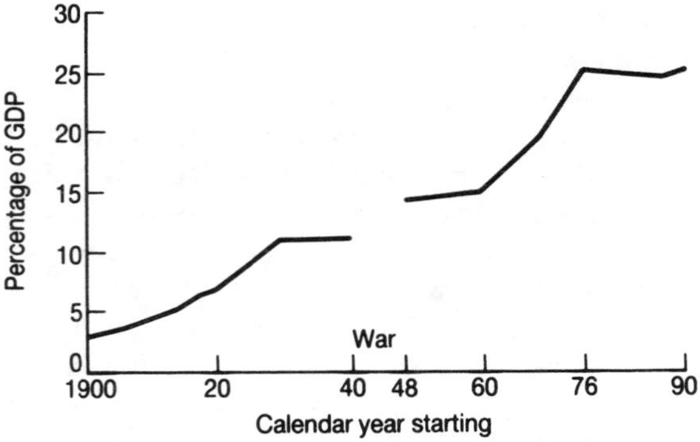

Figure 4.2 The cost of social services as a percentage of GDP in the United Kingdom 1900–90 (Source: Hills, 1990)

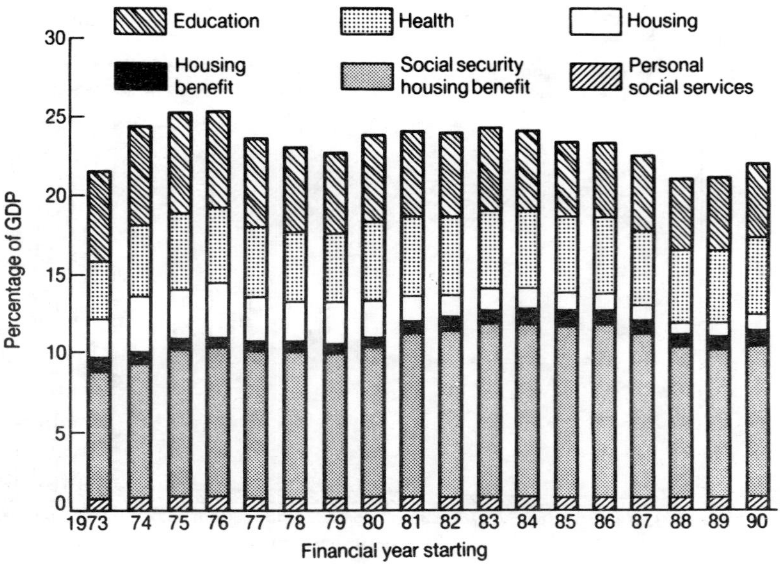

Figure 4.3 Public spending on welfare as a percentage of GDP in the United Kingdom 1973–90 (Source: J. Hills, LSE Welfare State Programme (Unpublished Figures.))

The year in which social welfare spending's rising share of the national income stopped rising was 1976. Figure 4.3 shows the recent story in more detail. It was not until 1990 that the share of the GDP going to the welfare state began to show a small rise.

Figure 4.4 shows how the absolute amounts spent on the services covered in this book stagnated in real terms after 1974. Only cash benefits grew. After decades of regular service growth this was a traumatic change.

The changes in public spending on welfare services since 1974 are examined in detail, with the outcomes for each service, in Hills (1990) and summarised in subsequent chapters in this book.

Less than Thatcher hoped

While the Callaghan Labour government broke the pattern of growth in 1976, by the end of its term, in 1978/9, it was planning to expand public expenditure again in line with economic growth.

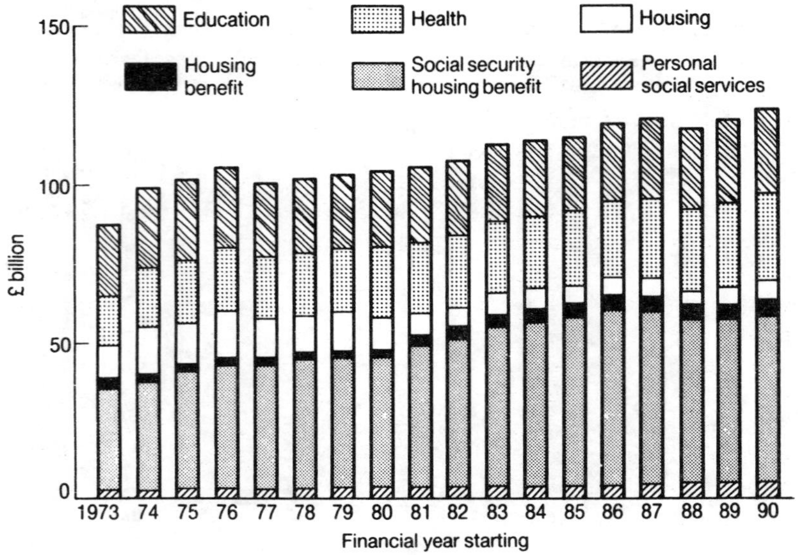

Figure 4.4 Public spending on welfare in the United Kingdom in £ billion (1990–1 prices) 1973–90 (Source: J. Hills, LSE Welfare State Programme (Unpublished Figures.))

The first Conservative Public Expenditure White Paper in November 1979 (Cmnd 7746, 1979) set its sights on a really radical change. It opened with a diagnosis of the United Kingdom's economic ills which put public expenditure 'at the heart of Britain's present economic difficulties' (p. 1). In the new government's first full review, presented in the 1980 Public Expenditure White Paper (Cmnd 7866, 1980), the stated intention was to reduce real term spending by 4 per cent in four years. The aim was 'not merely to halt the growth of public expenditure but to progressively reduce it' (p. 5).

It was to fail, partly because defence and law and order spending were committed to grow, but also because social security spending rose so rapidly, despite cuts in benefit levels. The other side of the government's economic policy, monetary restraint and unemployment, made its public spending goal difficult to achieve, so the goal was modified. The aim, after 1984, was to keep spending 'broadly at its present levels' in real terms and reduce it as a percentage of the gross domestic product (Cmnd 9428, 1985). As the economy grew that happened, although the goal of stable real spending can only be said to have been achieved up to 1990 if the returns from privatisation are included to reduce the total – essentially a cheat.

According to the government's figures (Cm 1021, 1990) public expenditure as a share of the GDP was 43.5 per cent in 1979/80. It rose to 46.75 per cent in 1982/3. It then fell to 39 per cent in 1990/1 (excluding privatisation proceeds in each case).

The 1990 White Paper (Cm 1021, 1990) contained another shift of the goal posts. Now, the figures reveal, the aim was to keep public spending roughly *constant* as a percentage of GDP. In short, public spending was to rise in real terms but no faster than the GDP. That was before John Major replaced Margaret Thatcher. The 1992 Budget Statement suggested that the government was contemplating an *increase* in the percentage of the GDP public expenditure would take – from 40 per cent in 1990/1 to 43 per cent in 1992/3 and 1993/4.

The ambitious goal of reducing *real* total public expenditure in *absolute terms* was never achieved. In 1991 total spending in real terms was about 18 per cent higher than in 1979. However, in breaking the presumption of growth and in forcing services to keep within a barely increased *volume* of resources, the Treasury had succeeded. It was no mean achievement, even if part of the success has been achieved by an almost continuous redefinition of the basis of the figures on which the White Papers are based (Thain and Wright, 1990).

Some criticisms and alternatives

Reforming PES again

Critics of the PES system in its latest form vary according to political persuasion. Those on the right believe it has been insufficiently successful in its control function. They argue that the main culprits have been local authorities and that their spending must be further curtailed. I shall discuss this position further in the next chapter. There are also those who would like to see changes that would redress the balance towards the Plowden objective of social planning (Walker, 1984).

The control function

The complete dominance of the control function over the planning function in the 1980s made service planning and efficient management extremely difficult. Cash limits are a healthy discipline for departments so long as they are realistic and are not used as a form of clandestine cuts in services. Since cash limits are set in advance of wage agreements and since wages and salaries are the largest element in social service costs, it is not easy to achieve 'realism' in the cash limits without some long-term understanding with the fairly cowed public sector unions about the scale of wage awards. If the latter is not likely to be a permanent feature, machinery for achieving some long-term pay agreements in the public sector becomes important for achieving efficient control (Heald, 1983).

The planning function

The publication of volume terms figures for past spending would make public discussion better informed. We tried to do this in Hills (1990).

Some longer-term, less detailed targets and stabler financial regimes for services are as necessary as Plowden recognised them to be. The continual changing of public expenditure targets in *real* terms, and the confusing changes in grant systems, have played havoc with local authorities' and services' capacity to plan.

The efficiency function

Blackstone and Plowden (1988) argue that the government was wrong to abandon CPRS and the PAR procedures, which provided the means to reassess programmes in depth from time to time.

Heald (1983) argues that the PES system should be 'rescued from despair and cynicism' by adopting some of these reforms and others. (Students should read especially Chapter 8 in his book.) Two more far-reaching reforms are now discussed.

Budget reform in 1993

The UK Parliament is unusual in considering expenditure separately from taxation. Public expenditure in Whitehall and the consideration of the public spending White Paper by Parliament were quite separate from the Budget discussions on taxation. This procedure made it impossible to discuss the government's income and expenditure in relation to one another, as any firm or household would do. In other countries the 'Budget' means a combination of income (that is, tax) and expenditure decisions. In a white paper on Budgetary Reform (Cm 1867, 1992) the Government proposed to combine the publication of expenditure plans with tax proposals as a new combined Budget in December. This will be done from December 1993.

Including tax expenditure

None of these changes fully gets to grips with the central weakness of the PES system as far as social policy is concerned – the failure to integrate tax expenditures into the system in an explicit way. It is the 'hidden face of public expenditure' (Hogwood, 1989). The consequences have been as follows:

1. The progressivity of the tax structure has been largely undermined so that the poor pay a very high price for their welfare.
2. More resources are devoted to aspects of fiscal welfare than to cash benefits or service delivery and they are allocated in ways that pervert what individual service policies are seeking to achieve.

The decisions that the Chancellor takes, to extend or limit the tax advantages people derive from certain life styles, amount to specific social policies. They may encourage home ownership, or private health insurance or personal pensions. They are not, however, part of the PES process. Indeed, even Cabinet ministers may not hear of them until they are told on the morning of Budget day by the Chancellor. The consequences are, firstly, poorly debated and largely hidden. There is no capacity to discuss a trade-off of £1,000 million between tax relief on pensions and higher cash old age pensions. Yet the tax consequences are essentially the same. Secondly, because a tax allowance reduces the total income on which a person pays tax, it has a greater value to a high-income person on a high marginal rate of tax than to a low-income one who may, if he or she pays no tax, not gain at all.

During the 1980s social policy-related tax expenditures tilted even more sharply in the direction of the non-poor. Housing expenditure on council tenants was cut but owner occupiers gained substantially, despite the limit imposed on the value of mortgage interest that could be claimed against tax (see Chapter 13). The main reason lay in the rising level of interest repayments home owners had to make. Private pension scheme tax concessions grew as part of deliberate policy. At the other end of the income spectrum, various social security benefits that were once relieved of taxation ceased to be so in the mid-1980s.

Despite the fact that Titmuss (1958) was one of the first commentators to appreciate the significance of tax expenditure, the United Kingdom has done little to tackle the problem. Other countries have been more enterprising. In what was West Germany some integration of tax expenditures into the Budget cycle was introduced in 1967. Budget estimates have to include their purpose and cost alongside the traditional expenditure items devoted to like functions – pension tax relief alongside pension expenditure. The US Federal Budget does something similar. Canada has gone further and the US Congressional Budget Office (1983) has been urging the US Congress to go in the same direction. The Canadian Parliament from 1980 on has discussed and voted on an estimates figure (an 'envelope') that includes both tax expenditures and traditional spending authorisation. This forces Parliament to consider, for example, the balance between housing subsidies and housing tax allowances, and a ceiling is put on the value of the total – tax relief cannot just grow without anyone noticing. France has gone some way towards the Canadian pattern. Separate votes are required for each item of spending and tax relief and they are published together. A reform of the PES system on the same lines is perfectly feasible.

Further reading

The following texts discuss the public expenditure control process and its reform in more detail:

Heclo, H. and Wildavsky, A. (1981), *The Private Government of Public Money* (2nd edn), London: Macmillan. Still the best and most readable account of the Whitehall process of expenditure control, though out of date in detail.

Heald, D. (1983), *Public Expenditure*, Oxford: Martin Robertson. Puts forward a set of reform proposals.

Hills, J. (1990) (ed.), *The State of Welfare: The welfare state in Britain since 1974*, Oxford: Clarendon Press. The most detailed account of public expenditure trends and service outcomes since 1974.

Hogwood, B.W. (1989), 'The hidden face of public expenditure: trends in tax expenditure in Britain', *Policy and Politics*, **17**, no. 2, pp. 111–30.

Likierman, A. (1988), *Public Expenditure: Who really controls it and how*, Harmondsworth: Penguin. The most up-to-date accessible account of the process of control.

Thain, C. and Wright, M. (1990), 'Coping with difficulty: the Treasury and public expenditure, 1979–89', *Policy and Politics*, **18**, no. 1, pp. 1–15. Brings the story of changes in Treasury control nearly up to date.

Walker, A. (1982b) (ed.), *Public Expenditure and Social Policy*, London: Heinemann. Discusses the first round of cuts in the early 1980s and has a chapter on each area of social policy. Now out of date in detail, but still useful.

Wildavsky, A. (1979), *The Politics of the Budgetary Process* (3rd edn), Boston: Little Brown. Gives the classic pluralist description of budgeting.

Wright, M. (1980) (ed.), *Public Spending Decisions: Growth and restraint in the 1970s*, London: Allen & Unwin. Discusses PES developments, especially the mid-1970s' changes and the reasons for them.

CHAPTER 5

CONTAINING THE LOCALS

Political scientists and economists differ in the views they hold about the extent to which central government ought to control the activities of local government. Actual practice changed fast in the 1980s as central government's desire to cut public spending overwhelmed all other considerations. The overall effect of these changes was largely to remove local authorities' financial independence.

Alternative theories of central–local relations

Four ways of thinking about the relationship between central and local government in Britain have been distinguished (Rhodes, 1979).

Local councils are the creatures of Parliament and they gain their powers only from Parliament. Nevertheless, historically, local authorities have had considerable independence, more at some times than others (Foster *et al.*, 1980). The *partnership model* reflected this tradition. It is still to be found in the rhetoric of ministers' speeches and circulars. Central government is there to set the boundaries to local government activity, to give advice, to set minimum standards and give financial assistance, especially to poorer areas, but local authorities have a distinct responsibility to develop services in their own way, setting their own priorities. Partnership theory stresses the following beliefs:

1. That a plurality of political authority is desirable, especially for such services as police and education.
2. That it is important to use local knowledge and reflect local preferences.
3. That to make these virtues real, local authorities must have significant independent sources of local revenue. This point was authoritatively argued by the Layfield Committee on local government finance (1976).
4. That there is, in practice, a large measure of consensus about the goals of social policy, so a degree of genuine independence can be tolerated by central government.

Proponents of the *agency model* argue that the partnership view is no more than rhetoric, for the following reasons:

1. The United Kingdom is a unitary and not a federal state, thus if central government is really serious about any policy it will get its way (Griffith, 1965).
2. Politicians are elected on party manifestos which have, increasingly since the Second World War, contained social policy commitments that must be carried out by local authorities but are often contentious. No minister can afford to fail to carry through his or her party's pledges even if this means forcing local authorities to comply – by creating comprehensive schools or selling council houses. Hence it is appropriate that local councils are dependent on central funds.
3. Since local authorities account for a quarter of all public expenditure, central government must control their spending. The more it wants to limit spending, the less freedom local councils can have to raise their own revenue.

Rejecting both views as over-simple, Rhodes (1979) produced a *competitors'* model. Central and local government compete for maximum advantage and possess different resources. While central government holds some of the cards, local authorities hold others, more in some areas of responsibility than others. Statu tory power and financial leverage lie with the centre, but local political legitimacy, accepted 'rules of the game' and professional knowledge lie locally. This model accepts the virtues of plurality and local independence, and argues that a competitive local government is in the end a more efficient system; nevertheless, it does not believe consensus on policy is realistic or desirable. Again, financial independence is crucial (Jones and Stewart, 1983).

The Marxist *conflict model* saw central government as the agent of capital class interests. It therefore sought to cut spending by forcing local authorities to reduce services. This would produce local protest and push more responsibilities to the centre, thus increasing government 'overload' (Gough, 1979; Offe, 1984).

In the 1980s the open conflict predicted by Marxists did result, but it did not end as they hoped. It was followed by a series of statutes that reduced local authorities to a *minimalist role* (Glennerster *et al.*, 1991). The essence of the Conservative government's case, as it evolved, was as follows:

1. Central government has a duty to contain local public expenditure and to determine what are the limits to any individual council's spending.
2. Only by centralising power can the role of the state be diminished.
3. Many services do not need to be *provided* by local authorities; they could and should be put out to competitive tender to be provided by private contractors – from refuse collection to school meals provision and old people's homes.

Increasing financial control

The years of growth

In the period broadly spanning the years 1948 to 1975, central governments of both parties gradually extended local authorities' social service powers, or encouraged them to use to the full powers they had already been given – achieving secondary education for all, creating a national pattern of further education, developing services for the elderly, sustaining a substantial housing programme. The emphasis differed between parties but the broad expansionary thrust held. Central government not only mapped out extended statutory territory for local councils to develop, but also provided a large financial incentive for them to cultivate the new territory.

In the early post-war years, *matching* or *percentage* grants by the centre met a share of approved local spending. *Unit* grants were given for housing – so much per house built.

Even after many of the separate grants were amalgamated in 1958 into a single general grant, government continued to expand its financial support quite rapidly to make it possible for local councils to fulfil the pledges which national parties frequently gave in general elections – to replace slums or old schools, to reduce the size of classes, and much else. Indeed, national politicians actually took much credit for the houses and schools built 'under the Conservatives' or 'by the Labour government'. It was in local politicians' interests to take these grants and develop services too. (For an account of this period of expansion, see Foster *et al.*, 1980, Chapter 4.) Yet the growth of local services promoted by central government in this way was not accompanied by any reform of local finance. The rates continued to be, in the words of the Layfield Committee (1976), 'an inflexible and politically sensitive local tax base'. The central government thus came to fund an increasing share of local services (see Layfield Committee, 1976, Chapter 5).

This expansionist financial relationship made it possible for central government ministers to use the rhetoric of partnership, while actually bribing local authorities to act as their agents. Layfield (1976) criticised this confusion and said that the centre must make up its mind whether it wanted to adopt a centralist or localist view. It must either be accountable for the consequences of its growing financial involvement, or give local authorities a larger independent source of finance – a local income tax or sales tax – and give local councils genuine financial accountability.

The party's over

The financial crisis of 1976 changed all this. Central government now sought to reduce local spending as part of its general public expenditure strategy. The Treasury saw local councils as part of that strategy just as much as spending departments in Whitehall or the nationalised industries – a very clear 'agency' view. Local authorities did not see things that way.

The Labour government between 1974 and 1979 took a number of steps that strengthened the centre's financial control, as follows:

1. It applied its new cash limits to approvals of local capital spending and to local grants. Instead of increasing grants during the year if prices rose or wage settlements reached were over the original target, the grant was fixed whatever happened.
2. The total share of local spending met by the centre was allowed to fall, putting more of the burden on the local ratepayer and giving local councils a financial and political incentive to economise. The share of relevant expenditure to be covered by central rate support grant fell from 66.5 per cent in 1975/6 to 61 per cent in 1979/80. The proportion of actual spending met was even lower.
3. A formal means of reaching 'gentlemen's agreements' between central and local government was created through the agency of consultative councils on local government finance.

The new Conservative administration in 1979 wished to go further. The Local Government Planning Act of 1980 introduced major changes in the structure of the rate support grant, as follows:

1. The grant was to be distributed between authorities on the basis of a set of detailed standard expenditure figures, set by central government for each service after discussion with local authorities on the consultative council.
2. Local authorities would get a *lower* rate of grant the more they let spending rise above these levels.
3. On top of this disincentive a *second* system of rougher *targets* and *penalties* was introduced, based on a council's previous spending. It aimed to fine or penalise authorities which did not actually cut their spending.

When this last measure failed to force some authorities sufficiently into line, the Conservative government, in 1984, introduced a measure called *rate capping* that made it illegal for authorities designated by the Secretary of State to levy more than a certain amount in rates, their only form of independent finance. When both the systems of targets and rate capping were enforced, a local authority was effectively told by central government the maximum it could spend. This amounted to the most profound change in the constitutional and financial relationship between central and local government since local government was introduced in the nineteenth century.

Central government loses patience

Local authorities did not respond in the way the government had hoped. Those, mainly Conservative councils, that were spending below the standard spending levels were tempted to spend more and gain more grant; those that were spending so much that government was giving them no grant could suffer no more penalties; and all kinds of ingenious methods were used to avoid the penalties through creative accounting. There were a series of confrontations with authorities, like Liverpool, faced with threats of central government taking over direct control of services. The government finally decided that the only solution was to introduce a form of local taxation that was very visible and unpopular to levy. So the *poll tax* was born (see below).

The central levers of power today

The legacy of decades of growing central financial control can be seen in the central levers of power that now exist (see Figure 5.1).

Statute

Local authorities can do nothing that is not expressly set out in some Act of Parliament. In this they differ from local authorities in many other countries, which have power to do anything which is not forbidden by the constitution or the national law. Every action of a social worker must be justifiable under some section of an Act of Parliament. In fact no recent government has reduced local authorities' statutory duties, only the money to perform them.

Legal action can be taken against an authority if it either goes beyond its powers – that is, acts *ultra vires* – or does not fulfil its duties – its *mandamus*. If a local authority persistently refuses to fulfil its statutory obligations, its powers can be taken over by

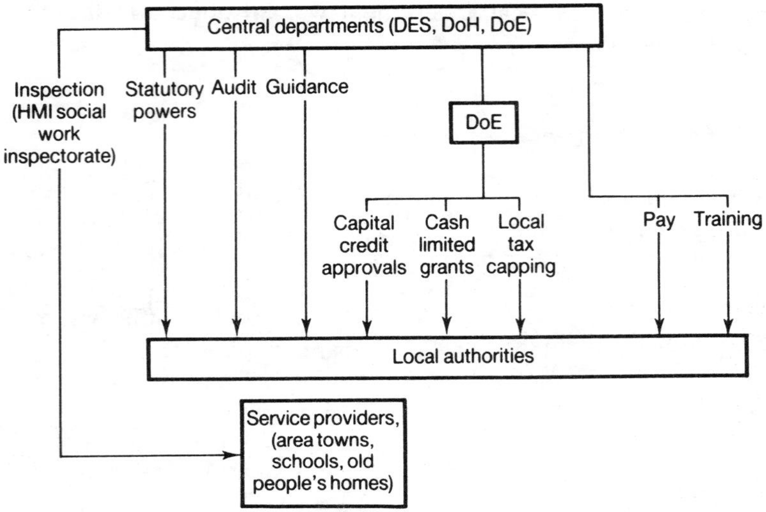

Figure 5.1 Central resource levers

officers of central government. This has happened in the case of civil defence powers on a number of occasions, and with the implementation of the Conservative Housing Finance Act at Clay Cross in the early 1970s. The Greater London Council (GLC) was ruled by the courts and finally by the House of Lords to be acting beyond its powers in lowering its public transport fares in the 'Fares fair' campaign of the early 1980s.

Local authorities were not always subject to such legal control. During part of the Middle Ages, and certainly between 1688 and 1835, local boroughs and justices of the peace had considerable freedom. The strict limitation of local authorities' powers to specific parliamentary approval grew up almost by accident in the nineteenth century as a result of Railway Companies and other private organisations abusing their powers under private Acts of Parliament. The crucial decision, indeed, concerned the National Manure Company (Robson, 1954). The courts ruled that such companies only had the powers specifically granted to them by Parliament, and the ruling was extended to local authorities despite the fact that they were independently elected, not mere private corporations. At various times proposals have been made to give local authorities general enabling powers akin to those of continental authorities – power to do anything not forbidden them.

Audit

Auditors are normally concerned with ensuring that the accounts of a firm are an accurate record of its financial position and that employers or directors have not been absconding with the funds or 'fiddling the books'. Local authorities must have their accounts vetted in the same way, but district auditors – appointed by central government – have additional functions. It has been *their* job to see that local councils do not spend money on activities which cannot be justified by statute.

The functions of the district auditor were reviewed by the Layfield Committee (1976) and revised by the Local Government Finance Act, 1982. This set up an Audit Commission for local authorities in England and Wales. It appoints auditors whose powers have been extended significantly. Section 15 of the Act sets out these powers. The first two incorporate existing practice, the third extends it. (Similar functions are performed in Scotland.)

1. Auditors must ensure that a local authority's spending falls within its statutory powers.
2. They must ensure that 'proper practices' are observed in drawing up their accounts.
3. They must assure themselves that the authority has made 'proper arrangements for securing economy, efficiency and effectiveness' in the use of resources. Section 26 gives the Commission power to undertake studies designed to enable it to make recommendations for improving authorities' 'economy, efficiency and effectiveness'. Such investigations have given rise to wide-ranging reports like those on housing management (Audit Commission, 1986a) and community care (Audit Commission, 1986b).

Guidance by circular

Every year all government departments send a score or more of circular letters to local authorities. The contents may vary from technical advice to general policy pronouncements. For example, the Department of Education has circulated local education authorities with technical scientific advice to beware of roofs containing a certain kind of cement in schools built in the 1950s.

Inspection

The Victorians invented an extremely effective system of central 'quality control' and 'information feedback'. The Poor Law inspectorate and the inspectors of schools were followed by others (Griffith, 1965). They inspected standards in schools and decided whether the schools were fit to receive grants, and they reported in detail on the activities of local Poor Law Guardians. In this century, and especially in the 1950s, the inspectors' functions became more concerned with giving professional advice and spreading good practice. In the 1970s, following growing public interest in the standards of education, Her Majesty's Inspectors of Schools (HMI) stepped up their activities. The old Home Office Inspectorate disappeared in 1971 when the new social service departments came into being and was replaced by a largely advisory Social Work Service. The Barclay Committee (1982) argued for the reintroduction of a formal inspectorate, and the Social Work Inspectorate followed (see Chapter 11). One of its concerns, unlike its predecessor, is the *efficient* and *economic* pursuit of their duties by local social services departments. (For a description of the forms of inspection that currently exist see Day and Klein, 1990.)

In 1991 the Conservative government proposed to privatise one of the oldest and most respected of the inspectorates – Her Majesty's Inspectors of Schools. Local schools were to be free to buy in the services of private organisations to inspect their standards. Many doubted the objectivity of the results.

Capital rationing

Control of local authority borrowing began in the nineteenth century when central government was suspicious of the new local authorities and their potential to borrow money they could not repay. Thus the Treasury had to give permission for all borrowing undertaken by a local authority, not merely in total but for each project for which money was borrowed. This weapon of control was elaborated and refined, especially after the Second World War, following the example of the Ministry of Education (Griffith, 1965). Since local councils borrowed to finance virtually all their capital expenditure, permission to borrow was used by central departments to set the total capital spending limits for local authorities, determine national service priorities for capital spending, and set common design standards and cost yardsticks which ensured a tight degree of economy in capital projects.

Under the 1980 Local Government Planning and Land Act the old loan sanction procedure disappeared, and with it some of the detailed controls. A council's total net capital expenditure for the year was controlled, not its borrowing or its project by project spending. Money raised from selling property or land could be added. Then that too changed. Government policy swung in favour of selling council houses and other assets on a large scale and this gave councils potentially larger freedom to spend the receipts in any one year. This freedom was rapidly curtailed in the 1980s and local authorities were only allowed to spend a fraction of their receipts from sales on new building in any one year. Then in 1991 a new system of capital spending controls was introduced.

The annual capital guidelines

The public expenditure limits published after the Autumn Statement (see Chapter 4) set out target figures for local authority capital expenditure, a separate target for England, Wales and Scotland. These are set three years ahead. There is an annual capital guideline (ACG) for each main service for each local authority. Part of these totals will include a figure for capital grants made by central government for a specific purpose or project. For the most part, however, local authorities will finance their own capital spending from borrowing. The amount they can borrow for the coming year is subject to approval by central government. These annual 'credit approvals' are split between what are called basic credit approvals (BCAs), which are total figures for each service and supplementary credit approvals (SCAs) which relate to particular projects. The final element in the total annual capital guideline is the amount the local authority is presumed to spend financed out of the money received by past or current sales of property – receipts taken into account (RTIA). Central government may assign a local authority a large guideline figure for capital expenditure but also assume it will finance a lot of it from sales of council houses, for example, and hence give a small credit approval. A local council can spend *more* than its total guideline if it finances more from sales than the government assumes. It can vary service spending within the total.

The ACGs for each local authority are distributed according to the measure of 'need' for capital spending determined by the central government. The scale of these controls had therefore increased substantially in the late 1980s.

Controlling current spending – capping

Controlling current spending by local authorities has been central government's major headache ever since it decided in 1961 that *local government* expenditure was part of *public* expenditure and therefore should be controlled by the Treasury. I discuss the merits of this argument at the end of this chapter. Essentially, until the 1980s, central government had no final sanction over an individual local authority's decision to spend and therefore no way, except persuasion or financial penalties, of achieving its objective. Central government tried both strategies after 1976, as we saw earlier.

Dissatisfied with its incapacity to make councils cut spending, the government adopted a final sanction – rate capping. The 1984 Rates Act introduced a constitutional change of the utmost importance – the principle that central government could set a limit to the amount of taxation a local authority could levy. By determining a local council's grant income from the centre and setting a ceiling to a local council's revenue raising, central government acquired the capacity to set a limit on any council's spending. It did not attempt to do so for every council in the country. It set up complex criteria. If a council crossed an upper threshold implied by them it ran the risk of being capped. The introduction of the poll tax or community charge was meant to replace this unpleasant practice but it failed. Thatcher's government had to use community charge capping to limit some authorities desire to levy a high poll tax, high; that is, relative to the government's somewhat ill-defined and obscure upper limit. These sanctions were usually threatened against no more than twenty councils; these had to be named in Parliament and special powers taken. Smaller authorities with budgets of less than £15 million were excluded before 1991.

Capping council tax
Under the new council tax announced in 1991 (DoE, 1991) the Conservative government proposed keeping the power to limit councils' right to cap the tax. Indeed, in Scotland Westminster's power to cap councils had been less powerful, but that will now change. Powers to cap in Scotland will be the same as in England under the council tax which will operate from 1993.

More from grant income

From 1976 through to the introduction of the community charge in 1990, governments had tried to curb local spending by reducing central government support. In 1975/6 central government met 66.5 per cent of local spending in England and Wales. By 1989/90 the Exchequer met only 43.4 per cent, with a further 4 per cent coming from a central grant that reimbursed authorities for part of the rate rebates that they gave to poor households. The rest, 52 per cent, was income councils raised themselves from the property tax or *rates*. Just over half of that, or 28.3 per cent of their total income, came from non-domestic rates, a tax on the value of shops, offices and industrial property. Rather less, 24.2 per cent of their income, came from rates paid by ordinary householders.

The Local Government Finance Act 1988 changed that balance. Not only did the domestic rates disappear (see below) but the non-domestic rates levied on shops, offices and industry became a national tax, determined by, and collected by, central government. The revenue was then returned to local councils in the form of a grant. This effectively *increased* the share of central grants to about three-quarters of councils' income. The poll tax or community charge had to meet the remaining quarter.

In 1990 the unpopularity of the poll tax made even that levy politically unacceptable. In 1992 the government made changes that cut local taxation to about 15 per cent of revenue income. It will be true of the council tax also.

Deciding the level of central government grant

The outcome of the public expenditure round each year produces the total amount of grant income local authorities are to receive. This is called the total aggregate external finance (AEF). There is a separate AEF for England, Scotland and Wales. In 1991–2 the English total was £30,550 million, with £4,790 million for Scotland and £2,210 million for Wales. This total 'envelope', as the Treasury calls it, is made up of three different kinds of grant, as follows:

1. The largest is the *revenue support grant* (RSG). This is allocated between local authorities on the basis of their population and a complex formula. This is what central government say that councils should be spending on its services given its populations' age and social conditions. It is called its 'standard spending assessment'.
2. The next largest is the payment to councils of the non-domestic rate income discussed above – the *national non-domestic rate* (NNDR). This is set at a uniform tax rate throughout the country, pooled and reallocated – so much per adult, with an adjustment for poorer areas.
3. There is a range of *specific grants* which meet a part of the costs of certain services that are particularly important to central government. The largest of these is the police force.

Beyond these three basic grants are several transitional measures designed to ease the introduction of the community charge and the new council tax. One is an *area protection grant* which gives extra to areas that suffered a substantial reduction in income from the business rate. It also gives especial aid to poorer areas that lost a lot of income in the changeover. There is, too, a grant to assist inner London boroughs taking on education powers. There was an even more temporary grant to ease the political problems the community charge caused – the *community charge reduction scheme* (previously 'transitional relief').

The poll tax and the 'son of poll tax'

The accountability case

A succession of measures to curb local authorities' spending in the early 1980s had thus failed. The government blamed this on the fact that only half the rates were paid by domestic ratepayers. Poor households had their rates bill reduced or remitted altogether under the housing benefit scheme. The government claimed that out of 36 million voters only 18 million actually paid rates. Voters were agreeing to high rates bills knowing that others would pay, the argument ran. This was largely specious. It took the head of household – the husband, usually – to be the tax payer and assumed that wives, for example, were somehow uninterested in the tax bill or did not contribute to it. In pointing to the large element of rates paid by local industry or commerce, the government had a stronger case.

The government concluded that if local voters were to appreciate the consequences of voting for councils that wished to spend more on local services every voter should be faced with the consequential bill – even those on low incomes. This would make local councils properly accountable to their local electorates.

Rates unpopular

Rates were unpopular. Although amounting to no more than 3–4 per cent of the average household's income, the rates bill arrived on people's door mat as a single lump sum annual charge. Even if paid in instalments it was very visible.

It was not directly related to households' capacity to pay. The more valuable the house, the higher the bill, but people's incomes do not necessarily match the value of their house. Some poor people live in houses that have become valuable through changes in the local property market. As we shall see, there may be good economic reasons to relate tax to property values, but this mismatch was perceived as unfair.

Single people living in a house on their own paid as high a rate bill as a family of four, all of whom were earning and using local services. This, too, was a popular criticism of the rates. It was used to argue that all members of the household should contribute to local revenue if they used local services. In fact, there is no reason to suppose that a household with four members is more able to pay than one with a single person, especially if three of the four are dependants. Its income is the real issue.

The unpopularity of the rates, very evident in Scotland in the mid-1980s, led the government to adopt the poll tax or community charge. The case for a poll tax (Foster *et al.*, 1980) was advocatedby the right-wing think-tank, the Adam Smith Institute, in 1985, and was then elaborated and presented as a 'Green Paper', *Paying for Local Government* (DoE, 1986). The Local Government Finance Act was passed in 1988. The poll tax was introduced in Scotland in 1989 and in England and Wales in 1990. (For a sympathetic and independent account of the case for reform see King, 1990.)

Poll tax revolt

The upheaval the new system caused meant that councils had an incentive to increase the tax levy and blame the government. The government had to give local authorities a succession of higher grants to buy off opposition. The task of registering every resident and tracking their movements proved intrusive and impractical. The government ended up both being unpopular *and* paying more for local government. Above all, the principle that the Duke of Westminster should pay the same tax as someone on below average earnings, despite relief for the very poor, was simply unacceptable to a wide spectrum of the electorate. When the Conservative government came to abandon the tax after Thatcher's downfall, however, many of the Conservative Party insisted on keeping some element of the poll tax for the accountability reasons set out above. The result was the council tax. (For a detailed account of the period see Gibson, 1990; for a brief evaluation of the poll tax see Glennerster *et al.*, 1991; Smith, 1988.)

Son of poll tax

The government proposed the outlines of a new tax (DoE, 1991) to come into operation in 1993–4. It would have two elements, combining the rates and the poll tax. Like the rates the tax would be based on the value of the property. As with the old rating system the occupier, normally the head of household, would be liable to pay. Unlike the old rating system there would be no attempt to value each property in the country. Instead, properties would be placed in one of eight broad bands each relating to a national average value. The bottom band might include properties falling 50 per cent below the national average, the top band those more than twice the average. The government left unresolved how properties would be valued. There were three main contenders – the *rental value* (what the property could be rented for), a *capital value* (what it could be sold for) and *rebuilding costs* (what it would cost to replace). Only a minority of properties are rented and few at a market price. Selling prices are at a market level and more readily available. Rebuilding costs might be calculated on a rule of thumb basis but the assumptions would be relatively arbitrary.

Like the poll tax, the council tax would also take account of the number of adults in each household. The basic tax would assume there were two or more in each household. If there were only one, that person could claim a discount, as could poorer households. If rebates are extensive this takes on some aspects of an income tax too.

Critics (Hills and Sutherland, 1991) claim that the administrative gains from the banding of property values will not be that great, as those near the band limits will have an incentive to appeal. The tax will be very sensitive to the valuation principles. Because the share of local councils' income contributed is small, small changes in spending by the council or grant by government will produce big changes in tax rates. There will be a lot of losers in changing from the poll tax, which will make the new tax unpopular too. The distributional effects will be very similar to a straight switch to a property tax.

The case for a property tax

The Labour Party alternative 'fair rates' also used a property valuation with rebates for the poor but without any element that links the *number* of people in the household to its tax liability regardless of income. The case for taxing property can be made on economic and practical grounds.

Economic theory suggests that all forms of economic activity should be taxed as equivalently as possible to prevent distortions in the market. (See Chapter 7.) If one activity is not taxed and everything else is, resources tend to shift to that activity in excess of what would happen if people had free choice. With the abolition of rates, ownership and use of property became the main economic activity that was not taxed, unless it was the income of private landlords. Taken in conjunction with the tax benefits owner occupiers receive (see Chapter 13) it can be argued that this was a major economic distortion.

Property and its owners are also relatively easy to trace and tax. Rates had very low administration costs; hence the case for reintroducing some form of property tax.

Local income tax

The case for taxing income as a form of local revenue is simply that it is most directly related to the capacity to pay. The Layfield Committee (1976) thought it the most feasible and equitable form of additional local revenue.

It does have serious administrative difficulties, though, unless the whole income tax system is reformed and further computerised. At present *individuals* pay tax in each of their employments and their tax is deducted by their employer. People live in *households* often in different places from their work. Adding up everyone's several sources of income and grouping it into a household income, related to where people live and the local rate, is a major exercise that our present income tax system is incapable of doing. The introduction of a local income tax therefore requires a major reform to income tax and one that points in the opposite direction to the recent individualisation of tax – with separate assessment for husbands and wives. Some move towards a local income tax remains the policy of the Liberal Democrats and would be feasible in the long term.

The centralist and the localist cases

The centralist case

The Conservative government set out this case in 1983 (Cmnd 9008) and again in 1986 (Cmnd 9714). Constitutionally Britain is a unitary state – not a federation like the United States or the former West Germany, where separate geographical units have reserved powers and can act independently within constitutional limits. Local authorities are creatures of central government. To pretend otherwise is to confuse the constitutional position. While local participation is to be encouraged, its purpose is to give local knowledge, not to be a rival to the authority of Westminster. Variations between local areas' needs can be measured and compensated for in national grants. Indeed, it can be argued that central government can draw upon and use 'superior intelligence and knowledge' (Foster *et al.*, 1980).

The government (Cmnd 9008, 1983) summarised its economic case thus: 'Ministers are accountable to Parliament for the broad conduct of the economy . . . For the business and for the individual it is the total level of tax that matters most, not who is imposing it.' In *Paying for Local Government* (Cmnd 9714, 1986) the government said:

> 1.13 Because Governments are responsible for the overall management of the economy they have to be concerned with the amount of local authority expenditure, borrowing and taxation. Local authority borrowing has implications for the Public Sector Borrowing Requirement (PSBR), the rate of monetary growth, and interest rates.
>
> 1.17 The arguments against high levels of taxation apply just as much to local taxes.

These arguments are not self-evident and it may be worth spelling them out. The nature of the basic theoretical argument clearly differs depending on whether the economic analysis is neo-Keynesian or monetarist (Jackman, 1982).

Traditional *Keynesian* analysis required government to intervene in the economy to affect the total level of demand for goods and services, and to ensure that this level was high enough to be consistent with full employment and not so high that inflation was generated or a balance of payments crisis precipitated. Aggregate demand comprised two basic elements, investment and consumption. It was crucial for successful demand management that central government generated or contained investment to an appropriate level. Local authority capital spending was used in this way as an economic regulator throughout the Keynesian period, 1945–76, by both Conservative and Labour governments.

For *monetarists*, control of capital spending was also important because it must be financed out of public borrowing, and that affects the money supply, interest rates and inflation. However, as we have seen, central government has always had power to control capital spending and still does.

It is over current spending that the debate centres. To neo-Keynesians it matters little what local authorities spend on revenue account. Since local authorities have no power to finance revenue spending by borrowing but must cover their expenditure from taxes, their revenue spending – on salaries, equipment and so on – would appear to produce little effect on aggregate demand in the economy. If they spend more and increase the local authority's contribution to demand they have to take more from local taxpayers, thus reducing *their* demand for goods and services. It is this last step in the logic that caused disagreement. Even some Keynesians argued that higher rates or local taxes could reduce the level of private savings, thus boosting demand above the expected levels. In fact this is an empirical issue – are taxes paid out of private savings or current consumption? If we know the extent to which changes in local spending affect savings and if government has some indication of the level of overall local spending during the coming year, it could make the appropriate adjustments to overall policy. Moreover, the effect seems likely to be small.

Traditional monetarist theory is also dismissive of the need to control local spending. On strict orthodoxy, control of the money supply will be enough on its own. If this results in high interest rates, local authorities like other corporate bodies may reduce their capital spending, as the costs of borrowing rise. That financial discipline is enough. Monetarists have been hostile to Keynesian attempts at demand management in principle, arguing that they are inflationary. Thus arguments for controlling local authorities' spending would appear to weigh even less powerfully within monetarist theory than in Keynesian arguments.

The *real* basis of the Conservative government's case then turns on the proposition that taxation is bad for the economy whoever levies it. Thus it is clearly in the wider national interest to reduce the scale of the public sector, whoever controls it, and 'where there is a clash between local and national mandates the national mandate must prevail' (Michael Heseltine, in Hansard, Vol. 16, No. 37).

The localist case

Those who favour local authority independence argue that: 'National financial controls will lead to nationally run services and that is politically dangerous' (Glennerster, Power and Travers, 1991). The spread of political responsibility throughout the population to local councillors, school governors and so on informs more people about the nature of the financial choices that have to be made, and thus produces a more informed electorate. This has been a traditional argument for local and participative democracy (Pateman, 1973). The larger the scope of welfare state activities, the more force it has. 'By providing a large number of points where decisions are taken by people of different political persuasions and different backgrounds, it acts as a counterweight to the uniformity inherent in government decisions. It spreads political power' (Layfield Committee, 1976, p. 53, para. 14).

Individuals and families differ considerably in what kind of education they want for their children and what kind of care for their dependants. At least the existence of a range of alternative modes of provision as between one local authority and another widens the choice available. Local independence generates alternative and innovative models of provision.

The needs of local populations, their service objectives and the most effective ways of achieving them differ between areas. They cannot be determined nationally; only a political and administrative system that is close to the local population, and responsive to it, can match services to this diversity of preference. In economic theory the more nearly expenditure can be matched to individual preferences, the more efficient the outcome. By analogy, the more nearly individual areas can match their populations' preferences for social spending to their expenditure, the more efficient will be the overall outcome – and the less 'coerced' local people will feel (Tiebout, 1956; Foster *et al.*, 1980). This requires the capacity to make local judgements about tax levels. Poor areas or areas with manifestly larger social problems can receive extra central help.

Those who provide and administer services must be available and open to local people's complaints and grievances. The further away the centre of power, the more difficult it is to complain. If local authority members are responsible for providing services but do not have to go to their own electorate to raise the money to pay for the services, they have less incentive to make effective use of these funds. It is always possible to blame deficiencies on central government. Proper local accountability requires a substantial source of revenue, and freedom to spend that revenue or reduce it.

This was essentially the Layfield Committee's (1976) case for a localist solution. Layfield argued that the extent and complexity of central government's controls and the grant structures were such as to confuse those immediately involved and the public as to who was responsible for what. The committee concluded that comprehensibility was a necessary characteristic for democratic and accountable service administration:

> It is inevitable that arrangements may sometimes be complex and that there will be some aspects that require specialist knowledge. But the main features of the system must be comprehensible to those Members of Parliament and councillors who are not specialists and to serious commentators and interested members of the public. The requirement of accountability cannot be met unless those who are responsible to the electorate for taking decisions are capable of answering for those decisions. (para. 11, p. 52)

Further reading

The best and most comprehensive account of the history and economics of local finance is still to be found in Foster, C., Jackman, R. and Perlman, M. (1980) *Local Government Finance in a Unitary State*, London: Allen & Unwin.

See also the Layfield Committee (1976), *Local Government Finance*, Cmnd 6453, London: HMSO, including the 'Note of Reservation' by Prof. Alan Day.

Travers, T. (1986), *The Politics of Local Government Finance*, London: Allen & Unwin, gives a good account of the post-war history of grant and other changes up to the mid-1980s

For an interesting account of the failure of central government's attempt to control local spending by negotiation in the 1970s see Rhodes, R.A.W. (1986). '"Corporate bias" in central–local relations: a case study of the Consultative Council on Local Government Finance', *Policy and Politics*, **14**, no. 2, pp. 221–45.

Proposals for a shift to greater reliance on local sources of revenue are spelt out in Jones, G. and Stewart, J. (1983), *The Case for Local Government*, London: Allen & Unwin, Chapter 12. The whole book is a useful summary of the localist case.

Cmnd 9714 (1986), *Paying for Local Government*, London: HMSO, sets out the Conservative government's case for the community charge in a glossy and colourful publication.

Criticisms are to be found in:

Easam, P. and Oppenheim, C. (1989), *A Charge on the Community*, London: Child Poverty Action Group.

Smith, S. (1988), 'Should United Kingdom local government be financed by a poll tax?', *Fiscal Studies*, **9**, no. 1, pp. 18–28.

The best academic defence is King, D. (1990), 'Accountability and equity in British local finance: the poll tax', in R.J. Bennett (ed.), *Decentralisation: Local governments and markets*, Oxford: Clarendon Press.

The new Council Tax is set out in DoE (1991), *A New Tax for Local Government*, London, Edinburgh and Cardiff: DoE/Scottish Office/Welsh Office. It is criticised in Hills, J. and Sutherland, H. (1991), *Banding, Tilting, Gearing Gaining and Losing: An anatomy of the proposed council tax*, LSE Welfare State Programme Discussion Paper no. 63, London: London School of Economics.

CHAPTER 6

SETTING THE LIMITS LOCALLY

Approaches to local budgeting

In the light of the leverage exerted on them, how do local authorities decide what it is appropriate to spend?

Follow central guidance

One view of local budgeting is that officials are largely influenced by the advice they are given from Whitehall and that local councillors largely follow that lead, tempered only by party politics. The public expenditure White Papers gave finance officers a broad indication of the government's medium-term intentions for local authority spending overall and for each service up to three years ahead. What finance officers will not know until much later is how these broad intentions will work out for their own authority, given the complex and changing allocations formula in the revenue support grant. As one officer put it in a local study (Glennerster *et al.*, 1983): 'Using the public expenditure White Paper as a guide to local planning is rather like using an atlas of the world to plan a journey to Liverpool.'

Outwitting the centre

In the 1980s conflict grew in local–central politics. 'Gentlemen's agreements' and understandings between local officials and central government might work with Conservative councils but not with most Labour ones. Officers, in both Conservative and Labour areas, became more dependent on radical local politicians to determine spending strategies and whether to cut or to devise ways of outwitting central government controls. Great ingenuity was expended in creative accounting to get round overall spending limits or capital allocations. Capital expenditure was switched to current accounts, and parking meters and town halls leased to private companies. These proved only temporary respites.

Overall, more diversity in local spending priorities emerged in the 1980s within the constraints central government imposed.

Told how to do it

Central government did not seek to affect merely spending priorities but also the manner in which services were provided. This, too, was new. The Local Government Act 1988 required local councils to put out to competitive tender the provision of a wide range of local services. Only if the council's own refuse department, for example, won the contract would it be able to continue to collect refuse. This process had begun under the 1980 Local Government Planning and Land Act, when councils were required to put out to tender certain housing maintenance and highways work. Under the 1988 Act the following services must be open to competitive tender if the council wishes to permit its own service departments to participate:

1. Refuse collection.
2. Building cleaning.
3. Street cleaning and other cleaning.
4. School and other catering (such as staff canteens).
5. Grounds maintenance.
6. Vehicle maintenance.

The Secretary of State can add to the list.

If the local authority knows that it wishes to privatise and not use local authority employees at all, it does not have to go through the compulsory tender procedure. In the first round of contracts in 1989, almost 75 per cent were won by in-house or direct service organisations (Painter, 1991).

A contest between competing departments

It is also possible to view the budget battle in local authorities, much like the parallel one in Whitehall, purely as an interdepartmental contest. The main protagonists are the chief officers and chairs of the committees. The pre-1974 local authority budget cycle was like this: each committee of a local council would discuss how much it would need to spend in the coming financial year, beginning in April. This long list of detailed items, agreed by each spending committee, was submitted to a finance committee. There the chairs of the various committees would haggle to bring the total additional claims down to some acceptable consequent rate increase and to decide whose budget was to be trimmed most. The modern form of this approach has been described by Greenwood (1979). Chief officers prepare their estimates for the coming year, setting out present spending plus price increases and what would be necessary to meet existing commitments. Then a list of possible new schemes dear to committee members' hearts is added and a list of possible economies and cuts, 1 per cent, 5 per cent or 10 per cent in total. The balance between additions and cuts will depend on the financial climate and the political complexion of the council. There then follows a 'Spanish Inquisition' procedure at which individual cuts and new schemes are considered on a one-off basis in private by a small group of senior politicians. The resulting bargains are then put to the policy and resources or finance committee. It is in the course of this bartering procedure that certain simple rules of battle will emerge (see below). The toughest chief officer, or the group with the most powerful chair, will usually win.

Incrementalism, or budgeting by habit

Another view of local budgeting is that it is dominated by habit, by small additions to or subtractions from the base budget. Authors have identified considerable consistency in individual authorities' spending patterns over time despite the variation between authorities. In statistical terms by far the best predictor of what an authority will spend this year is what it spent last year (Danziger, 1978). Nor is this surprising in itself. No council can hope to sack a large portion of its staff, who take the greater part of its expenditure. Many functions are mandatory. Nevertheless, over time many authorities' spending patterns do tend to be perpetuated; the high spenders on education remain high spenders, the low spenders on services for the elderly remain laggards. This reflects the traditions of an authority, or the lasting influence of a chief officer, but it may also reflect a natural desire by those involved to minimise the political conflicts that are generated when big changes are proposed in one department's budget compared with others.

There used to be an in-built assumption that the rate of increase in resources available to an authority would rise year by year. Chief officers became used to submitting last year's 'base budget', corrected for price and salary rises plus an extra *X* per cent. This may have held good in the palmy days of the 1960s for some authorities, but even then not for many (see Danziger, 1978). Since 1976 the presumption of regular growth has been rudely shattered and has lead to the emergence of new 'cutting strategies' (Glennerster, 1980).

Habits broken

In the short term local councils responded by making a series of adjustments, some short term, some longer term, as follows:

1. They sold their assets – empty sites, empty schools, council houses – in the hope this would permit them to continue to build with the money.
2. They charged for services or raised charges already in place to minimise real service cuts.
3. They cut capital expenditure before reducing current spending on staff.
4. They did not reappoint staff or slowed the reappointment process.
5. They cut administrative and research staff.
6. They cut someone else's budget – for example, grants to voluntary organisations from family service units to women's groups – before cutting their own staff.
7. They shifted the difficult and costly cases to other departments, usually social services.

Equal pain

Unless there are good and generally agreed reasons for doing otherwise, the rule which readily minimises conflict is simply to decrease each department's budget by the same percentage. This effectively retains their share of the total authority budget. Though this pattern is evident in some councils, especially in the less controversial services, it is by no means universal.

Your turn next

Some authorities have clearly operated a more variable rule. In some years a committee chair and his or her chief officer win a particularly favourable share of the pie, perhaps because they have a popular or long-delayed major scheme to launch. Then for the next year or two they do less well, suffering a declining budget. There seems to be a feeling that having done well one year you should then take a back place in the queue.

Fundamental change

It is also clear that there have been long-term shifts in priorities as the cuts became permanent. Even relatively small preferences made year by year by the same committee add up over a decade to a major strategic shift in budget priorities. Social services departments shifted their emphasis to community care for children and the elderly as part of an attempt to economise (Kelly, 1989). Cuts produced slower incremental growth in some parts of the budget and major shifts in others. A simple incrementalist model simply does not fit.

The demographic needs approach

One of the accepted reasons why most participants agree to such a major shift is that the population a department services has grown particularly fast. Education departments in the 1950s and 1960s, faced with rapidly rising school populations, were able to win the battle for funds locally just as the ministry did nationally. In the 1980s growing numbers of very elderly people were a similar justification for social services departments to receive a higher share.

Corporate rationality

In the late 1960s and early 1970s a reform movement spread, dissatisfied with the apparent arbitrariness of traditional forms of budget allocation. It paralleled the growing interest in planning and public expenditure control nationally and the spread of American ideas on budget reform (Stewart, 1974; Glennerster, 1975; Hambleton, 1978). A number of Conservative councils in the late 1960s began to introduce programme budgeting or its variants under the generic title of *corporate planning*, often on the recommendation of management consultants as a way of achieving greater efficiency. A number of Labour authorities did the same, believing it could help them plan service development more effectively. A national report (Bains Committee, 1972), *The New Local Authorities: Management and Structure*, recommended a revised committee and officer structure for the new local authorities that would replace the old in 1974. Bains quoted with approval the critical comments of the management consultants, McKinsey and Co. Inc., on one of the authorities they had studied:

> in common with many other authorities [it] finds itself with an organisation and a system of making decisions that has changed little since the present structure of authorities was created out of the tangled web of local boards and functional administrations in the latter half of the nineteenth century. The democratic forms of the Council and committees and the rigid hierarchical structure of the service have some great strengths but in many ways are not geared to the modern task of managing thousands of people and hundreds of millions of pounds of assets. (para. 4.11)

The committee went on to recommend 'some form of overall plan towards which the authority will work and against which it can measure its achievement'. Instead of the brief annual bargaining over estimates, each year's budget would be the outcome of a longer-term planning process which set authority-wide priorities. There should be fewer larger committees responsible for a whole range of related services – leisure, transport, education, housing, social services, for example. Most important of all, a central committee, rather like the Cabinet, would be responsible for key policy and spending priorities – the policy and resources committee. Most authorities lacked such a committee before this except in a shadow, non-statutory form within the majority party caucus. The policy and resources committee would have subcommittees looking at finance, staffing and land, and one that would review and monitor spending programmes to see that they were achieving results economically – a performance and review subcommittee. The changed committee structure was paralleled by a changed management hierarchy with a new chief executive, a managing director, at its head.

In other authorities corporate management was combined with a new system of *area management*. This was designed both to decentralise the delivery of services through mini-town halls, and to generate local plans which would feed into an overall local authority or corporate plan spanning a four-year period. This was perhaps the height of the reform movement's optimism.

In a study of which authorities had developed more sophisticated budget systems and corporate organisation, Greenwood *et al.* (1980b) test several interesting hypotheses. They suggest that the environment within which local authorities have to work affects their organisational structure and budgeting procedures. The more complex the social problems, the more elaborate the services provided – 'differentiation'. Greater social demands for services and the interaction of these factors produce a more complex organisational response. The greater the service complexity, the larger the authority and the tighter the limits to the budget, so the greater will be the organisational need for co-ordination and priority setting – 'integration'. Hence we would expect to see, and to some extent do see, the larger urban authorities with more social problems evolving more elaborate co-ordination and planning. Whether these will be centralised or decentralised depends on local circumstances. In some areas top-down systems with powerful central corporate planning groups and chief executives will not work. Instead, authorities develop matrix forms of management – specialist study groups, collaborating on particular issues, forming and reforming. Co-ordination takes place at all levels between departmental hierarchies.

Elsewhere, Greenwood (1979) suggests that tighter limits on spending enforced by central government encouraged more local authorities to move further away from the traditional incremental pattern of budgeting and introduce more 'rational' methods: strategic analyses of spending, attempts to forecast demands and changing needs, and new budget structures. However, in the 1980s, government's repeated sudden and confused demands for economy created a great deal of uncertainty which actually led many authorities to abandon what planning systems they had created.

On the other hand, many councils saw service decentralisation, area budgeting and community councils as a move towards involving local people in the difficult decisions that cuts involved, and as a way of improving their efficiency. Walsall, Islington and Tower Hamlets were all examples. Nationally the Priority Estates Project pressed for devolved budgets and management boards to run council estates (Power, 1987b, 1991).

Other authorities in England, and more in Scotland, have developed different variants. The authority is divided into smaller constituent parts with several wards grouped together. The administration of these services is decentralised as far as possible to conform with these areas in more accessible mini-town halls. An area committee of local councillors is responsible for overseeing these local services. A local budget can be drawn up with a degree of devolved responsibility. Meetings of local electors may be held to consider area priorities and identify issues of concern to that particular area. These may be formalised in neighbourhood or community councils. There may be local meetings to discuss services for particular groups in the community such as the elderly. At an early stage in the council's budget process these issues and preferences are fed into the consideration of next year's spending plans.

A modern local budgeting cycle

All these experiments have left their mark, as has central government's heavy hand. What has now emerged in most authorities is a budget cycle that includes some or all of the following features.

A central budget constraint

The Chancellor's Autumn Statement and subsequent central grant settlement sets financial parameters within which local authorities will have to work. So, too, does some guess about where the government may set a capping limit. The finance director gives committees advice on the authority's overall budget constraints for the next year. However, in many authorities, especially the larger ones, the process of thinking about next year's budget has begun months before.

The corporate function

Once one budget round is over in March, the chief executive and the chief officers' group will prepare papers for the policy and resources committee identifying key issues for deeper analysis, possible priorities for the next financial year, and areas for major economies. The finance officers will prepare an analysis of existing spending commitments and the costs of new schemes that will be complete by next year – the costs and loan repayments on the provision of a new home for old people, for example. The finance officer will also offer advice on the revenue the authority can expect from the government and from the council tax on various assumptions. The policy and resources committee will then set guidelines indicating clear policy priorities that should guide the preparation of the estimates, and initiate studies that will identify areas where cuts can be made, or expansion can be concentrated. In contrast to the 'Spanish Inquisition' method, a prior decision on priorities and cuts will have been made before the hectic bargaining about detail begins. Interdepartmental reviews of policy for particular groups like the elderly or the under-5s will be a continuing feature of the corporate process going to the parent committees. Thus by the time the size of the government grant is known in late autumn, the groundwork will have been done. A range of possible responses can be presented to members matching, some overall view of priorities.

Area reviews

Area priorities are discussed and fed into the budget review process from the area organisations, if they exist.

Departmental estimates

This more traditional process continues. Detailed work on drafting the initial estimates for the next financial year by departments takes account of the prior guidelines and studies that have been undertaken. They will be ready for November, before the government grant settlement arrives, and work will begin in the finance officer's department paring them down in bilateral discussions. Chief officers and chairs will begin the process of deciding the share of the budget that is to go to education, social services and housing in the light of the strategic analysis discussed above. The final decisions will be taken in January and February. After this the officers and the individual committees will be left to cut their estimates and keep within their given targets.

The policy committee resolution
This committee will have the initial task of resolving conflict between four policy streams – central government constraints, the authority's or governing party's collective goals, the demands of different geographical units and departmental interests. The final resolution will depend on the majority party group of members and the full council. It will inevitably be a political process but it will be a more informed political judgement, the reformers claim, than the pure bargaining process that preceded it.

In practice the procedures adopted by local authorities differ widely, and change in response to political control and financial stress. At one extreme some authorities still follow very traditional patterns, in others a more corporate approach like that just described has been sustained. Most are a mixture of the two.

Further reading

For a description of local authorities and how they work, see Byrne, T. (1986), *Local Government in Britain: Everyone's guide to how t all works*, Harmondsworth: Penguin.

The following have useful chapters which discuss the local budgetary process:

Booth, T. (1979), *Planning for Welfare: Social policy and the expenditure process*, Oxford: Martin Robertson and Basil Blackwell.

Wright, M. (1980), *Public Spending Decisions: Growth and restraint in the 1970s*, London: Allen & Unwin.

Hood, C., and Wright, M. (1981), *Big Government in Hard Times*, Oxford: Martin Robertson.

For a discussion of social service departments' responses to the harsher financial climate of the early 1980s, see Ferlie, E. and Judge, K. (1981), 'Retrenchment and rationality in the personal social services', *Policy and Politics*, **9**, no. 3, pp. 333–50.

For a discussion of their much longer-term, non-incrementalist responses, see Kelly, A. (1989), 'An end to incrementalism: the impact of expenditure restraint on social services budgets 1979–86', *Journal of Social Policy*, **18**, no. 2, pp. 187–210.

PART III

The sources of funds

CHAPTER 7

TAXES

Taxes form the lion's share of the revenue that pays for our publicly provided welfare services. In this chapter we begin to answer three general but basic questions. What form do taxes take? What economic effects to they have? Who bears the burden? There is a large and technical economic literature on these issues which I can only summarise here, suggesting where interested readers can continue.

The structure of taxation

Taxes are a *compulsory levy* on individuals and firms made by law and levied by government. Even with the legal penalties that exist, people go to great lengths to *avoid* paying taxes legally by finding loopholes in the tax laws; or they *evade* taxes by illegally cheating the tax authorities. One of the basic problems for any government is that the higher the level of taxation, the greater the financial incentive to avoid or evade it.

Taxes are thus to be distinguished from voluntary contributions. One particularly confusing term is used in the United Kingdom to describe one form of tax – the national insurance or social security contribution. I shall discuss its historical origins in Chapter 14. Briefly, however, the term derives from the state's gradual absorption of voluntary sickness benefit and pension schemes. After 1948 all workers had to be members of the national scheme and pay a fixed 'contribution'. The term then became a nonsense. It bears all the characteristics of a tax and is called a social security tax in other countries.

Taxes can be levied by *different levels of government* – central or local, federal, state or municipality depending on a country's constitution. Even prior to rate capping and the poll tax the United Kingdom had the most centralised revenue structure in the western world, with the exception of France and Belgium. From 1990 it has become the most centralised system of tax collection. Only 5 per cent of total tax revenue in the United Kingdom was raised by local authorities in the form of the community charge in 1990/1. In France the figure for local revenue is 8 per cent, but in federal nations like Canada and Switzerland it is well over 40 per cent, in the former West Germany and the United States over 30 per cent, and in Sweden over 25 per cent. Those countries with most fiscal decentralisation tend to expand their local service expenditures faster (Gould, 1983).

Taxes can be *earmarked* or *general*. An earmarked tax is one that is levied to cover the costs of a particular service, and national insurance contributions and social security taxes are an example. Since William Pitt's day, in the late eighteenth century, the British government has recognised the absurdity of keeping multiple accounts – the crown's revenue is the same whatever the source. Economists have usually held that trying to tie a government's hands to spend in line with revenue raised for particular purposes is impossible. Since *all* taxes are compulsory, earmarking is a pure fiction. More recently, however, some American authors have argued that there is a case for separate forms of tax linked to particular purposes. It enables voters to show some preference for different kinds of spending, for example, by campaigning to resist or increase the education or social security tax. Earmarking, they claim, increases the amount of information and leverage voters have on tax and expenditure questions (Brennan and Buchanan, 1980).

Payment of social security contributions over a given period 'entitles' the payer to a benefit, (though only until the law is changed!). Payment of other taxes is not linked to any right to benefit. Social security contributions are paid into the National Insurance Fund from which non-means-tested benefits are paid (see Chapter 14). All other central government revenue is paid into the Consolidated Fund – a 'common bucket' from which remaining expenditure is financed.

The next most basic distinction is between *direct* taxes levied on households' and enterprises' incomes and *indirect* taxes levied on expenditure.

Direct taxes

There are various forms direct taxes can take and in theory they can be levied by either central or local government.

Poll tax

The earliest and simplest form of tax was to oblige every person to pay so much each. The tax was used by the ancient Greeks; the levy of 1380 led to Wat Tyler's rebellion in the Middle Ages; and the tax was used by southern states in the United States to exclude black people from voting. It was discussed by Thatcher's government (DoE, 1981) as a new source or revenue for local government, and was initially rejected. Then, as we saw in the previous chapter, it was introduced in Scotland in 1989 and in England and Wales in 1990, but it lasted for a very short period. Under poll tax, the poor pay a higher proportion of their income than the rich, and the share of income taken in tax falls as incomes rise, a characteristic we call 'regressive'.

Income tax

This more modern tax, dating in Britain from the Napoleonic Wars, is now the main *direct* tax on households. In 1990/1 it contributed 27 per cent of all tax receipts – not more, it is important to note. It is levied on all those with incomes above limits which Parliament sets each year, and the amount paid varies with people's income above that level – their 'taxable income'. Over the long term, income tax has moved from being a tax paid only by the rich to one levied on quite poor people. The share of a person's income paid in tax could be a flat percentage. In practice, in this and in other countries, rich people pay higher rates of tax on their marginal earnings above a given level. Those with lower incomes pay, or should pay, a lower share of their income in tax. This characteristic makes income tax a 'progressive' tax. In some countries the percentage tax paid on the first slice of taxable income is quite low, say 15 per cent, and rises steadily as income rises. In the United Kingdom most people pay a common basic rate of tax, 25 per cent in 1991/2. Higher earners move on to a higher rate – in 1991/2, a rate of 40 per cent for that taxable income which topped £23,700. Most people's income is taxed directly by their employers and handed on to the Inland Revenue, an arm of central government, under a system called Pay As You Earn (PAYE). In many other countries in Europe and in states and cities of America, local income taxes are levied.

Corporation tax

This tax is the equivalent of income tax on enterprises or firms. A firm pays tax on its profits but that part of the tax paid on distributed profits – dividends paid to shareholders – is counted towards the individual shareholders' tax bill – a 'credit'. Profit – the company's net income – is measured as the difference between its revenue and its costs. This sounds simple enough, but defining costs, especially those of capital equipment that wears out, is a very complicated business. Historically governments gave firms very generous allowances and permitted them to offset the costs of new capital equipment against profits, so that in practice the total revenue from corporation tax has been relatively low as a share of all revenue. In the 1980s the Chancellor reduced the rate of corporation tax companies paid but also reduced the allowances on new investment. The main rate of corporation tax was reduced to 33 per cent in 1991/2, the lowest rate in Europe (*Economist*, 23 March 1991). The total revenue from this tax was 10 per cent of government income in 1990/1.

Taxes on capital

So far the taxes we have discussed (except the poll tax) have been assessed on the size of an individual's or firm's income. Another way to measure an individual's capacity to pay tax is the amount of capital assets he or she may have. Wealth, or the ownership of capital, is far more unequally distributed than income and is more unequal in this country than in many others, though wealth data in general and international comparative data in particular are deficient (Regional Commission on the Distribution of Income and Wealth, 1979). Hence, governments interested in reducing these disparities have introduced various taxes on large wealth holders, directed in particular at reducing the extent to which large accumulations of wealth can be passed on to the next generation. A tax on inherited estates began in 1894, though death duties can be traced back much further. The modern form of death duties is the inheritance tax. If you died with assets worth more than £140,000 in 1991/2 you paid tax at the full rate. If you gave your money away seven years before you died you paid no tax. There was a sliding scale in between. Large owners of wealth with good tax advice largely avoided paying this tax. It falls most heavily on people with very modest savings or houses who have not taken appropriate advice. In 1990/1 this tax raised only £1,300 million, compared to the £55,000 million raised from income tax.

Stamp duty

Another central government tax raised on transfers of ownership is stamp duty. Before 1992 it was levied on the sale of securities, other property and land and buildings. After April 1992 duty on securities and property, other than land and buildings, was abolished.

Capital gains tax

Here a tax is imposed when individuals part with an asset and make a capital gain on it. The gain is measured as the market price minus the price at which it was bought, indexed to take account of the general price increase in the period. Owner occupied houses are exempt. Once more, people can successfully avoid the tax and the revenue is comparatively small – £2,000 million in 1990/1.

Property tax

The old rates and the new council tax were, or will be, the *only* form of tax revenue available to local government. The tax liability is based on the value of the property the householder is occupying. Rates developed as a direct tax on an individual's income levied so as to take into account his or her capacity to pay. In the days before PAYE there was no easy way of determining an individual's or family's income. The value or size of the property a person lived in was the next best indicator. Today the value of property is assessed by the Inland Revenue – central government civil servants – a process which (in theory) is repeated at regular intervals.

National insurance contributions

These are levied on employees, employers and the self-employed. They are paid into a fund specially earmarked to meet the costs of the national insurance scheme – the National Insurance Fund. We discuss this system of funding in Chapter 14.

Expenditure taxes

Some reformers (Kaldor, 1955; Meade, 1978; Pechman, 1980; *Economist*, 17 September 1983) have argued that instead of taxing an individual's income, it would be better to tax his or her expenditure. It would be simple. It would not, they argue, be such a disincentive to work as progressive income tax. It would be less easy to avoid and it would be an incentive to save. Other economists are less sure (Atkinson and Stiglitz, 1980, pp. 563–6).

Indirect taxes

These taxes are levied not on particular households or firms but on the goods they buy or sell. They include the following.

Customs and Excise duties

These are some of the earliest forms of revenue. Imports from non-EEC countries carry a tax or customs duty. The EEC itself levies a tax on imported food which will vary according to its price. Basically, the levy will bring the price of food up to the level set for that product by the agricultural policy of the EEC, a price the EEC will pay European farmers. This protects the farmers and produces revenue – but the revenue goes to Brussels, not to the British government. Customs duties also perform the function of keeping out expensive foreign-produced goods. They are raised by a separate arm of government – Customs and Excise. This is concerned with levying tax on certain items – many of them previously imported – such as tobacco and spirits, beer, wine and oil, including petrol.

Vehicles

Cars and lorries are taxed before they can be driven legally on the roads.

Value added tax (VAT)

This is now the major source of indirect taxation. It is essentially a sales tax levied at a percentage of the final price of the product

(17.5 per cent from 1991), but is collected at each stage in the production process. The shopkeeper pays tax on his or her sales of all taxable goods, minus the tax paid by those who sold him or her the goods wholesale, and so the chain goes back to the producer. Each stage in the production process thus pays tax on the value it has added; hence the tax's name. Charities and small firms are exempt, as are certain essential items, such as food as a product.

Total tax shares

We can see from Table 7.1 that the structure of taxation has changed substantially since 1948. Contrary to popular belief, income tax provides only just over a quarter of all tax revenue. That share has fallen. It is the national insurance contributions that have become the second largest element, with 17 per cent of the total. Tobacco has collapsed as a primary source of funds. Local government taxes once formed 11 per cent of all tax income, a share that is down in 1990/1 to 5 per cent. VAT, which replaced purchase tax, has become the other major revenue raiser. In 1979, the Conservative government reduced the standard rate of income tax from 33 per cent to 30 per cent but nearly doubled the standard rate of VAT. Then in 1991 VAT was raised again to pay for the reduction in community charge. That rise is not shown in the table, which predates the change, but it was expected to increase VAT's share of tax revenue to 17 per cent.

What effect do taxes have?

Allocative efficiency?

For the government to raise large sums of money and redistribute them to purchase social services must have profound effects on the economy. These matters are the subject of a large and technical literature. The student with an interest and a good grounding in the principles of economic theory should pursue that literature beginning with a standard public finance text (Musgrave and Musgrave, 1980; Prest and Barr, 1985). The best advanced text is

Table 7.1 Sources of tax revenue in the United Kingdom 1948–91

Tax	Percentage of total taxes					
	1948	1956	1964	1972	1982	1990/1
Income tax and surtax	31.8	36.1	32.1	27.8	26.5	27.4
Tobacco	14.3	11.4	9.7	5.4	3.3	2.8
Beer, wine and spirits	10.2	6.9	5.7	4.9	3.1	2.4
National insurance*	8.0	10.7	14.8	15.3	20.2	17.2
Local authority rates/ community charge	7.6	9.3	11.3	11.1	11.2	5.1
Purchase tax	7.2	7.6	6.5	6.5		
Value added tax					12.8	15.2
Profits and excess profits	6.8	3.3	4.2			
Corporation tax				6.7	5.0	10.6
Death duties/ inheritance tax	4.4	2.8	3.2	2.2	0.5	0.6
Customs duties**	2.7	2.1	2.0	1.7	1.8	0.8
Stamp duty	1.4	1.0	0.8	1.0	0.8	0.8
Petrol and diesel	1.3	5.5	6.6	7.1	4.7	4.7
Vehicle licences	1.2	1.5	2.0	2.3	1.7	1.7
Entertainment tax	1.2	0.7				
Selective employment tax				2.1		
Capital gains				1.3	0.6	0.9
Petroleum revenue tax					4.7	0.4
Other	1.7	0.9	0.9	1.2	1.9	9.6

* Includes payments by employers, employees, self-employed and the old national insurance surcharge.
** Includes customs duties and miscellaneous Customs and Excise revenue.

The table excludes interest and trading surplus and rent – all small additions to total government receipts.

Sources: *Economist*, 17 September 1983; *Financial Statement and Budget Report 1984–5 1991–2*, HM Treasury.

Atkinson and Stiglitz (1980). However, the issues are of central importance and can be simplified to some extent.

Classical economists begin from a model of a free market interchange of goods and services with no monopolies or imperfections in the capital market or the labour market. In such a free market, goods and services would be efficiently allocated. Everyone's preferences would be reflected in their purchases of goods and their productivity in wages paid. In economic terms, resource allocation is optimal. Economists can then theorise about what happens when we remove those assumptions one by one. The introduction of governments that tax goods and incomes in various ways is of course one of the major 'imperfections', and economic theory is concerned to show what kinds of tax would interfere least with allocations that would arise in a free market. One of the difficulties with classical theory is that there are so many other interacting 'imperfections' at work that to measure the impact of a single tax is all but impossible. Some general principles can, however, be deduced.

Direct and indirect taxes: is it better to tax incomes or goods?

Let us first consider the impact of imposing a proportional income tax, that is, one that taxed a constant proportion of one's income however high, and raising the same revenue as a tax on one particular product, or a narrow range of products. To take a similar proportion of everyone's income away will not affect individuals' capacities to express their preferences between goods or services though it does bias their choices between goods and leisure. However, to raise the same revenue by concentrating all the tax on one particular product or narrow range of products would change its relative price. This in its turn would change people's pattern of purchases *away* from that which reflected their true preferences. In theoretical terms this results in a loss of welfare for individuals.

However, this does not necessarily prove that direct taxes are more efficient in economic terms than indirect taxes, for the following three reasons:

1. It is possible for indirect taxes to be levied at an even rate across all goods and services; a sales tax with a single rate of, say, 5 per cent, or value added tax, are examples. If these taxes increase the price of all products in proportion to their original price, they distort market preferences relatively little.
2. A tax on a particular product may be justified on efficiency grounds if heavy 'external' costs are involved in its production or use . Tobacco or alcohol are examples. The public is not faced with the true cost of these products because their use costs lives and uses public health resources. Leaded petrol, too, has pollution costs. A higher tax rate on such items can be

justified if it faces consumers with the true costs, private and external, of producing and consuming the product. A tax on smoke or water-polluting production processes, or a higher tax on leaded petrol or a congestion tax on vehicles in city centres, or a duty on heavy lorries that badly damage road foundations, could be justified in these terms. A pollution tax could theoretically be set at a level that would exactly match the external costs involved. The practical difficulty lies in deciding how to value the external effects.

3. An indirect tax could be justified in terms of pure allocative efficiency if a product were produced under conditions of severe imperfect competition – a monopoly, for example. In the real world it is difficult to see how such a tax could be imposed or calculated, and it would make much more practical sense to tackle the offending firm under monopolies legislation.

Taxes for the future

These arguments are not mere economic theorising. Their logic is reflected in the kinds of indirect tax that are levied. We have seen that VAT is levied at a common standard level, with food and a few other items exempted. That aside, VAT does fit the rules of allocative efficiency quite well. We also tax tobacco and alcohol separately, and government has raised the possibility of extending the principle of environmental taxation even further, to face consumers with the true social costs of driving their cars into crowded city centres or polluting the atmosphere. It is becoming clear that taxation in the 1990s could be used as a major tool to promote a more efficient allocation of resources in society, forcing consumers to take account of the long-term implications of their actions. Taxes are not just a way of paying for welfare: they can be a way of promoting welfare too.

So far we have discussed the impact of indirect taxes on allocative efficiency. Direct taxes can also affect the 'efficient' distribution of resources. At the extreme, a 100-per-cent tax will remove all financial incentives to move to the new job in a new industry that requires a particular kind of skill. At the other extreme, a poll tax that takes the same amount from everyone will keep the same absolute difference between the rewards in one job and the next. As so often, we have conflict between equity or fairness and efficiency. A poll tax takes a larger proportion of poor people's pay, but does least 'damage' to the 'efficient' allocation of labour. Just how important efficiency considerations appear will depend on how far the reader accepts the basic theoretical framework. However, while it is possible to discount the efficiency consequences at low rates of tax, it becomes less and less easy to do so as the rates of tax get higher.

Taxation and the supply of labour

The relevant economic argument that reaches the notice of even the ill-informed newspaper reader is the proposition that high taxation, or indeed any taxation at all, is undesirable because it limits the extent to which people work, produce and add to the 'wealth of the nation'. This standard economic theory refers to what is called the 'substitution effect'. It can be stated simply. Individuals could spend all their time at work or play. In practice, life is better with a mixture of work and leisure. The worker trades (or *substitutes*) one for the other until he or she is satisfied with the mix. At this point the marginal pound he or she earns from an hour's work is just more than equal to the value of that hour in watching TV or pottering in the garden. Wages, in a purely competitive labour market, would reflect that trade-off (or marginal rate of substitution). When an income tax is levied, it will reduce the return or rewards for labour. At the margin, leisure will be more attractive. The individual will work less and give more hours to leisure, but this is not what he or she originally wished to do, and his or her satisfaction or welfare is thus reduced.

This view visualises workers and potential workers weighing up the pleasure gained from an hour of gardening, balancing it against an additional hour in the office or on the production line. The focus of this theory is upon the comparison individuals are presumed to make between the *marginal* value of an extra hour of work or leisure. Clearly, then, a progressive income tax which makes individuals pay a higher marginal rate of tax as they earn more will penalise work. This has serious implications for the whole economy. A low-tax economy will therefore, other things being equal, be a more efficient economy. That is the conclusion from this part of the theory.

The first standard problem is that the market is not perfectly competitive. Workers are not able to choose to trade small adjustments in hours worked against take-home pay. Fixed hours and production processes, and negotiated wage rates with limited opportunity for overtime, all reduce the flexibility of the trade-off between leisure and work. Nevertheless, some workers do clearly have some freedom, to earn bonus payments and undertake piece-work, to vary effort with reward. Moreover, the major choices that face individuals are about what kind of job to enter. Young people may very well judge that a job in a demanding high paid position is not worth it because the financial rewards are taxed away. Secondly, for some people work and leisure may not be clear alternatives. Work itself may be a pleasure and the monetary reward may be of limited importance after a minimum income is gained. Thirdly, economists often implicity assume that more labour supply is a good thing. In a fully employed economy, this is reasonable. In the recent period of excessive unemployment and weak demand for labour, the validity of this assumption is less clear.

So much, then, for the 'substitution effect' theory. A second perspective emphasises the 'income effect'. This postulates that people have in mind a target income they would like to receive – set by the life style of their neighbours or those just above them on the social ladder. Households will do their best, with the main earner searching for a good job, undertaking training and pursuing overtime, while the second earner goes out to bring the household income up to that socially approved target. If a worker's earnings are taxed, his or her motivation to work *longer* hours, to buy the prized new car or video, is *increased*. This theory counterbalances the other. It predicts precisely the *opposite* human response to the substitution effect – higher taxes increase incentives to work. To put it another way, reducing income tax will increase people's capacity to afford more leisure. Some writers (Musgrave and Musgrave, 1980) have put the two theories together, claiming that in the *low* range of income workers are motivated by the second effect, but later as basic necessities have been bought, and 'social' necessities too, then the trade-off between leisure and work becomes dominant and the first effect predominates. Taken to its logical conclusion, this suggests that to maximise work one would need to place high taxes on the poor and low taxes on the rich! These issues and many more are discussed in Atkinson and Stiglitz (1980), Chapter 2, and in Atkinson (1981).

It is not enough, however, to argue that these two effects simply cancel one another out and we can therefore forget about them. If an individual works longer hours than he or she would wish to do in the absence of taxation, that involves a loss of welfare.

Public finance economists often stop at this point, leaving the impression that all taxation does is to introduce inefficiency. They ignore the efficiency gains that flow from providing the services which the taxation makes possible (see Chapters 2 and 3). However, in the reverse way, social policy writers tend to ignore the efficiency consequences of taxation and concentrate on the benefits of service provision. It is, therefore, important to know how big the effects may be.

Evidence on the effects of taxation

Evidence of the impact of taxation on incentives to work is fully reviewed by Brown (1983). The evidence is of several kinds. There are, for example, interviews. Brown and Levin (1974) undertook an interview survey of workers to test their views about the impact of different levels of tax on their willingness to undertake overtime. The results suggested no strong association. Most workers were unclear about what their marginal tax rates were, and consequently did not have any very clearly calculated response. Low-earning workers seemed least affected, but on higher earnings some evidence of a small disincentive was discernible.

There are also econometric studies using panel data on individuals' labour supply, wages and personal circumstances. Houseman (1981) is perhaps the best known. Overall, the results do suggest that high taxable rates have some impact on men's working hours and quite a lot of impact on women's. By comparing the labour supply data of different groups facing different tax rates over time, it is possible to build statistical models that include a measure of labour supply response. This has been done in the United States (Hall, 1973). These also show that the measurable effects of different rates of tax were very small for most types of workers. Some workers did, however, appear to respond as the substitution effect predicted. Mothers, younger people, pensioners – those without primary family supporting roles – did work less when faced with higher tax rates.

Some further evidence can be gained from a series of very

interesting experiments undertaken in the United States in the 1960s and 1970s. They were unusual for social science research: attempts at controlled experiments in selected communities of different kinds in different parts of America. Their aim was to see what incentive effects financial aid to poor families would produce. As a family's income rose, so the cash aid was withdrawn at different rates for different members of the sample. There was a matching sample that received no grants. The effect of withdrawing state income as earned income rises is precisely the same in economic terms as an ordinary tax on additional earnings. Moreover, a cash *supplement* to income would also be expected to lead to a fall in work effort. On both counts these experiments might be expected to show strong disincentive effects on work.

The first of these experiments was in New Jersey (Pechman and Timpane, 1975). Later experiments were undertaken in Gary, Indiana (Burtless and Housman, 1978), rural areas of North Carolina and Iowa, and the western and north-western cities of Denver and Seattle (Robbins, 1982). A summary of the results is to be found in Brown (1983). All are subject to fierce statistical debates about the methods and whether the results can be extended to a national scale. Different experiments also produced somewhat different results. The earliest experiment in New Jersey suggested that the reduction in working hours produced by relatively high tax rates was small – a 0.5-per-cent reduction in hours worked by men who received a cash supplement and had it withdrawn at a 50-per-cent tax rate. However, wives were affected. They used their extra income gained to stay at home to look after children. The same result showed up in rural experiments. The largest experiments were the last, at Denver and Seattle. They suggested that, faced with high tax rates of 50 to 80 per cent, husbands in poor families worked less – a total reduction of 5 per cent. Wives' reductions were greater – 22 per cent – while single mothers cut their hours by 11 per cent.

How far is it reasonable to extrapolate these results to the non-poor is a highly debatable point.

In brief

Overall, it is difficult to avoid the conclusion that high tax rates do reduce labour participation, certainly for poor households doing unpleasant jobs and for women. But the scale of these effects, especially for married men, is small.

None of these studies, however, deals with the issue raised earlier. How far does the knowledge that the state will tax away high salaries deter people from entering high-earning and demanding jobs? Since tax avoidance is so effective, the answer is probably not much. However, that is not a good reason for trying to levy high tax rates that no-one can enforce.

Who pays taxes?

Like so many questions about taxation, this is deceptively simple. If the government puts an extra tax on whisky, who pays it – whisky drinkers? If the government puts a tax on employers for every worker they employ, who pays – the employers? A little more thought suggests that the interactions are more complex. What if the price of whisky is already so high that no-one is prepared to buy any more if the price goes up again? In that case, shopkeepers and manufacturers might be prepared to drop their profit margins, absorb the tax and go on selling at the same price. In this extreme case, the tax would be paid by the producer or seller of whisky. In the same way, if employees and unions have already squeezed as much out of the employer as they possibly can, the employer cannot pay higher labour costs without going bankrupt. Then the effect of raising the employer's social security tax will be for the employer to pay lower wages than he or she otherwise would. These are extreme cases, but in most situations part of the cost of taxation will be passed on or 'shifted' in this way. In short, the economic incidence of taxation will not be the same as the 'statutory' incidence. By 'incidence', economists mean where the tax burden falls – who pays. Public finance theory sets out the possibilities more formally.

The theories show that the incidence question is complex, and that precise calculations of who pays and who benefits are very difficult to determine. One lesson seems to be that we cannot tell anything about the consequences of taxation. That would be too pessimistic. It turns out that the theoretical 'shifting' effects are less important than they seem in theory. (The relevant findings and theories are accessibly discussed in Pechman and Okner, 1974; Pechman, 1985.) Pechman's study attempts to show what difference alternative economic assumptions about the incidence of various taxes make. It illustrates the difficulty of such studies, and also suggests some broad conclusions.

The combined effect of federal, state and local taxes in the United States in 1985 fell heavily on the poorest. The share of income paid in taxes was more or less proportional to income for most families (about 20–5 per cent of income) and then rose for the top 10 per cent of highest income earners. The progressivity of the tax system had been reduced between 1965 and 1985. That pattern was not very different whatever theoretical assumptions were used. Remarkably similar results have been obtained by studies in the United Kingdom and other countries. Taxes do not fall more and more heavily on people the more they earn. The outcome of the political merry-go-round that sets nominal tax rates has produced a roughly *proportionate* tax structure. That finding is certainly borne out in the United Kingdom, where the shift to a less progressive tax structure has been even more evident than in the United States (Hills, 1988). As can be seen in Figure 7.1, the combined effect of the tax and benefit changes in the period since 1978–9 have been dramatic. The gains recorded by the top 10 per cent of households amounted to £40 a week, mostly in lower taxes, while the middle income groups were little affected and the poorer ones lost over £10 a week in benefits and higher VAT.

Findings for the United Kingdom

For many years the UK statistical service has estimated the burden of taxation and the value of benefits which households pay and receive. It is based on a national sample of households' income and expenditure. It does not attempt the economic sophistication of the American work we have described – there are no alternative sets of theoretical assumptions. In most cases it assumes that the burden of tax falls where the legal form says it falls. But intermediate taxes on production costs, like the property tax, commercial vehicle licences and employers' national insurance contributions, are assumed to be passed on in consumer prices.

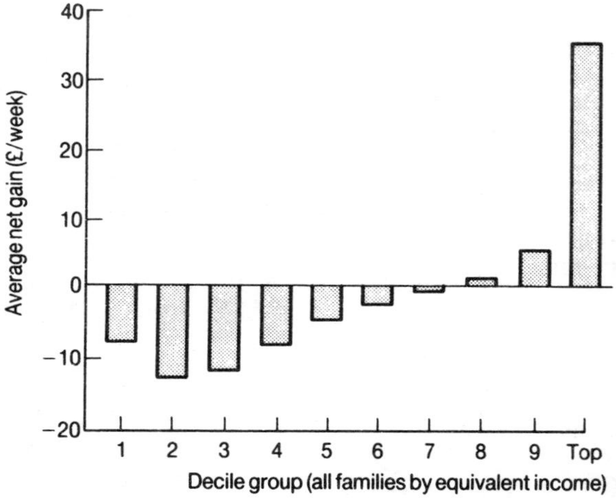

Figure 7.1 The effect of direct tax and benefit changes in Great Britain since 1978–9 (Source: Hills, 1988)

They are treated like VAT. From households' expenditure patterns it is possible to deduce how much indirect and intermediate tax is paid, and there is a straightforward entry of the direct taxes each family pays. There are many theoretical difficulties with the whole study (see O'Higgins, 1980), notably on the allocation of benefits (Evandrou *et al.*, 1991). However, given the nature of the overall bias, and the fact that the broad outline of the tax conclusions would probably not change dramatically under different assumptions, the results are worth examining (see Table 7.2).

Table 7.2 shows very clearly what a *proportionately* high price the poor pay for their social services through the tax system. The reasons are clear. The poorest fifth pay nearly a quarter of their income in indirect taxes if you include in that the assumption that employers pass on their taxes in higher prices. This figure falls away to 12 per cent for the highest income group. Average income tax actually paid rises from 4 per cent of the income of the poorest to only 16 per cent of the top fifth in the income range. This is a tribute to how effectively the rich use the wide range of allowances available to them and other forms of tax avoidance. National

Table 7.2 Taxes as a percentage of gross income by income group in the United Kingdom 1988

Taxes	Quintile group*				
	Bottom	2nd	3rd	4th	Top
Direct					
Income tax (less relief)	4	7	10	13	16
National insurance	1	3	5	5	4
Domestic rates (gross)**	10	7	4	3	2
Total direct taxes	15	17	19	21	22
Indirect					
VAT	8	7	7	7	5
Tobacco and alcohol	5	3	4	3	2
Other (including intermediate)***	11	10	8	7	5
Total indirect taxes	24	20	19	17	12
Total taxes	*39*	*37*	*38*	*38*	*34*
Average gross income including cash benefits (£/person)	4,426	7,239	12,501	17,336	29,881

* All households are ranked from poorest to richest. The bottom fifth is the lowest quintile and so on up to the highest fifth. Income is 'equivalised' to take account of the size of family.
** Intermediate taxes include taxes on employers passed on in prices.
*** Excludes the offsetting housing benefit poor households can claim, to meet rates then and community charge later, which is included in gross income.

Source: *Economic Trends*, March 1991, London: HMSO.

insurance contributions rise to their peak with the third and fourth quintiles. At that point there is a ceiling on contributions. They, therefore, form a smaller share of total income for the highest income group. The official figures now show what a family would have to pay in rates or community charge if they paid the full amount. The housing benefit they can claim to offset that bill is added to the total income. The overall result suggests that the total tax burden faced by the UK population ranges from about 39 per cent of income for the very poorest down to 34 per cent for the richest fifth. If we net out rates and the rebate on rates in 1988, the poorest fifth paid about 30 per cent of their adjusted income in taxes.

The striking feature, as in the United States, is how similar is the share taken by taxes across the income range.

Taxes paid in other countries

Britons have a deep-seated belief, fostered by the popular press and some politicians, that they are more heavily taxed than anyone else in the world except perhaps the Swedes. It is true that before 1979 the marginal rates of income tax on the very rich were high (marginal tax rates are the percentage of the last pound earned taken in tax). At 40 per cent they are now one of the lowest in the western world (Hills, 1988). It is true that the rate of income tax is high compared to other countries. In the United States, for example, people began to pay tax on the first slice of their income at 14 per cent, then 16 per cent for the next band, and so on. We begin paying income tax at 25 per cent once we move into the tax bracket. But, *on average,* people in the United Kingdom do *not* pay more tax than the average European. Indeed, we are now one of the least taxed nations in western Europe, though we are still more heavily taxed than the average American or Japanese. Table 7.3 sets out the international tax league table and compares the changes since 1971.

In contrast to most countries in Europe, again, we put heavy reliance on expenditure-related taxes, like VAT, and less reliance on social security contributions paid by employers. As we can see from Table 7.3, the share of total incomes going in tax and social security contributions increased sharply to take nearly two-thirds of all income in Denmark and Sweden. It is perhaps not surprising that this caused a political backlash in the early 1990s. France also saw a large increase in public spending and taxation in the nearly two decades from 1971, as did Italy from a lower base. In contrast the United Kingdom and what was West Germany saw a small increase in the 1970s and then stabilised their share through the 1980s. The United States under Reagan reduced its share, but only at the cost of a large budget deficit.

Table 7.3 Taxes and social security contributions as a percentage of GNP at factor cost in various countries 1971, 1981, 1988

Country	1971	1981	1988
Denmark	51	55	65
Sweden	50	58	63
Norway	52	56	57
Netherlands	47	51	53
France	40	48	51
Belgium	40	49	49
Austria	44	50	49
FR Germany	41	46	45
United Kingdom	40	44	44
Finland	38	41	43
Greece	28	30	41
Italy	31	39	40
Canada	37	38	40
Australia	29	36	36
Japan	22	24	34
Switzerland	25	30	32
United States	32	34	31

Source: *Economic Trends*, July 1990, London: HMSO.

In conclusion

Students of social policy often concentrate their attention on social benefits and social services and forget about how they are paid for. We have seen in this chapter how wrong that is. There is little point in mildly pro-poor benefits if the tax burden is heavily anti-poor. The structure of taxation matters.

During the 1980s the level of income tax for high income groups was reduced substantially. Value added tax was increased sharply, the national insurance contribution rose. Benefits were made less generous for some, but the major changes affected the tax structure. The poorest groups have seen their incomes fall. This has been done to increase the incentives the higher income groups have to work harder.

Taxes into the 1990s

If we wished to pay for welfare in a way that was less burdensome on the poor without being massively destructive to the higher income groups what might be done? A programme for reform might include the following:

1. Reform local government taxation to link the local tax to capacity to pay. In the short run this could mean a property tax with substantial rebates for poor households. In the longer term it would mean adopting a local income tax.
2. Levy the social security tax at the same percentage right to the top of the income range. National insurance contributions now have a ceiling: higher earners pay no more than average earners.
3. Make a wide band of incomes carry no income tax, and marginal rates begin at, say, 20 per cent. That would, however, have to be accompanied by the abolition of tax relief for most present purposes, including owner occupation. This would permit a much lower marginal rate of tax.
4. Introduce a tax to repay the costs of higher education for those who take courses.
5. Abolish the present inheritance tax and make recipients pay on gifts above a certain band as income.

Reforms of this kind would go further towards making the welfare system more redistributive than any likely changes in the structure of services or benefits.

Further reading

The simplest and most lucid account of taxation in the United Kingdom and its impact on different income groups is Hills, J. (1988), *Changing Tax: How the tax system works and how to change it*, London: Child Poverty Action Group. It also discusses a range of reforms.

The best written longer account of taxation is Kay, J. and King, M. (1989), *The British Tax System*, Oxford: Clarendon Press.

CHAPTER 8

FEES AND CHARGES

Fees and charges are payments made to service providers for services rendered. The term *fee* is usually used to mean a payment that covers the full cost of the service provided. It is the market price of a professional's service – the doctor's fee, an architect's fee, school fees. In a profit-making enterprise like a private health clinic, this will include an element of profit, a return on the capital invested. If the organisation is a non-profit charity, like a private school, the fees will merely cover the cost of the service minus any income the school will receive from other sources. Public sector pricing raises more complex issues but it, too, is based on the idea that the price is fixed at least to cover the marginal social cost of producing the service. (For a general introduction to the economic theory of public sector pricing students should read Musgrave and Musgrave, 1980, Chapter 34; Judge, 1980.)

The term *charge* implies some rationale for fixing the levy other than pure pricing criteria. Charges for social services cover from 5 per cent to 20 per cent of the full cost, depending on the service or part of the service (see Table 8.1). Why? Though some economic texts suggest that the case for charging is essentially the same as that for any price mechanism, the history of charging suggests the motivation has usually been quite different.

Table 8.1 Revenue from charges as a percentage of total current income in the United Kingdom

Social service	Percentage	
National Health Service		
Total charges to patients (prescription charges, etc.)	4.5	(1990)
Personal social services		
Charges to users (home helps, old people's homes, children's homes, etc.)	11.2	(1990)
Universities fee income		
Home students	6.4	(1988/9)
Overseas students	5.4	(1988/9)

The history of charging

Parker, in a seminal article in the *Journal of Social Policy* (1976; see also Judge, 1980), summarised the reasons legislators had invoked for charging in the social services. They were:

symbolism – expressing an ideological position regardless of the economic value of the charge itself;

abuse – to reduce the cost of a service to the general taxpayer by raising the revenue from users;

deterrence – to reduce the cost to the taxpayer by reducing demand for a service;

priorities – to concentrate available funds on priority services and charge for less urgent facilities.

Judge and Matthews (1980) examined the history of charging in the personal social services, where many activities still carry a charge, and identified an even more varied selection of motives. It is instructive to look at some particular examples, because they show that the simple economic case for pricing turns out to be only part of the story.

To avoid stigma

In his second reading speech on the National Assistance Bill in

1947, for example, Aneurin Bevan argued that the accommodation in a local authority old person's home should be charged for in just the same way as that in a private hotel or nursing home, 'so that any old persons who wish to go may go there in exactly the same way as many well-to-do people have been accustomed to go into residential hotels' (HC Debates, 1947, Col. 1609). This was a clear example of the phenomenon discussed by Pinker (1971). People in a capitalist or free market economy, he argued, tend to feel stigmatised when they receive something free. The prevailing value system suggests that it is only if you have paid in full for what you receive that you fully deserve to have it. Otherwise there is an element of charity and hence stigma in the exchange. Bevan seemed to be saying just that. Charges have also been advocated for precisely the opposite reason.

A symbolic deterrent

Mary Carpenter, in 1851, argued that charges would be necessary in her proposed reformatory schools because otherwise unscrupulous parents would 'throw the charge of their children's bodily wants [and] those of their moral training . . . on the State' (Judge and Matthews, 1980). Though reformatory schools were later transformed into approved schools and community homes, the principle of charging never seems to have been seriously questioned. It was raised in the committee stage of the Children and Young Person's Bill of 1969 by a Conservative member who questioned whether charging should be mandatory, given the widespread variation in the levels of charging practised by different authorities. The reply by the minister was a direct echo of Mary Carpenter: 'The principle behind this provision in the bill is that parents should be required – if their means so permit – to pay for their child's board and lodging, so that they are in no way better off as a result of the child's being in care.'

The practical effect of the charges is, however, trivial. Even in the nineteenth century the total revenue raised from parents in industrial schools only amounted to between 2.5 and 5 per cent of expenditure, while in the period 1948–69 the parental share of the costs of children in care amounted only to between 4 per cent and 6.5 per cent. The most recent figure (1990) is 12 per cent. Most parents whose children are taken into care are extremely poor, either permanently or as a result of the crisis that has led to their being unable to look after their child. One is driven to the conclusion that here, too, the charge has most to do with symbolism.

A real deterrent against disapproved behaviour

There is no better example of the logical and ideological confusions into which we have fallen over the charging issue than in pre-school provision. Local social services departments (formerly local health departments) provide day nurseries for some up to the age of 5. They provide care and not education; at least, that is the theory. Day care is in very limited supply. In general, only high-priority cases are able to gain a place. There also exist private day-care facilities and child minders who provide a comparable service and who are registered and inspected by social services departments. Quite separate and distinct, so we are told by the professions concerned, are the pre-school facilities run by local education authorities – nursery classes. These take children only from the age of 3, and are staffed not by nursery nurses but by trained teachers. The schools are open for limited hours. Most children attend only part-time – morning or afternoon.

Local authority nurseries charge, nursery classes do not. Why? Again we must delve back in history to understand how we got to this position. Day nursery provision by local authorities was strictly limited in the 1930s and charged for, as a result of the cuts in local spending introduced as part of the National government's economy drive, but when the Second World War came and women were to be mobilised in large numbers for the war effort, the government gave local authorities a 100-per-cent grant to cover the costs of day nurseries, merely charging parents for the cost of food served to the children. When the war ended, however, the policy changed. Women were no longer needed in the factories, and the traditional view that a woman's place was properly in the home and that young children were best cared for by their mothers reasserted itself. Government cut the grants to local authorities, arguing that nurseries were now required only for families in particular need (Ministry of Health Circular 221/45, 1945). Many were closed, but local authorities began pressing government to permit them to charge and reduce the cost of providing the new nurseries that did continue. The Labour government resisted this pressure, but the next Conservative government, in the 1952 National Health Service Act, obliged authorities to charge the economic cost of such provision but to apply a means test. This further reduced demand and put state nurseries on a par with private ones except in the case of poor parents. Thus state day nurseries became confined very largely to the children of poor and needy parents, often single parents. Free day-care provision was, and still is, seen by many as an incentive that would attract women away from their proper caring duties. In 1989, 780,000 children under 5 were receiving day care in the United Kingdom, only 34,000 of them in state day nurseries (50,000 were in private nurseries and the remainder with playgroups and child minders).

A way of relaxing public spending limits

Pre-school education was quite different. Legislators in the 1944 Education Act looked upon nursery education in a positive light and indeed laid a duty on local education authorities to provide enough to enable any parent who wanted it to send their child to a nursery school. The same Act, as we shall see later, abolished fee paying in schools as being a barrier to equal educational opportunity – *ergo* nursery education must be free. In fact, the resources, notably teachers, were not to be available after the war. There was a rapid increase in the number of primary school children, with very overcrowded primary classes, and governments pushed all the available teachers and capital into primary education, limiting local authorities' right to provide nursery education even when they wished to. It was not until the 1960s that pressure began to mount on government to lift that ban and expand pre-schooling (Blackstone, 1971). The Plowden Committee Report (DES, 1967) contains an interesting discussion on whether there was a case for introducing charges for nursery education. A minority report signed by several distinguished social scientists argued that there was. The main stumbling block to expanding nursery classes as a right, which they and the majority of the committee favoured, was the limit on public spending. By reducing the net cost to the public purse by charging on a means-tested basis, it might prove possible to persuade the Treasury to expand provision. Without that incentive government would not implement the majority's recommendation. Moreover, they argued, very similar provision in day nurseries already carried a charge. Unless the state expanded its pre-school facilities, children would be catered for in the private sector, *increasing* class divisions. The majority of the committee did not accept these arguments. Essentially they retained the belief that nursery education should be free (even if that meant there was little of it) and that to charge for nursery classes would be the thin end of the wedge, soon leading to charges for ordinary schooling. The teachers' unions strongly supported the majority report. Margaret Thatcher, the Secretary of State for Education in 1972, encouraged authorities to expand provision, but did not accept the suggestion of charging. (Students may like to consider where they stand on this issue.)

Avoid cuts

In the 1980s many local authorities faced the opposite kind of dilemma. Faced with cuts in grant from central government, they tried to preserve services by charging users. Councils argued that rather than run down the home-help service it was better to charge those who could afford to pay and keep the total level of service. Museum charges and higher fees for adult and further education were all defensive responses to the cuts, as well as being supported for political reasons by some councils. Some writers feel that there is much more scope for local authorities using their wide powers to charge to enhance their revenue (Blair, 1991).

To prevent abuse or reduce demand

When the National Health Service Act of 1946 was passed it was envisaged that medical care should be freely available at the point of need. Related activities provided under the Act by local authorities, like home helps and day nurseries, raised different issues, but all medical care, whether in hospital or general practice, dental care and opticians' services were free. So, too, were the appliances prescribed, teeth and spectacles, or surgical appliances.

It was not long after the Health Service came into being that the economy began to go into one of its periods of crisis. The cost of the service turned out to be much higher than had been predicted. There was a particularly high demand for the dental and ophthalmic services which had not been included in many of the pre-war insurance schemes. There was thus a very big backlog in demand from people who no longer faced a price barrier. It was this aspect of the new service that critics attacked most sharply. Popular newspapers were able to find or invent a few examples of 'frivolous' applications for dentures or spectacles. The Labour government took powers to introduce charges for dentures, spectacles and appliances, but it was not until the financial crisis of 1951 that the government finally brought itself to introduce charges for these items, in the wake of the economic crisis brought about by rearmament and the Korean war. It provoked a major split in the Cabinet and the resignation of the Minister of Health and architect of the Health Service, Bevan, as well as that of Harold Wilson. The charges would prevent abuse: that, the Labour Prime Minister Attlee argued, was the main reason for them (*HC Debates*, Vol. 495, Col. 374).

We have seen, then, that the historical reasons for charging in the social services are diverse and often contradictory, but a case can still be made for charging on *a priori* grounds. I shall now set out the case for and against the extended use of charging.

The case for charges

Revealing consumer preferences

The most basic case for charging is the general case for pricing in a competitive economy (Seldon, 1977). People who wish to consume a service know what resources it uses because they are faced with a price which just covers the additional resources that are needed to provide it. If that price is too high people will not purchase it. The pricing system thus reveals people's preferences in a realistic way. Faced with a zero price a consumer may opt to have the service just because it is free, while not really feeling very strongly about it one way or the other. Bleddyn Davies (1978), in his study of school meals charging, illustrates the force of this argument. When school meals were heavily subsidised there was little pressure to change the traditional pattern of meals, or to worry too much about quality. When the price was raised, parents and children asked whether it was really worth it, or sandwiches would do just as well. Many authorities had to respond by modernising their service and providing quick self-service and more popular food.

Encouraging efficiency

When a service is free it is difficult for consumers to express dissatisfaction. If they withdraw their *cash* from a particular school or college, when they are not getting what they want, the teachers will have to respond or lose their jobs. There is a direct sanction the parent or student can bring to bear. (I reviewed these arguments in Chapter 3.) Instead of the public sector having the advantage of free or subsidised services, the higher the charge the nearer it will be to the private alternative. This will put the public provider in direct and healthy competition with its private counterparts.

Social services are not different

Although some activities cannot by their very nature carry charges, there is nothing about social services that leads to such a conclusion. Most are not pure public goods and charging for them is technically possible. (See Chapter 2 for a discussion of public goods.) Foster *et al.* (1980) use this point to argue that there is a case for more extensive charging for local government services.

Charging brings appreciation and self-respect

It was argued by some on the Public Schools Commission (DES, 1970), for example, that parents and children would appreciate the value of the education they received and not simply take it for granted if they actually had to part with some money. Faced with the full cost of schooling, parents would ensure that their children made good use of it.

The same case has been made for social work. Free advice is largely ignored. If you pay good money to a psychiatrist or counsellor for advice you are likely to take it seriously. Moreover, as we saw earlier, it is possible to argue that to pay for a service produces an equal exchange relationship. The recipient feels no obligation, or sense of charity, in a market exchange. Pruger (1973) and Uttley (1980) argued that those who receive free services perceive themselves to be in debt in two senses:

1. They are in a vague way in debt to society or the state. This induces a sense of compliance.
2. Professionals who are already in a powerful position over their

patients or clients because of their superior knowledge can also induce a feeling of deference because the client has not paid for the service. If a free service builds up a high demand and a waiting list, that too increases a professional's power to humiliate or increase the client's dependency. A paying consumer at least feels he or she can say, 'I am paying for this service. If I do not like it or you keep me waiting, I will take my custom elsewhere.'
3. The professional may make more effort, knowing that the client is paying good money for his or her services, in a society that values things that are paid for and tends to devalue those that are not.

The poor need not suffer

Those who favour charging reject the claim that free services are the only way of ensuring that the poor benefit from them. It is possible to adopt any of the following strategies to give the poor access:

1. To vary the charges with the income of the recipient and, if the recipient is poor enough, to waive the charge.
2. To enable the poor to recover the charge from an agency like the DSS.
3. To provide everyone with a voucher that can be used instead of money to purchase a minimum amount of that particular service.
4. To ensure through general redistributive tax and cash benefit policies that all families have sufficient resources to purchase these services if they wish.

All these arguments, it should be noted, make the case for *pricing*, or *fees*, at cost. What they do not do is to make the case for charging token sums to a small minority of users.

Raising revenue – the pragmatists' response

Although many politicians have not been prepared to accept the thorough-going case for pricing advanced above, many have, under the practical pressure of public spending constraints, been prepared to accept charging as a supplementary way of raising revenue, or to see charges increased as the only way of preserving a service.

Public expenditure bargaining in Whitehall is conducted in terms of *net* spending by the departments – that is, spending after receipts from charges have been deducted. Thus at any particular point in that debate ministers will have to weigh the merits of cutting the hospital building programme or holding down nurses' salaries against raising the prescription charge, or of reducing the number of home students against charging a higher fee to overseas students. The DES managed to fend off pressure to increase the size of classes and other cuts in the standard of the education service by permitting the price of school meals to rise, and then by charging overseas students the full economic fee. The DHSS and DoH defended the Health Service in the same way by being prepared to see prescription and other charges rise.

The case against charging

Social service consumers are different

The opposing view holds that social service consumers are not like consumers in a supermarket. They are not able, or are less able, to express their preferences through a market mechanism for at least three reasons (Titmuss, 1968, Chapters 10 and 12).

Enforced consumers

Perhaps the extreme examples are the offenders who must make use of the probation officers' services. They are scarcely free to shop around for the officer who would give them the easiest time. Many of the social workers' functions require them to act as controlling agents, or in the interests of children against irresponsible or cruel parents, or to safeguard the community against a dangerous or disruptive mentally ill person.

The state forces children to be educated for a given period, if necessary against the parents' wishes or indifference. The notion of giving money or quasi money to a family to spend in a way they would not otherwise choose to do is very far from the assumptions of a free market in which people spend their own money on something they want.

Vulnerable consumers

Many recipients of the personal social services are very old, or mentally ill or handicapped, or disabled. Moreover, these dependent people do not reach a social services department in most cases unless the family cannot care for them without help. As a consequence, such people are weak and potentially exploitable recipients of service. The model of equal bargaining partners scarcely holds. Many old people are as good a set of consumers as anyone else, but the very old and frail are at risk.

Second-hand consumers

Patients are not merely vulnerable: they or their relatives are not really consumers at all. The medical professional is in an overwhelmingly powerful position. The doctor is essentially the 'demander' determining whether treatment is necessary, what kind and for how long the 'consumer' shall receive it. The phrase 'under doctor's orders' expresses a real situation that is different from a normal market. Many services like medical care are not bought in a normal commercial transaction by a user, but are bought via an intermediary or a third party, the insurance company. The consumer is often not even aware what the bill is, and if he or she is, merely posts it off to the company to pay. The disciplines of a market do not apply. None of these are an arguments against market allocation as such; they merely suggest that the market's virtues apply in a strictly limited range of circumstances.

Markets can be inefficient

While there is a good deal of intuitive sense in the observation that social workers and teachers respond to financial and other economic incentives like most workers, it is a hypothesis rather than an empirically supported contention. We do not know that market motivation is more effective in promoting high standards of care than professional value systems, ethical standards and organisational traditions of public service, professional and peer review, inspectorates, public criticism and evaluative research. We know little about the way in which workers' motivations are affected by the creation of a powerful market test. The economic literature largely ignores the fact that the public sector has devised its own alternative modes of efficiency incentive. In many respects these are deficient and could be extended and improved, but it is misleading to suggest that no incentives to good performance exist except market forces. There are grounds for suggesting that the market test can produce perverse incentives, as we have seen in Chapter 3.

Social services can be different

While there are close affinities between education provided in a state and a private school, much of the argument does in the end turn on the belief that there is something different in kind in the educational experience gained by a child in a local community school and one in a private school catering for a particular income group. These views depend on political values and preferences which we are not going to explore here, but clearly if you believe that society as a whole will gain by children from all income groups being educated together, or children from a local community or religious group being educated together, you will prefer a system of finance that favours such provision. Different financial incentives change the *nature* of the educational experience and are not merely alternative ways of financing the same service. Finance and provision are seen as interdependent, not independent.

Charging need not enhance a consumer's view of a service

It can do the reverse. In a largely market economy, individualistic values predominate. In general we value goods with a price, and devalue the 'free lunch', but it is possible for some institutions and professional and personal relationships to be viewed in different terms. As Hirsch (1977) points out, sexual relationships that are bought tend to be looked down on in our society compared with those that are freely chosen. Social institutions of long standing sustain their own value systems. People's attitudes to the Health Service expressed in opinion poll findings suggest it is extremely popular in comparison with the health care system of the 1930s.

The poor can suffer

The process of reducing charges for low income groups may not be effective. Precisely because 'paying your own way' is seen as the socially acceptable thing to do, where some do this and others do not the non-payers distinguish themselves as undeserving or in receipt of special favours. Even if they are not inhibited from applying for special treatment they may suffer some loss of self-respect in receiving the service free. Evidence on this subject is extremely difficult to gather and interpret. People do not readily admit to feeling stigmatised.

Probably the most decisive argument for the free personal social services is that most of their recipients are already so poor that charges bring little revenue.

In brief

There are contested arguments for and against charging for social services, which resemble the more general argument about markets we reviewed in Chapter 3. In practice, the origins of charging are diverse and often little more than symbolic. They raise little revenue because so many of the recipients are poor. Some services, however, are exceptions.

Further reading

A polemical case for charging is well advanced in Seldon, A. (1977), *Charge*, London: Temple Smith.

The case for pricing local services is set out briefly in Foster *et al.* (1980), *Local Government Finance in a Unitary State*, London: Allen & Unwin.

The Layfield Committee (1976), *Local Government Finance* (Cmnd 6453), London: HMSO, discussed the wider use of charging for local government services.

Charging, its origins and theory as applied to the personal social services, is excellently set out in Judge, K. and Matthews, J. (1980), *Charging for Social Care*, London: Allen & Unwin.

CHAPTER 9

CHARITY AND GIVING

Giving as a form of finance

Taxes are a compulsory levy to finance services. Charges often amount to the same thing. Fees are payments made, more or less voluntarily, depending on the circumstances, for a service you buy. A gift or donation is, at its best, a payment made voluntarily so that a service may be given to others. Of course, it would be naive to claim that all gifts are made with no thought of any benefit that might accrue to the individual or his or her family at some future time, or to deny that gifts are often a reflection of gratitude for past services rendered to a member of the family or the donor him or herself. Relatives may make a gift to a local hospital that has cared for a loved one. Parents or relatives often make donations to their old public school or college as some repayment for what it has done for them, or in the hope that it may give their child a better chance of entry! Many donors lay down more or less stringent rules about the use of their funds and these are legally binding on the body that receives them. They do not change as society changes and this may be an embarrassment to the organisation or trust that administers such income.

It is quite wrong to associate 'charity' or voluntary giving exclusively with 'voluntary' or non-profit organisations. As we shall see later, National Health Service hospitals obtain an important share of all monetary gifts and other voluntary help. But while public provision does not preclude charitable giving, the existence of the profit motive in any service usually does. It seems improbable that donors will be motivated to give time or money to a profit-making hospital or home, on the grounds that it would be difficult to ensure that the patients or residents received the benefit, not the owner.

Forms of giving

Unpaid caring

It is possible to distinguish many different forms of giving in the field of welfare. First, and most important in relation to the personal social services, is *caring within the family* – services given without financial reward to other members of the household, including children, or to relations outside the household. A number of points can be made about this form of giving, as follows:

1. If it were not for such giving the burden on the formal services and on tax payers would be far greater.
2. Much of the most personal forms of care is done by women, but both men and women contribute a lot of time.
3. Most of the burden falls very heavily on a small number of people.
4. The motives and felt obligations that lie behind such giving are complex (Finch, 1987; Lewis and Meredith, 1988).
5. Much of this care is not voluntary; it is enforced by lack of other services and is sometimes resented by those doing the caring. In so far as this is the case, the result is similar to a tax on the carers concerned.

Studies in the 1980s revealed the scale of unpaid caring. The General Household Survey's special analysis of carers in 1985 (Green, 1988) suggested that: 1.7 million adults are caring for someone living with them; 1.4 million are spending at least twenty hours per week doing so; and 3.4 million are bearing the main responsibility for the care of someone. Overall, about one adult in seven was caring for someone who was sick, elderly or handicapped. Although some of the early literature suggested this was a largely female responsibility, a reanalysis of the General Household Survey suggests that this is not so. 15 per cent of women are caring for someone, but so are 12 per cent of men (Evandrou, 1990). It is true that women live longer when more of such caring is undertaken hence there are more women carers in absolute terms – 3.5 million compared to 2.5 million men.

The type of care given is gendered to some extent; 28 per cent of women are giving personal care, as against 19 per cent of men. Men do more physical work. And Parker (1990) points out: 'The costs to informal carers of caring for dependent people can include economic, physical, emotional and opportunity costs: loss and reduction of employment; reduced income; increased expenditure; restricted family and social life and physical and emotional strain': where families had a severely disabled child, mothers' participation in the labour market was lower, they worked fewer hours and were paid less. Fathers' employment was not as affected. The same kinds of effect can be seen in studies of families with disabled young adults (Hirst, 1984) and a disabled spouse (Martin and White, 1988).

Putting a cash figure to the loss of employment that results from caring responsibilities is far from straightforward. It is estimated that for women to give up work to look after disabled relatives cost earnings of £8,500 if they had no children and about £7,000 if they had. Family income in families with dependent children is lower (Smyth and Robins, 1989). Evandrou (1990) showed that, nationally, the equivalent income of carers (taking account of family size) was somewhat lower than for non-carers, but the real drop in income was experienced by those caring for someone in their own household. While non-carers' individual equivalised median income was £87 in 1985, carers with a dependant in their household had a median income of only £64 a week. This drop in income can be seen as a private contribution to the cost of care by the family itself. The policy question is how far families should bear the burden themselves and how far the state, through social security, or otherwise, should pay for the costs of disability (see Chapter 14).

Giving human capital to voluntary organisations

Giving skills

Many voluntary organisations depend heavily on those with

technical, secretarial, accountancy, fund-raising, carpentry, building or professional skills giving their advice free of charge.

Giving time

Volunteers who give their labour free provide an important part of work done by Citizens Advice Bureaux, law centres, marriage guidance, youth work and teaching English to foreigners. The Wolfenden Committee's (1978) survey of voluntary work in the social service field showed that 14 per cent of the national sample reported undertaking some work of that kind in a twelve-month period. Just over two-thirds of the total, or 10 per cent, worked with some identifiable voluntary organisation. On average these people claimed they spent about six hours a week on such work, and this was equivalent to about 400,000 full-time workers. Later surveys of voluntary work have produced varied results (Halfpenny, 1990), but it seems that about three in ten adults undertook voluntary work on behalf of an organisation in 1990, a figure that had not changed much throughout the 1980s.

Giving in kind

Anyone who has ever participated in a voluntary organisation, youth work or parents' association will know what a central place is taken by jumble sales and selling raffle tickets (see Table 9.1). Whether you see jumble as giving or refuse disposal, the fact is that it makes up a significant part of the income of small local organisations. Gifts in kind on a larger scale by local shops or firms also exist on a large scale. Unlike America, Britain has nothing equivalent to the 'food bank', through which gifts of food can be distributed on a community-wide basis to poor people. The most highly organised and valuable system of giving in kind is the gift of blood. Titmuss's famous book *The Gift Relationship* (1970) used the example of donating blood to raise the whole discussion about giving and social welfare on to a philosophical level. He argued that there were some peculiar features of blood as a commodity that made the donating of blood efficient. Since blood could be infected and since detection was both difficult and expensive, the best guarantee of purity was the screening of donors who had no monetary incentives to lie about their past medical records. (Titmuss's work pre-dated AIDS, which reinforced his message.) However, Titmuss's argument was deeper and more general. Donating blood was an example of a social institution that

Table 9.1 Voluntary fund-raising and other activities of households in Britain 1987

Activity	Percentages		
	Male	Female	All
Raising money			
Jumble sale helper	6	10	8
Selling raffle tickets	8	12	10
Selling tickets for events	3	6	5
Collecting things to be sold	7	10	8
Making things to be sold	3	6	4
Sponsored event participant	6	8	7
Sponsored event organiser	3	3	3
Organising fund-raising event	2	5	4
Doing things to help			
Visiting elderly/sick	8	8	8
Blood donor	4	4	4
Other	15	20	17

Source: Central Statistical Office, 1991a.

embodied non-selfish actions by individuals without demeaning the recipient. It was important to provide an opportunity for that to happen in all welfare organisations, for it sustained an unselfish motivation which was in the end necessary to sustain social institutions.

Giving cash

The only form of giving that shows up in formal accounts is cash. It comes broadly from four sources: direct giving by households and enterprises, indirect giving by tax payers, and charitable bodies' own income from property trusts or investments.

How much does the ordinary household give in cash to charity? The Charity Household Survey, the Family Expenditure Survey and Inland Revenue figures give us some rough guide. From July 1989 to June 1990 a national sample of households was asked to record their charitable donations of all kinds (*Charity Trends, 1990*). In line with other previous studies the total level of cash giving revealed was very small. Half the respondents gave £1 per month or less, and only 6 per cent gave £30 or more. The mean or average amount was nearly £8 a month or about 0.76 per cent of average earnings. This means that the total household cash contributions to every form of charity, of which social services are only a small part, was not more than about £5,000 million, or one fifth of the cost of the NHS. The level of giving has not increased in real terms at all significantly in the late 1980s despite attempts to increase its attractiveness through various tax reliefs.

Any income a charity receives is not subject to tax. Charities are also exempt from paying various taxes such as VAT. Taken together these are a significant help and in effect constitute an indirect government subsidy. In so far as the levels of government expenditure are fixed by general political considerations, if one group is expressly given favourable tax treatment the value of tax revenue lost is a cost that must be financed by other tax payers. An individual can also trigger tax help by making a covenant to a charity. If he or she undertakes to make a part of his or her income over to a charity for four years or more, the tax the individual pays on that income is given by the tax authorities to the charity concerned.

The charity does not pay tax on its income. Thus the *price* of giving is reduced for tax payers, especially higher-rate tax payers. If I want a charity to benefit by £100 and I am paying tax at 30 per cent, I need only give up £70. If I pay at 50 per cent, I only need give £50. The higher the tax rate the more incentive there is to give to charity. The lower the tax rate the more costly it is to give to charity compared to ordinary spending. The lower marginal income tax rates of the 1980s made giving to charities relatively more expensive.

In America there are more generous tax advantages for giving to charity, since individuals and firms can offset any one-off gift against tax, whether in cash or in kind. The inducement to give is greater, but by the same token there is a cost to the Exchequer in lost revenue. Some early work in the United States (Feldstein, 1975; Clotfelter, 1985) has suggested that the scale of charitable donations increases faster than the reduction in tax revenue and that the level of giving increases sharply if tax reliefs are given. Some have therefore concluded that such a tax deduction system would increase the flow of revenue to charities by more than the tax loss and hence produce an increase in social service provision. There are, however, several assumptions in that argument.

The first is that the donations that would be made would go to charitable social service agencies providing for the same groups as statutory agencies. If tax-relief-induced donations did not go to pay for mainline social service functions and elected representatives still felt it necessary to continue to provide them, they would have a lower tax base on which to raise the revenue.

The second assumption is that additional tax relief will indeed increase the level of giving. During the 1980s the Conservative government took several steps to increase tax relief on gifts with this in mind. After 1980 it was possible for charities to reclaim tax paid on money covenanted to them for four years or more, not just at the standard rate of tax, but at the higher rate if individuals paid tax at the higher rate. The 1986 Finance Act introduced tax relief on regular giving to charities deducted from the giver's pay packet. In the 1983 budget, gifts to charities were exempted from capital transfer tax. In 1990 the Gift Aid Scheme allows tax relief on single cash gifts to charities. In short, a lot was done to increase the level of charitable donations from individuals in the 1980s. Does it provide a new way of paying for welfare in the 1990s?

Jones and Posnett (1990) examined the relationship between the level of covenant giving and the tax price (that is, the tax relief you gain if you give through a covenant). They were unable to find any link when other variables like prices and incomes were taken into account. They also point out that more recent American work has cast doubt on the relationship there too. In short, the latest evidence does not suggest that giving more tax relief will promote much more giving.

Companies are another source of cash aid. Again, the Conservative government tried to encourage such activity by enabling them to make one-off tax deductible donations of up to 3 per cent of annual dividends. The level of corporate support is low. A survey in *Charity Trends* (1990) of the top 400 companies in the United Kingdom showed corporate support as a share of profit running at about 0.6 per cent. This figure had not changed much on previous surveys. Amongst those who did give, education, health and general welfare came out as top recipients, but the top 200 corporate donors altogether only gave £150 million for all purposes – a trivial sum in comparison with any social spending total: £25 billion, say, on the NHS or education (see Figure 9.1).

About 80 per cent of all giving in the United Kingdom comes from individuals, not very different from the percentage in the

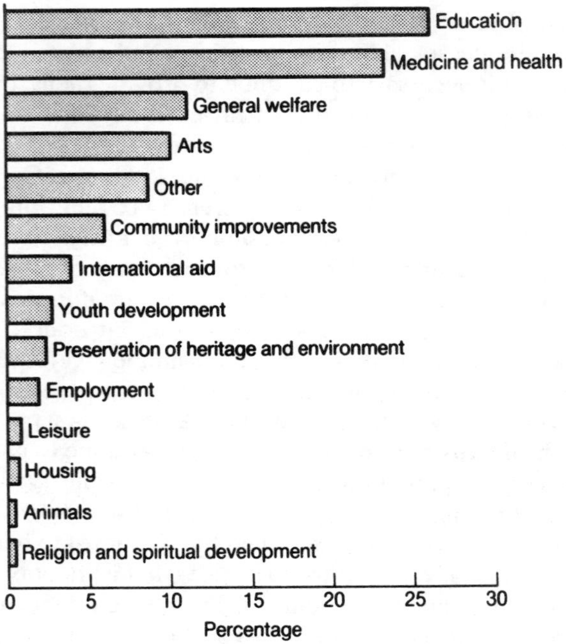

Figure 9.1 The uses of corporate contributions: percentage share of total contributions by top companies by purpose of gift in the United Kingdom 1990 (Source: *Charity Trends*, 1990)

United States and Canada, but in the United States gifts amount to about 2 per cent of the GNP, in Canada 0.7 per cent and in the United Kingdom only 0.55 per cent. Individual contributions fell sharply in the recession of the early 1980s. They were equivalent to 0.57 per cent of an individual's income in 1975 but fell to 0.35 and 0.4 per cent in the early 1980s. By 1988 they had recovered to 0.75 per cent.

The limits of giving

We have seen that gifts of time, skills and even blood can be a significant component in the income of social service organisations, especially in the personal social service field. Private money is less important, but still significant for some areas of voluntary non-profit social service. Giving is also qualitatively important for the giver. It is a means by which a person can express concern and gain satisfaction, especially if the gift takes the form of personal involvement. Nevertheless, there are limits to the extent that charity can be an effective form of financing social welfare.

Prejudice against giving

The Victorians were much concerned with pauperisation. They feared that well-meaning people giving out money to the poor would merely encourage the 'non-deserving' poor to pursue their lazy and irresponsible ways. It was this fear, indeed, that lay behind the creation of the Charity Organisation Society, whose aim was not to prevent charity but to curb its excesses and 'irresponsible' hand-outs. Though such fears may be associated, possibly wrongly, with Conservative values, a contrasting attitude is expressed by many on the left. They do not feel that charity is an appropriate response to poverty. The causes, they believe, are social and political and should be tackled as such. Hand-outs to the poor will merely reduce the pressure for such change and are particularly pernicious if they are given by the rich, who are in effect purchasing their own privilege at a small price. Both sets of attitudes reduce the motivation to give.

Reluctance to receive

To give usually brings status. To be a recipient is normally to put oneself in a subordinate position. It is not until that gift has been repaid and the exchange relationship put in balance again that a person will feel no sense of obligation. The more sensitive we are to the possible stigmatising consequences of charity, the less motivation there will be for giving. The more remote the relationship between the giver and the receiver, the less these inhibitions may be. Perhaps that is why there is so much voluntary help given to local hospitals. No-one supposes that because volunteers help out in the pathology laboratory, or carry tea round or give blood, the patients will feel stigmatised. That is because giving is being undertaken within the context of a service that caters for everyone, and the gift is granted by what Titmuss (1970) called the 'unnamed stranger'. Nevertheless, such impersonal giving has its disadvantages. There are, we may postulate, different kinds of giver. Some people may be pure altruists. They merely require the knowledge that they have given to their fellows, but most people will wish to have a closer involvement. The more remote the giving, the less they will be motivated.

'Free-rider' problems

If we could be sure that everyone in the community was equally generous, it might be possible to finance social services by announcing how much it would cost to run the Health Service per head in the coming year and then leave it to individuals to post an appropriate sum to their local health authority. We would all act on the assumption that others were acting in a similar manner. The problem is that it would be in the self-interest of any one of us to withhold our contribution, let everyone else contribute, gain free health care *and* keep the cash. We would get the ride free, as the economists put it. (For a fuller discussion of the economic theory see Collard, 1978.) If we know the tax inspector will force compliance if our neighbour tries to gain a free ride, we may more willingly pay our taxes. By the same reasoning, individuals would be unlikely to donate to an activity that the state was already undertaking unless they could be sure that their gifts were not merely being used to reduce other tax payers' liability. Arguments of this kind are very evident in discussions about how parents' associations should respond to education cuts. If they do come in and give a computer or prevent the school library closing by providing books, may the council not simply take the opportunity to make more cuts in the hope that the parents will pay up?

The unevenness problem

If giving is specific, its spread will tend to be uneven. If a millionaire has a mentally handicapped child, services for such children in his or her home town may be superb, regardless of how many such children there are in that town.

The problem of fluctuating incomes

Economic crisis (as we saw earlier) or simple chance factors like media coverage and fashion will affect the scale and permanence of giving for particular purposes. Charities therefore face fluctuating incomes that make it difficult to offer consistent and continuous provision, unless they are big and have endowment or trust income to draw upon – and even then unwise investment policy or a fall in dividends or share prices may affect the level of the service offered.

These inherent limits to voluntary or charitable giving apply most directly to basic, mainline social service provision where the state accepts a clear residual responsibility. It *will* provide if no-one else does. In this situation the 'free-rider' problem becomes dominant. If I wish to maximise my impact on improving human life, I can do so best by putting my effort into activities I know are unlikely to take place otherwise and into small-scale ventures where I can actually see results for my efforts. It was for these reasons that Beveridge (1948) saw the role of voluntary activity fitting best *on top* of a sound comprehensive foundation of public social services. Voluntary action could provide innovation, experiment, specialist extra help and the filling of gaps left by the state.

The economists' case for a third sector

Arguments about voluntarism and giving are apt to get confused with arguments about mixed economies of welfare and plurality of provision. They are, in fact, quite distinct. A non-statutory, non-profit agency may well have volunteers working for it and receive donations. These factors will affect its organisational structure and ethos (Billis, 1989) but are not crucial to its essential characteristic – it is not a profit-making agency and it is not under direct political control. Why should such a third sector exist? Is it merely a remnant of the past? Weisbrod (1986), an American economist, produced a theoretical justification. He argued that since there was evidence of market failure (Chapter 2) and public sector failure (Chapter 3) it was logical to expect there to be room for a third kind of organisation that served purposes which public and market institutions failed to do. He was not able to deduce what these purposes might be, but the persistence of a third sector suggested they must exist.

Wolfenden's case

One attempt to generalise the distinct contribution of the voluntary sector was made by the Wolfenden Committee on the future of voluntary organisations (1978). The committee argued that the two main agents for providing social care were the state, local and national, and the 'informal' sector, families and individuals helping one another. It stated: 'Although the voluntary system, as we have shown, was once the chief form of collective action outside the Poor Law, it can now best be seen in terms of the ways in which it complements, supplements, extends and influences the informal and statutory systems' (p. 26). The voluntary non-statutory sector was able to extend provision because it could attract the services of people who would not be prepared to work for a public authority. Not being bound by statutory rules and political control it was better able to innovate – perhaps trail-blazing for local authorities to take up when the experiment was seen to work. Voluntary bodies could provide alternatives to local council or NHS provision, thus giving clients a choice of some kind. Some kinds of social need may not be met by the state because the groups involved are too small or too unpopular for politicians to be prepared to incur displeasure helping them – alcoholics, drug addicts or battered women. A non-statutory body with gifts from concerned members of the public can fill such gaps.

Running through much of the public debate on voluntary organisations, and not entirely absent from the Wolfenden Report, is the confusion between a non-statutory organisation that provides services and can have significant or even total support from state funds, and the notion of voluntary donations of time or money, which are not exclusively given to non-statutory bodies. Many voluntary bodies became heavily dependent on grants from central government under the urban aid programme and the Manpower Services Commission schemes for unemployed young people in the 1980s. There are some good arguments for tax payers' money being channelled to social service providers that are not statutory bodies. They may be freer to experiment or help unpopular clients, and the government can then disown them or cut off funds more readily if it is attacked. This kind of tactical reasoning must, however, be sharply distinguished from the argument for voluntary or charitable sources of income with which we are concerned in this chapter. By a similar slip of logic it is sometimes presumed in such discussions that voluntary bodies are the only or the main beneficiaries of voluntary help and cash aid. But much volunteer help now flows to statutory services, like hospitals and old people's homes. The NHS has more volunteers working for it than any other agency. One rationale for the non-government *sector* is that it can more readily mobilise 'voluntary' help, but this is not necessarily so. The state sector could, if it wished, make a good deal more use of voluntary help.

Some of these issues were explored in a useful international study by Kramer (1981). He compared the role of voluntary organisations for the physically and mentally handicapped in Britain, the United States, the Netherlands and Israel. Their scope and role were very different in many ways but, as he argues, there were more basic similarities than differences. The unique features he identified were rather different from those identified by Wolfenden, Beveridge and other writers, such as experimentation or innovation. These were actually relatively infrequent in the voluntary sector, which was often conservative in its approach, while the state sector could be innovative. What the voluntary sector did, which democratic government could not do, was the following:

1. To provide *specialist* care on a selective or *exclusive* basis – for example, for families of a particular religious denomination or area. Governments, rightly, find it difficult to be overtly discriminatory, or to specialise in idiosyncratic ways. Voluntary organisations attract support from such narrow groups and enthusiasts precisely because their constituency of appeal is a narrow one. In a pluralistic society this is to be welcomed.
2. To act as *advocates* or defenders of the specialist care of the group for which they are working. 'The mission of defending and articulating the interests of undeserving populations at risk takes on more importance as the social services in the welfare state become universal' (Kramer, 1981, p. 261).

3. To provide a vehicle for *self-help* or *consumerism*; that is, groups of families, dependants or sufferers who seek mutual support or a means of articulating their concerns. In practice, Kramer argues, the older traditional voluntary organisations gave little or no place to the consumer. They were typically paternalistic. The newer, smaller, spontaneous groups – of parents with mentally handicapped children, for example – must be voluntary and self-help to retain their independence and to enable them to build the self-respect of their members. To achieve these purposes, such organisations must be free from government interference or control.
4. To *provide main-stream services*, not distinctively different in kind from those of state welfare; to supply supplementary services, complementary services or services on a cost basis to agencies of government. Kramer points out (as I have done) that there may be the particular advantage of wider choice or plurality in these cases, but they are the advantages of a private or mixed market, not of voluntarism as such.

Kramer also adds some warnings. If voluntary organisations expand, especially if largely in receipt of public money, they tend to take on all the disadvantages of size and age – bureaucratisation or 'creeping formalisation', as he calls it. Agencies can become dependent on public finance and subservient to government or those who give the funds, such as large corporations. In this case they are less able to perform their exclusive and critical functions 1–3. They suffer from 'donor dependency'. Their very idiosyncratic and undemocratic nature, which is part of their strength, can lead to their rule by a narrow and self-selecting group. Since they are subject to the disciplines of neither the market nor the ballot box they can become *ineffectual*.

We shall be returning to these arguments about the mixed market for personal social services and recent government policy in Chapter 11.

Further reading

Economics students should consult Collard, D. (1978), *Altruism and Economy: A study in non-selfish economics*, Oxford: Martin Robertson.

An excellent American text is S. Rose-Ackerman (1986), *The Economics of Non-Profit Institutions*, Oxford: Oxford University Press, which contains an article by Weisbrod and much else comprehensible to social policy students. This could be supplemented by Jones, P.R. (1983), 'Aid to charities', *International Journal of Social Economics*, **10**, no. 2, pp. 3–11.

Social policy students should certainly read Titmuss's classic exposition of the case for donating blood, set out in Titmuss, R.M. (1970), *The Gift Relationship*, London: Allen & Unwin, and comments on his thesis, such as Pruger, K. (1973), 'Social policy: unilateral transfer or reciprocal exchange', *Journal of Social Policy*, **2**, part 4, pp. 289–302.

Parker, G. (1990), *With Due Care and Attention: A review of research on informal care*, 2nd edn, London: Family Policy Studies Centre, is the best overview of research on informal care.

Two general discussions of voluntary organisations which should be read are the Wolfenden Report (Wolfenden Committee (1978), *The Future of Voluntary Organisations*, London: Croom Helm) and Kramer's international study (Kramer, R. (1981); *Voluntary Agencies in the Welfare State*, Berkeley, C.A.: University of California Press).

A useful US discussion of the use of informal helping networks in social care is to be found in Whittaker, J. K. and Gabarino, J. (1983), *Social Support Networks: Informal helping in the human services*, New York: Aldine.

The case for more charitable effort is to be found in Gerard, D. (1983) *Charities in Britain: Conservatism or change*, London: Bedford Square Press.

For information on levels of giving by individuals and firms see the latest edition of *Charity Trends*, Tonbridge: Charities Aid Foundation.

PART IV

Financing the services

CHAPTER 10

PAYING FOR HEALTH SERVICES

The history of health care finance

It is impossible to understand why health care is financed the way it is in the United Kingdom without looking briefly at its historical origins. Moreover, they illustrate many of the theoretical points that have been raised in previous chapters.

The hospitals

By the early part of the last century two kinds of hospital had emerged that set the pattern for finance and provision for the next 150 years (Abel-Smith, 1964). The *voluntary hospitals* were private charities. They ranged from ancient foundations, like St Bartholomew's and St Thomas's, to smaller local charities. Most hospitals in the provinces relied on donations or regular subscriptions to keep going. Such giving was not unconditional. Sometimes the hospital was obliged to purchase goods from the traders who were subscribers, and donors also had the right to nominate people whom they wished to receive attention. One group that was frequently excluded was the poor – those who could not be guaranteed to be able to pay their own funeral expenses. Those with infectious diseases, too, were excluded, and children who were vulnerable to them. The chronic sick, the elderly and others who would need long-term care were a drain on the hospitals' budgets and of little interest for teaching purposes. So they were increasingly excluded. It was not only gifts of cash that kept the voluntary hospitals going, but the donation by leading doctors of their services. What these men gained in return was the prestige and professional recognition that came from practising at one of the teaching hospitals.

Despite these developments, charitable subscriptions supplemented by local appeals could not keep pace with rising demand and increasingly expensive treatments. One obvious way out was to charge richer patients a fee, but the hospital governors feared that this would deter charitable donations. In smaller towns where the general practitioners ran the hospitals (often called cottage hospitals), patients were already charged. So, reluctantly, the larger voluntary hospitals followed. Financially squeezed by the depression of the 1880s, they began to accept paying patients. They were treated in a quite different way and in separate wards – the forerunner to the modern pay-beds. In 1895, the Royal Free appointed an official 'almoner' to ensure that patients were genuinely poor and that they contributed what they could afford to their treatment. The practice became widespread and a new profession emerged to administer the process – the precursors of modern medical social workers. Yet payments of fees on a means-tested basis changed the nature of the voluntary sector and caused widespread resentment.

After the First World War the voluntary hospitals faced a severe and growing financial crisis. An immediate Exchequer grant was provided to tide the hospitals over the emergency. Moreover, people who covenanted money to the hospitals for over six years secured income tax relief on the sum (1922 Finance Act). Thus an indirect form of Exchequer aid began. Another new source of income was the contributory schemes, the largest being the Hospital Saving Association. In return for paying a small weekly contribution the contributor and his dependants acquired a presumption that they would be treated free without a means test – though this was never a legal right. The association usually paid the hospital a weekly flat rate. These schemes were very unpopular with the medical profession as they limited the number of private patients who would pay the doctors direct. In short, voluntary hospitals that began as charities had, by the 1930s, developed an enormous variety in their forms of income. There was also great variety in the standard of treatment they offered. Since consultants gave their time free they were more available in more wealthy urban areas which could support the private practices that provided their income. By the Second World War, many of the voluntary hospitals were still in serious financial trouble, a problem the war helped solve, at least temporarily, as the government paid large sums for the treatment of war casualties (Titmuss, 1950).

Alongside the voluntary hospitals there had gradually developed a state-provided hospital sector. Its origins lay in the Poor Law and it was never to lose that association. The Poor Law workhouses came to accommodate growing numbers of sick, elderly and infirm paupers, and a medical officer was employed, along with nursing staff, to care for these people. Under the Metropolitan Poor Act of 1867 and a Poor Law Amendment Act of the following year, Poor Law Guardians were able to create separate infirmaries – pauper hospitals. They were to be equipped like any other general hospital ward. The association with the stigma of poor relief remained, however, and to a very large extent these hospitals became the home for the long-stay patients and the elderly who were such a drain on the finances of the voluntary hospitals.

In 1929, as part of the larger reform of the Poor Law, these hospitals became the responsibility of local authorities – the county councils. They also had control of the hospitals that had been provided under other statutes to treat the mentally ill, those with infectious diseases, tuberculosis and the mentally handicapped. Moreover, several of the more ambitious authorities, like London and Middlesex, developed their own acute hospitals. During the war the Coalition government produced a plan to reorganise completely the chaotic system of hospital finance and provision. The local authorities were to be the main organisers of hospital provision, combining together in joint authorities to plan care in their areas, including the voluntary sector. They would have no direct control over such institutions except that they could pay them for particular services. It had some similarities to the Conservative reforms of 1990. Such a system would not have reduced the wide disparity in standards of care or the process of means testing or the financial difficulties of the voluntary hospitals. When the Labour government was elected in 1945, it produced more radical proposals – nationalisation of the local authority and voluntary hospitals. The 1946 National Health Service Act was the result (Webster, 1988). Hospitals were to be wholly *funded* from taxation, *provided* by statutory bodies – Regional Hospital Boards – and managed by hospital management committees, with nominated members. That change was carried into effect on 1 July 1948 and remains the basis for hospital finance today.

Primary care

The finance of primary care has had a very different history (Eckstein, 1964; Gilbert, 1966; Stevens, 1966; Honnigsbaum, 1979). Medical practitioners began as individual private entrepreneurs selling their skills and medical knowledge, such as it was. But theirs was never a free market. The Royal College of Physicians, incorporated by Henry VIII in 1518, established a monopoly of medical practice in London by licensing registered physicians in the area. Surgery grew as a separate profession under its own royal charter. Both groups sold their services mainly to the rich and the upper classes, *giving* their service to the voluntary hospitals in the large cities.

It was the apothecaries who were the originators of what, today, we call the family doctor, or the general practitioner, and the dentist. They were shopkeepers who sold medicines or cures and established their right to treat the sick during the plague. They extended their functions to holding surgeries with dispensaries and to visiting the sick at home. They became 'the doctor' for the working class, but they remained private entrepreneurs who had to make their living by charging for their services. At the same time working people developed their own form of voluntary associations – the friendly societies – that enabled the better-off sections of the working class, at least, to receive cash benefits when the wage earner was ill, with the illness certified and treated by a doctor paid by the society. By the beginning of the twentieth century they had about six million members. Commercial insurance companies also grew and some doctors in poor areas ran their own sick clubs, to which the poor contributed on a regular basis to obtain free treatment when they were sick. That system and the friendly societies were needed to keep doctors in business at all in the poorest areas of the industrial cities.

By the end of the nineteenth century the friendly societies were also in financial trouble. Their members were surviving longer. Instead of dying by the age of about 40, more were living to an age at which they could not continue to work and had to be supported. It was a burden their funds could not bear. Moreover, few schemes covered women or children. This threw growing numbers on the Poor Law and added to a rising poor rate. Lloyd George's attempt at a solution was to copy from Germany's social insurance scheme and create a British variant – National Health Insurance (Gilbert, 1966). This provided sickness benefit and the right to free treatment and drugs for members, as well as the choice of a local doctor from those who practised in the scheme (1911 National Insurance Act). It was essentially an extension of the friendly society schemes – the societies helped administer it – but it also covered occupational groups that had never been able to be members. It covered all manual workers and those earning up to a given sum – £430 a year by 1942. Each employee and his or her employer had to contribute so much per week to the scheme. The doctor received a *per capita* payment for each of those registered with him or (rarely) her. Once established there was natural pressure to extend the scheme. Excluded groups and those just above the income limit always felt aggrieved and pressed for inclusion. Though workers were in the scheme, it excluded children, non-working wives, the self-employed and the elderly. This illustrates the difficulty of confining provision of a sought-after service to low-income groups (Goodin and Le Grand, 1987).

Two other features of the scheme were both bitterly resented by working people. First, the flat-rate contributions required were the same for each person. The incomes of similarly sized approved (friendly) societies were the same, but those which covered miners or those in more dangerous or unhealthy jobs had a high call on their benefits. White-collar societies were thus able to be much more generous, covering members of the worker's family and dental treatment, convalescent care, ophthalmic care and more. The resentment arose from the concentration of high-risk categories in particular occupations and the reluctance of insurance companies or societies to include them – a perfect example of cream skimming and adverse selection, discussed in Chapter 2. Attempts to extend the scope of risk pooling by using richer schemes' surplus funds to help poor schemes failed. (There is a debate between historians of this period as to whether the government or the societies were to blame: (Honnigsbaum, 1983; Whiteside, 1983; Whiteside and Krafchik, 1983).

The second unpopular feature of the system arose from the different attention doctors gave to members of the state scheme compared with their private patients, often even segregated in different waiting rooms. These perceived injustices led the trade union and labour movement to campaign vigorously for an end to the insurance system and for a single universal, Exchequer-funded scheme to cover all forms of primary care. This solution was to be embodied in the 1946 Act. The general practitioner, however, retained his or her claim to be 'an independent contractor' by receiving a sum of money from the Central Exchequer for each person who signed on to the practice. The doctors in poorer areas, in particular, were major beneficiaries of this arrangement, which gave them a secure income for the first time. They were private individuals or partnerships, paid by the state to provide a universal service free at the point of use.

The third leg of the 1948 tripartite structure to the NHS was the community health service administered, as it always had been, by local authorities and hence financed like any other local service partly by central government grant and partly out of local revenue – the rates. The services included midwives, health visitors, district nurses and various clinics. In 1974 the structure changed and they were taken from local authorities and amalgamated within the new health authorities – first area, and then later (1982) district, health authorities. The community health services then came to be financed wholly by central government.

Expenditure on the National Health Service

From 1948, when the Health Service began, to 1990, current expenditure in real terms (excluding price increases) rose more than two and a half times. Total spending on the NHS represented about 4 per cent of the gross domestic product in 1948, and rose to 6 per cent by 1990, stabilising in the 1980s. Compared to most other advanced economies, that figure is low (see Table 10.1).

Table 10.1 Total expenditure on health care, public and private, as a percentage of GDP in OECD countries 1989

Country	Total expenditure, public expenditure and private house-holds	Public only	Public expenditure's share (excluding charges)
Australia	7.6	5.1	70
Austria	8.2	5.7	67
Belgium	7.2	5.5	89
Canada	8.7	6.5	75
Denmark	6.3	5.2	84
France	8.7	6.7	75
Germany	8.2	6.3	72
Greece	5.1	4.0	89
Ireland	8.6	6.4	84
Italy	7.6	5.4	79
Japan	6.7	5.0	73
Netherlands	8.3	6.6	73
Norway	7.6	7.4	95
Portugal	6.3	3.9	62
Spain	6.3	4.3	78
Sweden	8.8	8.2	90
United States	11.8	4.6	42
United Kingdom	5.8	5.3	87
All OECD	7.3	5.6	76

Source: *Health Care Financing Review*, 1989 Annual *Supplement*, Schieber *et al.*, 1991.

Public expenditure on health care is similar to the OECD average, but our overall expenditure including private is lower.

The low spending figure is, in part, a tribute to the way the NHS has been able to keep down health costs which have increased much faster in other countries, most notably those with insurance-based systems of finance (see below). Nevertheless, strong underlying trends have been pushing up costs in the United Kingdom as they have in other countries – the increasing sophistication of medical treatment, the survival of those who would have died in an earlier decade, new and expensive drugs, the growing awareness amongst the public of potential treatments, a reluctance to merely grin and bear pain and discomfort, and above all the ageing of the population. It is twenty-three times as expensive to provide health care for those over 85 as for people aged between 16 and 44 (see

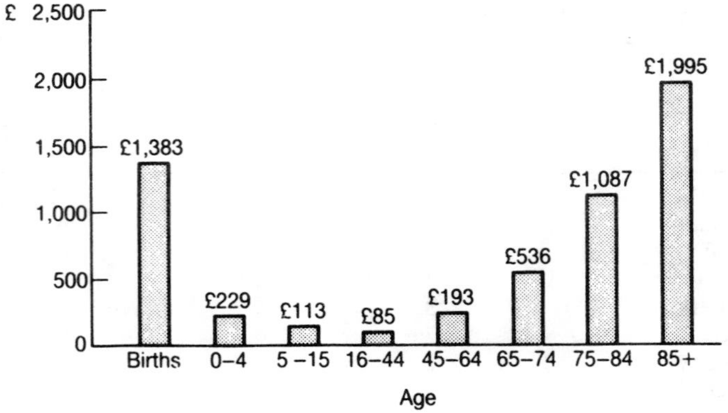

Figure 10.1 Estimated gross current expenditure per head by age in hospital and community health services in the United Kingdom 1988–9 (Source: Cm 1513, 1991)

Figure 10.1). About half the total expenditure of the hospital and community services goes on the care of people over 65.

If we take account of the changing age structure of the population and the rising relative costs of the elderly, NHS expenditure on an age-weighted basis fell in volume terms in the 1980s. Sixteen per cent of the budget goes on the care of the mentally ill and mentally handicapped. None of these categories of patient so far are likely to get private insurance cover.

Nearly two-thirds of the total budget is used to pay for staff. The largest part of that – nearly half – is on nursing staff. Medical and dental staff take only about one-eighth of salary costs. Drugs, dressings, X-ray and laboratory expenses take the largest share of the non-salary costs. Hospitals take the lion's share of the NHS budget. Family practitioner services take just over a fifth of total NHS spending. They comprise the services of general practitioners, opticians, dentists, and the cost of drugs dispensed by chemists.

Despite the growing demographic and other pressures on the NHS, it has reduced the real costs of treating patients in the last ten years. Taking account of the general increase in prices, the price of treating each acute in-patient fell by 12 per cent from 1978/9 to 1988/9 as the length of stay fell. It fell even more for geriatric patients – by no less than a third in the same period (Cm 1513, 1991).

The present system of finance

The National Health Service claims its funds from three sources. General taxation provided about 77 per cent of the total in 1990–1 (Cm 1513, 1991); about 9 per cent came from a small addition to the weekly national insurance contribution; and the remaining element came from charges (6.5 per cent) and other receipts like land sales (1.7 per cent) (Cm 1513, 1991). The National Health Service contribution is really an historic relic of the pre-1948 insurance-based system. Beveridge thought a small part of the new scheme's income should go to the NHS as it had under the old. Since everyone has a right to treatment whether they have been contributors or not, it is difficult to justify.

Charges to patients are made for drugs, appliances, dentistry, spectacles and, most recently, opticians' services. Though patients were exempt from all charges under the 1946 Act, the Labour government amended that Act in 1949 to give itself the power to levy charges if it wished on prescriptions and appliances. Prescription charges were not actually introduced until the next Conservative government in 1951. Apart from a brief period after 1964 when prescription charges were removed, these charges have remained ever since and been increased regularly. In 1991 the charge was £3.40 per item on a prescription. The figure was 25p in 1979. The scale of dental charges has risen sharply since the 1970s and now approaches the economic cost.

Those on low pay or receiving income support are exempt from all the charges. Those excluded from paying for prescriptions are: hospital in-patients, those suffering from diseases that need continuous medication, expectant mothers and those with a baby under 12 months, children under 16 (or under 19 if they are in full-time education), men over 65 and women over 60. Expectant mothers are exempt from dental charges, as are children at school and those on low incomes; similar exemptions apply to sight tests, glasses or contact lenses. Young people up to 14 qualify for free treatment but not dentures. These exclusions make the charges an inefficient way to raise revenue. Over three-quarters of the prescriptions are issued free to those exempt groups we have listed.

Road traffic casualties

This is a relic of the attempts to provide an income for the voluntary hospitals in the 1930s. The Road Traffic Act of 1933 obliges motorists or their insurance company to make some contribution to the expenses of treating the victims of an accident if the driver is liable. The sums involved are very small and do not cover anything like the cost to the NHS of car accidents.

Private pay-beds

One of the concessions Bevan made to the consultants in 1946 was that they could keep their separate private pay-beds in NHS hospitals. Private patients can occupy separate accommodation and be treated by the specialist of their choice, in return for paying a fee. Under the 1977 Health Service Act this is meant to be a 'full cost' fee which the Secretary of State fixes. The 1978–9 Labour government tried to phase out these beds, but under the 1980 Health Service Act they were extended. It is probably not the case that the fees are fully economic. Many feel they do not reflect the valuable back-up services a modern hospital and trained staff provide.

Amenity beds

An ordinary NHS patient can ask to be given a greater degree of privacy in a separate room if it is not needed on medical grounds for other patients, and can pay for the privilege.

Overseas visitors

Under regulations introduced in 1982, any overseas visitor who falls sick and requires treatment other than in an accident or emergency will be charged for his or her treatment on a special scale of charges reflecting the 'full cost' of the care. Various visitors are exempt: students here for more than a six-month course, EEC residents and those from countries who give UK residents free treatment (reciprocal arrangement nations).

Other income

Most of the old teaching hospitals inherited from pre-NHS days have trust fund and endowment incomes that they were allowed to keep and administer. These are regularly supplemented by new gifts and bequests. Other voluntary hospitals with such funds lost them to the Exchequer, which pooled them in a central fund. In 1974 this fund was allocated to the regional and area health authorities, and in 1982 it was once again reallocated to the new district authorities. Many hospitals have a League of Friends that raises money on their behalf.

This is how the National Health Service's money is raised. How is it allocated?

Allocating the money

Of the total NHS budget, as we can see from Figure 10.2, a small part – less than 3 per cent – is taken by the central department to provide central administration, supply a few specialist services and give a few specific grants. The Department of Health, for example, manages the NHS superannuation scheme. It meets the running costs of the Public Health Laboratory Service, which gives technical assistance, for example, to local districts facing an outbreak of an infectious disease, perhaps spread from abroad. It meets the running costs of limb and appliance centres for the disabled. It finances the Dental Estimates Board and the prescription pricing authorities that keep a check on dentists' and doctors' prescribing habits in order to contain costs.

The rest of the budget is allocated in two parts: that which pays for the hospital and community services – three-quarters of the total – and the remainder, which goes to the family practitioner services – the GP, the dentists, the opticians and the cost of drugs dispensed by GPs.

We look first at the way the main block of money is allocated.

Financing hospital and community services

In the early years of the Health Service the ordinary hospitals, the community health services and the teaching hospitals had been separately financed. Variations between the hospital regions

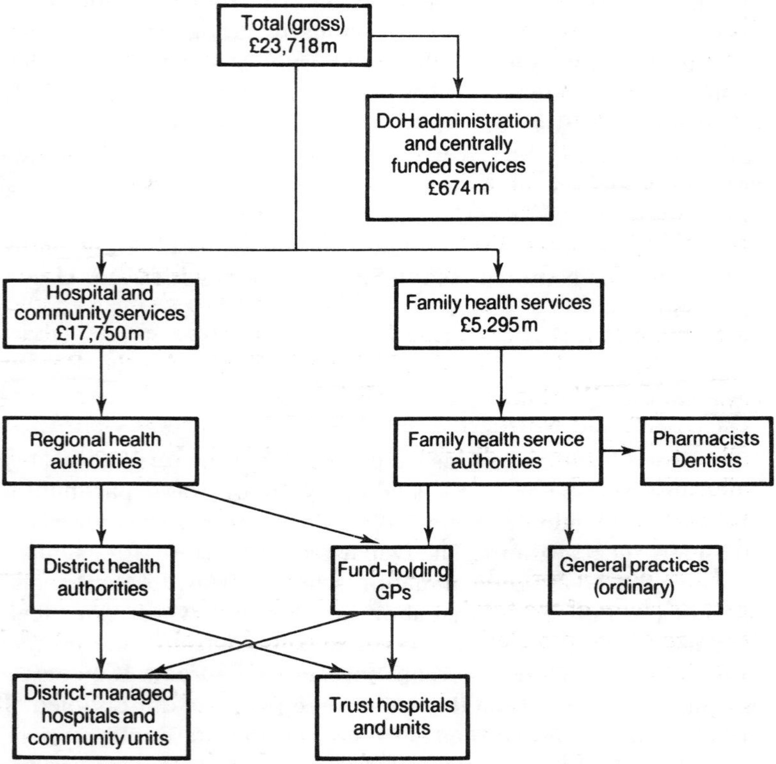

Figure 10.2 Allocating the Health Service budget in England 1990/1

remained wide. The reason lay in the budgeting procedures. Every year each region's allocation was merely rolled forward with small additions to the previous year's spending and extra to meet the current costs of new hospital premises. The spending patterns of the 1970s still reflected the inequalities of the pre-war system. The NHS had failed to produce 'a uniform standard of service for all', as Bevan put it in 1945. Variations within regions were even greater (Buxton and Klein, 1975, 1978; Jones and Masterman, 1976; Culyer, 1976).

After the 1974 reorganisation, the new regional health authorities took over responsibility for all hospital and community health expenditure. The reorganisation presented an opportunity to redress some of the old inequalities. The difficulty was partly political; the favoured regions, London notably, had powerful friends in the major teaching hospitals. An important first step was to include these hospitals in the budgets of the regional health authorities, so that their claims had to be considered alongside everyone else's. The next step was to devise a budget allocation procedure that reflected the health needs of different areas. It was one thing to agree that this was desirable, another to agree a measure of need. A working party was appointed in 1974 to produce one. It reported in 1976 (DHSS, 1976d) giving its name to a formula that was to decide how much revenue money (that is, not capital) each region should have in England – the Resource Allocation Working Party (RAWP), Scotland and Wales (SCRAW) and Northern Ireland (PARR). Regions were free to allocate revenue to districts as they wished. In practice these allocations reflected the scale of existing facilities and their resident populations. Under the 1990 reforms, districts will be financed on a pure formula basis too.

How does a formula work? In essence each region or district gets its share of the total amount of funds available on the basis of the size of the population served, weighted to take account of the use different sections of that population can be expected to make of the service. If a region has more old people, those people each count for more than one because they use services more frequently than average. National data on the use of each part of the service by age and sex, married persons and unmarried persons, is used as the basis of these weightings, but they are only the first stage. What the original working party wanted were local measures of ill health – morbidity – by age, sex and marital status. In fact, there were no reliable district data. Hence the study had to fall back on a proxy for measures of ill health – standardised mortality ratios (SMRs) or death rates from different diseases standardised by age. There were many arguments about the validity of taking death rates as a proxy for ill health, but in the absence of agreement on anything better, they remain (Mays and Bevan, 1987).

There was also criticism that SMRs did not take account of the health-care costs of social deprivation. People with poor housing conditions have to stay in hospital longer. Old people with poor housing and with no families or supportive neighbours fill more geriatric beds. The official review of the RAWP formula in 1989 accepted that there should be some weighting for social deprivation (DHSS, 1989). The *Working for Patients* White Paper later that year (Cm 555, 1989) proposed to abandon the RAWP formula and rely instead on a 'simpler' weighted formula for regional allocations, moving gradually to apply a similar formula to the cash districts were allocated. See Carr-Hill (1990). District formulae will be fully in place by 1993–4.

Purchasers and providers

Under the changes introduced by the 1990 Health Service and Community Care Act, implemented from April 1991, the District Health Authorities have become 'purchasing authorities'. They use the money they have been given to buy services from hospitals or community units either in their own districts or elsewhere. These hospitals and units may be of two kinds. Some are managed by the districts themselves, others are self-governing trusts. These latter are run by boards whose chair is appointed by the Secretary of State and whose members are appointed partly by the regional health authority and partly by the Secretary of State after consulting the chair. The trusts have to finance themselves from contracts made with district health authorities, fund-holding GPs (see below) or private insurance companies. The trusts are independent public corporations whose assets, like their buildings, are owned by and can be sold by the trust.

The Act also created a quite new form of purchaser of hospital and community services – fund-holding general practitioners (Glennerster *et al.*, 1992). Under this scheme, groups of family doctors who have more than 7,000 patients can opt to become fund-holders. In this case part of the hospital and community budget allocated to the region is transferred to the family doctor. The amount depended initially on the number of patients referred in the previous year multiplied by the actual cost of those referrals in the hospitals concerned. In future the plan is to move to a formula-based allocation. These doctors then make their own contracts with whatever hospitals or other providers they wish to and pay them from their larger budget. They continue to be funded like any other GP for their own practice work (see below).

Fund-holders' budgets enable them to purchase a range of non-emergency, mainly surgical procedures, outpatient care and laboratory tests from whichever hospital or provider they choose. They are given a budget to spend on the drugs they prescribe for their patients. They must keep within the budget, but if they spend less than their limit they can reallocate it to other purposes within the practice.

Financing the family practitioner services

The family *practitioner* services comprise not only the cost of the family doctor service – about 30 per cent of the total – but medicine prescribed by GPs, (nearly 40 per cent), pharmacists' costs (10 per cent) and opticians' (3 per cent). The cost of this sector has risen faster than any other – a more than 40-per-cent increase in real terms from 1978/9 to 1987/8. The system of paying the family doctor retained the pre-1948 idea of a payment per patient registered with that doctor. Gradually there was added a whole range of extra payments to give doctors financial inducements to provide adequate surgery facilities and to encourage them to practise in unpopular industrial and inner-city areas, and in remote rural areas.

Thatcher's government sought to extend the financial incentives, encouraging doctors to undertake preventative health checks and reach immunisation and vaccination targets. It also sought to tighten up what it required of doctors who received the basic NHS practice allowance for the upkeep of their premises. If they were to be paid this sum the doctor should in return guarantee to keep the premises open at certain convenient hours. A much fuller 'contract' was discussed with the profession. No full agreement was reached and the contract was imposed on GPs in 1990.

The notion of paying GP's to provide certain specified standards of service and undertake certain preventative health measures was a step forward, in terms of both public health accountability and *promoting better health*. The usefulness of certain of the activities, like visiting old people once a year or screening, was disputed by the medical profession.

The complex form of funding family doctors in 1991 is set out in Table 10.2. These payments are found in what GPs call the 'red

Table 10.2 Payments to general practitioners per annum in the United Kingdom 1991

Item	Payment
Basic practice allowance	
(£2,500 for the first 1,200 patients rising to a maximum)	£6,000.00
Additions to the basic allowance	
Designated area payments where there is a shortage of doctors (more than 3,000 per doctor):	
Type 1 (for three years the case)	£3,125.00
Type 2 (for one year)	£4,765.00
Associated allowance	
To employ an associate in the case of a single-handed practice in a rural area to allow the practitioner to attend training and refresher courses	£19,310.00 (first year)
Deprivation payments	
For each resident in an area of:	
high deprivation	£8.80
medium deprivation	£6.65
low deprivation	£5.05
Capitation payments	
Each patient: under 65 yrs	£12.40
65–74 yrs	£16.30
75 and over	£31.45
Child health surveyance fee	£5.00
Registration fee	
Night visit fees	Up to £45.00
Child immunisations (if a target level reached)	
Pre-school boosters	
Vaccinations for public health reasons	
Cervical cytology, smear tests	
Contraceptive services given	
Health promotion clinics	per clinic £45.00
Maternity services provided	
Payment for temporary residents	
Emergency patient – night visit, etc.	Up to £20.25
Minor surgery	
Extra for being a rural practice	
Other minor items	

book' – a statement of fees and allowances payable to medical practitioners in England and Wales.

Essentially the Conservative government said to family doctors, 'You want to remain private practitioners on contract with the NHS. So in return we shall specify in more detail what we expect from you. We expect surgeries to be open certain hours, and for you to undertake certain preventative health measures for all your patients whether they normally come to the surgery or not. If you see and screen more than a certain target number of patients you will get paid more.' These targets were more difficult for some doctors to meet in deprived areas or in practices where the population moved frequently.

Dentists

Most dentists are paid on a fee-for-service basis. They claim for each piece of work done and are paid according to rates laid down by the Dental Estimates Board. They then receive a net sum that takes account of the sums patients pay. Dentists in health centres can be salaried.

Chemists

Chemists are paid for the costs of the drugs they dispense on an NHS doctor's prescription. On top of that a percentage is added to cover the chemists' overheads and profit. They are paid for remaining open after normal hours on a rota basis and sums are paid to keep chemists open in remote areas. From this gross total is deducted the amount they collect in prescription charges.

The private sector

The private health market is largely confined to a narrow range of relatively uncomplicated surgery for those who require speedier treatment or more attractive surroundings than an NHS hospital – about 'two dozen procedures accounting for 70 per cent of expenditure' (Propper and Maynard, 1990). About 10 per cent of the population in 1988 had some form of private health insurance cover (Propper and Maynard, 1990; Laing, 1990). The scale of private cover has grown. From 1971 to 1989 the number of people insured with the largest insurers, British United Provident Association (BUPA), Private Patients' Plan (PPA) and the Western

Provident Association (WPA), rose from 2.1 million to 5.2 million (Central Statistical Office, 1990). Nearly half of these had their contributions paid in whole or part by their employers, a third having them paid in full. In 1990 the Conservative government introduced tax relief for private health insurance for people aged 60 and over.

In the late 1980s the expansion of the sector slowed. Costs rose and premiums were difficult to increase. The recession made companies less keen to support their employees' premiums. The optimistic invasion by American companies receded and even the long-established British insurers faced financial difficulty in 1992. Many private hospitals had low occupancy rates. Private pay-beds in UK hospitals remain and the new trust hospitals may be in a much stronger position to compete with the private sector.

Into the 1990s

The Conservatives' reforms

In the 1980s the Conservative government succeeded in checking the growth of the NHS budget. Demographic trends required more resources if the service was merely to stand still – an increase of about 1 per cent a year in the mid-1980s. In the period from 1960 to the mid-1970s the purchasing power available to the NHS rose by 4 per cent per annum on average. Then it dropped to roughly 2 per cent. But in 1983–7 the real (volume) increase in funds first fell to zero, then fell absolutely, then rose at a rate lower than 1 per cent – that is less than the increasing trend to an ageing population required to sustain standards (Kings Fund Institute, 1988; Owens and Glennerster, 1990). The consequent growing delays and a series of scandals put such pressure on the government that the prime minister, Margaret Thatcher, took the radical way out. She set up a fundamental review of the way the NHS was financed and organised. This at least diverted political attention from the funding issue. In the debate that followed, right-wing think-tanks pressed for radical changes: from introducing a requirement that people insure themselves against health bills and the state should merely help poor individuals, through tax relief to encourage private insurance, to the introduction of competition into the health market (Letwin and Redwood, 1988; Pirie and Butler, 1988; Willetts and Goldsmith, 1988; Robinson, 1988).

More private finance?

The radicals proposed to shift the source of *funding* from the public to the private purse. This option largely failed to make headway for many of the basic theoretical reasons that were outlined in Chapter 2. At the time, in evidence to the review, Barr *et al.*, (1988) argued:

> private medical insurance has efficiency problems of two kinds: gaps in coverage and incentives to excessive consumption of medical care. Gaps arise, first, because private policies generally offer incomplete (or no) coverage of chronic or pre-existing medical problems because the likelihood of treatment is too high, nor of the medical costs associated with pregnancy because this is the result of deliberate choice not a random risk. In addition the elderly, if they can obtain insurance at all, pay very high premiums. (These groups take perhaps two thirds of the cost of the NHS.)
>
> In addition to such gaps, private medical insurance can also face third party payment problems, leading to exploding costs: where doctors are paid a fee for service, and treatment is paid in full by their insurance company, both doctor and patient can act as if care were free, which encourages excessive use of expensive medical resources.

The theoretical arguments receive empirical support from private systems elsewhere. It is not sufficiently appreciated that the American private medical system is buttressed by government spending on a very substantial scale in precisely those areas where private medical insurance has gaps: Medicare (for the elderly), Medicaid (for the poor), veterans' benefits (often chronic health problems) and maternity and child welfare. Equally predictably, given the third party payment problem, the cost of those publicly funded has come close to running out of control.

Inspection of the comparative figures is both instructive and startling. The UK currently spends around £400 per person per year on medical care, about £360 via the NHS, the rest private. In the USA *public* spending on medical benefits (ignoring tax relief) is around £470 per person per year and private spending about £640, giving a total of three times the UK figure. *Public* spending in the

> USA is higher than in the UK; the US spends nearly one and a half times that amount *in addition* on private medical benefits, yet health outcomes in the two countries are broadly comparable. (pp. 7–9)

The fear of the cost consequences of third-party health insurance no doubt worried the Treasury most. For whatever reason, the government chose to accept the case for retaining an Exchequer-financed service free at the point of use. However, they also accepted the case for major change, in particular the case for an internal or quasi market within the NHS (see Chapter 3). Some Conservative critics from the think-tanks were disappointed that consumer choice and true market solutions had not been taken further (Green, 1990).

An internal market: the case for change

In 1985 an American health economist, Alain Enthoven, had published an influential critical analysis of the NHS. It was also publicised in *The Economist* (22 June, 1985; see also Enthoven, 1991). He argued that the NHS suffered from the following:

1. *Gridlock*. 'It is more difficult to close an unwanted NHS hospital than an unneeded American military base.'
2. *Inefficiency*. There were no incentives to run a ward or service more efficiently except persuasion. Consultants were on lifetime contracts and had no reason to change.
3. *Perverse incentives*. A consultant who treated more patients would shorten the queue and attract more patients without attracting more resources – more anxiety and no reward or means to do the job.
4. *Overcentralisation*. National pay settlements meant staff were difficult to attract in areas with high demand for labour – especially nurses in London, for example.
5. *Accountability*. No-one knew what anything cost or whether they were keeping within their budget.
6. *Free capital*. Since central government had always paid for new building, local districts and services did not have to face the cost of using buildings and capital, and hence tended to waste space and capital assets.
7. *Customers not being central*. Patients are so grateful to get treated they do not complain or get taken seriously.

None of these points was new but Enthoven's solution, drawn from recent American reforms, was – introduce competition and an internal market. District health authorities should cease to have direct responsibility for managing the hospitals and units. They should become purchasing bodies, buying services from whatever hospital or unit could give the best deal.

Contracts could be with a specialist unit outside the area, which would be able to keep its facility going by attracting patients needing that care and bringing with them the cash to pay for their operation. Contracts would be made on a competitive basis with the hospital providing the 'best buy'. Contracts would be of three main kinds, as follows:

1. *Block contracts*. These would provide accident and emergency service for everyone at a given sum per year and meet certain quality criteria.
2. *Cost and volume*. These would undertake so many operations for half a million pounds. If 10 per cent more were done, the payment would increase by 12 per cent; if less than the volume target were done, the payment would go down.
3. *Cost per case*. In more specialised units, each operation, episode or visit might be paid for separately.

Hospitals could lose their monopoly status: The market incentives would encourage consultants to do more, to get more resources, to offer a good service, to win the contract. Information would have to improve and with it accountability. Services would be charged for the value of the buildings they occupied to encourage economy. The basic idea of a *purchaser–provider* split, with the district health authority as purchaser, was the crux of the Enthoven plan and became the basis of the working party's plan. How was it to be achieved? Hospitals might be privatised or turned into voluntary hospitals, as the Conservatives had favoured before 1946. In the end a compromise emerged under which some – eventually most or all – hospitals and community units were to be allowed to become 'independent trusts' owning their own buildings and having their own governing bodies. Those that did not survive in the market-place would close because they could not attract the revenue to survive. The logic of the purchaser–provider split and the American model suggested that all units should be independent. For some this had the additional attraction that the hospital trusts could, at a future date, be simply floated off as private bodies.

An alternative model for the internal market

There was an alternative model on offer, this time advanced by an English professor of health economics – Alan Maynard of York University (Maynard, 1986).

Maynard's analysis of the NHS failings was similar to Enthoven's. He too wanted to distinguish purchasers from providers. The difference lay in his choice of purchaser. The district, he argued, was too distant from the consumer. The GP was nearer to the patient, knew more about the practical needs and family situation and was in a good position to act as the proxy but expert consumer. If cash followed patients in ways that reflected the preferences of consumers informed by their family doctor, it would be possible to combine the virtues of consumer choice and free access to health care, and avoid the high cost of the American system of private health insurance. This view was favoured by the new Secretary of State for Health, Kenneth Clarke, who came into office late in the discussions of the working party on the reform of the NHS. Giving the GP power to buy hospital services for his or her patient might help redress the relative loss of status and power of GPs and primary health care in general compared to that of the hospital consultant, and be a strong corrective to some inefficient practices within hospitals. The consultant in the old voluntary hospitals (see above) depended for his or her income on patients referred by the GP. In the post-1948 NHS the consultant was paid a salary and could pick and choose patients from his or her waiting list. The GP became a supplicant. If GPs had the purchasing power they could redress the balance again.

There were, however, major problems with the idea. Most practices were too small and had too little managerial capacity to manage a large budget. A small budget might be swallowed up with a few very expensive cases. Patients who cost a lot might be turned away by a GP. The idea was, therefore, modified. Only large practices would be allowed to opt for the scheme. Only cheaper procedures would be included. High-cost patients would have their higher costs met by the district – patients who cost more than £5,000 a year would have the extra met by the district initially. The result was the General Practice Fundholding Scheme – see Glennerster *et al.* (1992) for a full history. There were, therefore, two competing ideas for the finance of hospitals and community services – contracts set and paid for by districts and contracts set and paid for by GPs. One was top-down funding, one bottom-up. The government went for both at once.

The merits of districts and GPs as purchasers

The merits are as follows:

1. *More explicit accountability*. Hospitals and community units have to say exactly what they can do in a year, and districts and GPs can specify the quality criteria and kinds of service they want.
2. *Incentives for districts to rationalise their services*. Districts can buy what they want from a nearby district or a teaching hospital rather than attempt to provide everything in their own area.
3. *Districts have a clear task*. Their primary job is to measure local health needs and monitor the quality of the service. The management of the hospital or service can be left to the unit manager or chief executive of a trust.
4. *Poorly run services face sanctions*. These units will fear they may lose their contracts and close. This will make them perform better.
5. *GPs may be in a better position*. Fund-holding GPs in the first year were less afraid to switch contracts to better units or consultants, could make more flexible contracts, demand more attention, and use their funds to encourage consultants to come to the surgery rather than rely on patients to go to outpatients in the hospital. They had a strong incentive to ensure hospitals made efficient use of their money on behalf of their patients (Glennerster, 1992).

Difficulties with districts and GPs as purchasers

These illustrate many of the theoretical points in Chapter 3, as follows:

1. *Costs*. Accounting information needed for contracting has been costly to obtain.
2. *Outcome measures*. Measures of quality and outcome barely exist, making it difficult to make good judgements about the 'best buy'.
3. *Competition absent*. In many areas and for many services there are few real competitors. The local district general hospital is the only possibility. This leads to districts asking hospitals to do as before with the same money and little changes.
4. *Measures of need and priority*. These are poorly developed. Some districts are relying on minimum cost rather than good value. As a result, GPs with funds and negotiating power may get a better deal for their patients than those with no funds.

The future

The changes to the NHS outlined above were controversial. But every health-care system is facing similar pressures and the need to improve efficiency is important, without sacrificing equity and free access, which the NHS has in larger measure than most other health care systems (Le Grand, 1989b).

The Labour Party have rejected trusts as partly privatised entities. They have rejected an internal market as such, but they have proposed funding hospitals on the basis of the work they do – if they do more they will get more – up to a point. Whatever government is in power in the 1990s, the purchaser–provider split is likely to remain.

A possible future is that regions will pass away and districts amalgamate to make contracts for more specialist services – tertiary care . They could approve providers' capital plans. Groups of GPs will negotiate and buy from the hospitals of their choice the ordinary range of services their patients need. They may also come to contract for the community health *and care* services their patients need, taking over from the social services departments or competing with them.

Further reading

The financial history of voluntary and public hospitals is to be found in Abel-Smith, B. (1964), *The Hospitals 1800–1948*, London: Heinemann.

The best brief history of the NHS including the Conservative reforms is to be found in Klein, R. (1991), *The Politics of the National Health Service*, London: Longman.

The in-depth standard history of the early years is Webster, C. (1988), *The Health Services since the War*, Vol. 1, London: HMSO.

For a comparative account of many of the issues discussed in this chapter see: Abel-Smith, B. (1976), *Value for Money in Health Services*, London: Heinemann; McLachlan, G. and Maynard, A. (1982), *The Public/Private Mix for Health*, London: Nuffield Private Hospitals Trust; OECD (1987b), *Financing and Delivering Health Care*, Paris: OECD.

For an account of the recent reforms to the finance of health care in different parts of the world see special issues of two journals that are worth a regular perusal: *Health Affairs*, **10**, no. 3, 1991, and *Health Care Financing*, 1989 Supplement on International Comparison of Health Care Financing and Delivery.

CHAPTER 11

PAYING FOR PERSONAL SOCIAL SERVICES

It is difficult to draw any clear dividing line between health care and the personal social services. This makes their separate systems of finance a problem. Again, history helps us to understand how this came about.

The personal social services as a distinct category really only date back to the 1970 Local Authority Social Services Act in England and Wales and slightly earlier in Scotland. The new social services departments inherited a diverse range of powers and duties drawn from many existing Acts of Parliament previously administered by different local authority departments. They shared responsibility with the National Health Service for the care of groups like the elderly, the mentally ill and the mentally handicapped where the boundary lines of responsibility were extremely vague. In addition, non-statutory or 'voluntary' organisations have continued to be more important providers in this field, partly because it is nearer its pioneering stage than other services, partly because the services cater for specific categories of 'deserving' people who attract charitable help and encourage the creation of small specialist organisations. They are also services in which lay people can still play a part. Charging is widespread for the diverse reasons I discussed in Chapter 8. The private for-profit sector provides a great deal of residential care. Changes to the social security rules in the 1980s led to an increase in social security payments to meet the costs of care in private homes. Informal care is more important than all these. Overall the services present a complex picture – the most mixed form of finance of any we shall study. To simplify matters I shall distinguish briefly several groups of responsibilities and outline the forms of financial support that have grown up in each case.

The history of personal social service finance

Residential provision

The largest part of a social service department's budget is still devoted to residential care for the elderly, children, mentally ill and handicapped people and the physically disabled. The residential bias dates back to the 1834 Poor Law Amendment Act. The Local Boards of Guardians were responsible for providing workhouse accommodation for the poor and these included a growing number of elderly who had no independent means, children and the homeless. This responsibility passed to the welfare committees and children's departments of local authorities in 1948 and on to the social services departments in 1970. Throughout, local revenue and central government grant have been the main sources of finance, but, as we saw in Chapter 8, charges were introduced in 1948 in a deliberate attempt to break with the Poor Law tradition of free accommodation for the destitute. The public sector provides only about half of all places in old people's homes. The rest are provided by charitable or private for-profit organisations. Local authorities have a duty to inspect such accommodation.

During the 1980s the number of private old people's homes and the number of places in them began to rise sharply. Some increase had been discernible from the mid-1970s, when local authority spending on residential care was reduced and individual families began to pay for their own or relatives' care. Then in the early 1980s, as a by-product of changes to the social security regulations, poor residents began to be able to draw more readily on social security funds to help them pay the fees. Under regulations that governed the old supplementary benefit system, and the national assistance scheme before that, payments towards the cost of care in a private or voluntary home were extremely rare. In 1979 they amounted to only £10 million. The changes of the early 1980s extended the duty of local social security offices to meeting fees if residents had no resources of their own. This led to a rapid rise in the finance of such homes through the social security budget. By 1989 the figure had reached £1,000 million (DoH, 1989). Central government was financing an increase in private residential care while encouraging local authorities to place more people in the community. The perversity of this approach was first criticised by the Audit Commission (1986b). Roy Griffith's report on Community Care (DoH, 1988a) proposed ending the payments by social security, placing all the responsibility for *funding* such care on local authorities (see below).

Protection and care of children

A second source of statutory responsibility derives from the powers given to the courts at the end of the nineteenth century to prosecute parents for wilful cruelty and to commit children to the care of 'fit persons', including local authorities. Councils' powers were gradually extended so that they could take children into care if they were deprived of a normal home life because of the death or illness of parents, homelessness, or unsatisfactory home conditions that put the child at risk. This activity, too, was primarily financed from the rates with general Exchequer support, but, as we saw in Chapter 8, governments from the mid-nineteenth century onwards were anxious to deter irresponsible parents and insisted they must contribute on a sliding income scale to the cost. This does not mean that a local authority has to provide care itself. In practice it will frequently place children in ordinary households that are paid to look after them, or it may pay a non-statutory body to take the child. The authority's task is then to inspect those arrangements to safeguard the child, but no more. The new basis of parental responsibility and the state's role in protecting children is defined in the Children Act 1989.

The Act extended local authorities' powers to help prevent family breakdown. They have a duty to 'safeguard and promote the welfare of children within their area who are in need'. That term is closely defined to mean a situation in which a child is unable to achieve or maintain a reasonable standard of health or development without services being provided by the local authority, or where the child is disabled. Local authorities must 'take reasonable steps' to identify children in need and prevent them suffering ill treatment or neglect. They must open family centres and provide day care for children under 5 who are in need. (For a discussion of the new law see Harwin, 1990.) Whether local authorities will have the resources to implement the Act fully remains to be seen. In 1986/7 the total amount of money spent on preventative work in social services departments was £9 million. The sum spent on residential care was £434 million. These activities are financed, like all others in the departments, out of the general central government support for local authorities and local revenue. The claims of the elderly, the new community care responsibilities and the Children Act 1989 will compete seriously in the 1990s.

Meals on Wheels

This service began as a voluntary activity in the Second World War, run by the Women's Voluntary Service (now the WRVS) or a local old people's welfare committee (Slack, 1960). For many years it was merely an activity that authorities could support financially. It only became recognised as a mainline statutory function in 1962, and more fully in the 1968 Health Services and Public Health Act. Voluntary bodies had made some charge to cover their costs. Local authority grants merely covered their overheads, or any shortfall that arose from the proceeds the WRVS gained from selling their meals. The practice of charging continued when local authorities began to provide the meals. Ministerial advice made it clear that even if the revenue were tiny and administrative costs high some charge should be made. '[Authorities] will no doubt bear in mind that for many elderly people it is important to pay at least in part for any such service' (DHSS Circular 5/70, 1970, *Organisation of Meals on Wheels*).

Home helps

Local authority provision of this service grew up in the 1920s and 1930s to assist mothers of young children who needed domestic help. The service carried a charge though the precise rationale was never spelt out. The issue was, however, debated when provision was included as a function of the new local authority health departments. Bevan was pressed to allow free service in line with the general principle of free health care. He resisted, using the following argument:

> It is a perfectly reasonable proposition that, where domestic help is needed and the persons concerned are able to provide it for themselves, they should do so, and where they are able to make a contribution they should make it . . . it seems to me wholly unjustifiable that we should provide a service of this sort without any payment whatever. (HC Debates, 1946, Col. 1562)

What Bevan was arguing by implication, it seems, is that many people already provided themselves with an almost identical service out of their own pockets – a 'char-lady' or 'domestic help'. A local authority could not simply begin providing a comparable service free without undermining the private service and landing itself with an intolerable demand for the public equivalent. Because most users are now old people unable to afford other help, they are mostly not charged or charged very little on a sliding scale. The share of costs met by charges never rose above 13 per cent (in the 1950s) and then fell steadily to less than 5 per cent in the mid-1970s. In the wake of the 1976 public expenditure cuts even Labour councils raised their charges to preserve the service.

The promotion of welfare

In 1920 local authorities were given powers to promote the welfare of blind people, and in 1948 welfare authorities were given a more general duty to promote the welfare of the handicapped. This was later extended to cover the deaf, and powers and duties were set out in more detail in 1970. These powers have always been used not merely to provide services but to fund local organisations that are in various ways providing support through social clubs, training workshops or day care.

The voluntary origins of social care

So far we have looked at the origins of particular statutory duties, but in many ways the origins of social work lie not in statute but in the activities of volunteers – do-gooders, some would say – who pioneered helping activities in a variety of ways. The Charity Organisational Society sought to organise and co-ordinate charitable activity and developed social case-work methods as a way of making such help more 'effective'. Residential care for children, housing management, work with offenders, prison visiting and after-care are all examples of statutory services that had voluntary origins. In the 1970s and 1980s a new and much wider range of non-profit and non-statutory agencies developed self-help groups, and began to act as advocates for many groups from battered women and AIDS sufferers to disabled children and the mentally ill.

Expenditure on the personal social services

These services are small in public expenditure terms. If we take the current range of activities covered by modern social services departments, their predecessors in the late 1940s and early 1950s spent about 0.2 per cent of the GNP. Over the whole of the 1950s that total grew by about 7 per cent in real terms. Several factors accelerated that growth rate: Peter Townsend's horrifying accounts of conditions in the old workhouses that posed as old people's 'homes' (Townsend, 1962), and the growing numbers of very elderly, concern with juvenile delinquency in the late 1950s, the development of preventative social work with families, and political interest in 'community' services as an alternative to expensive hospital care. In the 1960s spending just about doubled in real terms (Ferlie and Judge, 1981; Wistow and Webb, 1982). The new amalgamated departments were set an expansionary universal role by the Seebohm Committee (1968). The Department of Health and Social Security encouraged them to expand. During the period 1970–5 real spending doubled again. Then local government finance changed for the worse. The pace of expansion slowed sharply, but did continue. There was 11 per cent real growth in the last five years of the 1970s.

Thus by 1979 the services took the equivalent of about 0.9 per cent of the GDP – a near five-fold increase in their share since 1950. In the 1980s that share remained more or less static

(Evandrou *et al.*, 1990). Nevertheless, the demands on these services have been growing sharply too. Fewer of the mentally ill and those with learning difficulties are in long-stay hospitals; there are more families at risk, and there are more very elderly people. For many years government claimed that a 2-per-cent per annum growth in the real volume spending was necessary for the personal social services to meet the needs of an elderly population. An analysis of the replies to the General Household Survey shows that while the percentage of old people receiving personal social services rose from 17.7 per cent in 1974 to 22.4 per cent in 1979, it fell back to 21 per cent in 1985 (Evandrou *et al.*, 1990).

The share of spending allocated to each of the groups of clients is broadly shown in Figure 11.1.

Standard setting and inspection

The central departments have inherited various powers to inspect local standards of service from the old Poor Law days. They were

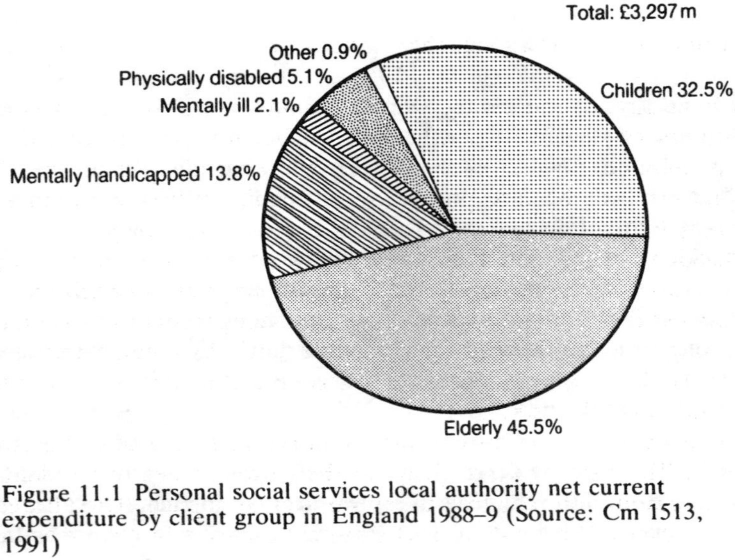

Figure 11.1 Personal social services local authority net current expenditure by client group in England 1988–9 (Source: Cm 1513, 1991)

included in the 1948 National Assistance Act, the Children's Act 1948, the later Children and Young Persons Act 1969, and the Mental Health Act 1959. In 1971 a new Social Work Advisory Service was formed to take over these functions, but primarily its task was to provide professional advice on social work to local authorities and the Secretary of State. The report of the Barclay Committee (1982) recommended that the service be transformed back into a full inspectorate, comparable to Her Majesty's Inspectors of Schools, monitoring the general standards of professional practice in the social services departments and residential establishments. The government accepted this advice and added its own gloss: the new Social Service Inspectorate was also to monitor 'the efficiency and effectiveness' of social services departments. Its most high-profile activities have been to mount investigations of various child abuse cases and instances where local authorities have come under particular investigation (DoH, 1988b, 1988c). For a brief account of the Social Work Inspectorate's work, with others, see Day and Klein (1990).

Into the 1990s

A new basis for funding community care

I have already mentioned that the rapid growth in social security funding of private residential care was beginning to create a large, open-ended flow of money from the central Exchequer. The Treasury was keen to put a stop to this flow. Private homes and many families were keen to see it continue. Which agency should decide whether a family or elderly person was in need, and of what services? The conclusion that it had to be local authority social services departments was one that Thatcher personally resisted for a long time. In the end, aided by the Griffiths recommendations (DoH, 1988a), the government accepted that this was the only solution (DoH, 1989).

This was not the only absurdity in the financing of community care. The care of those living in their own homes or residential accommodation falls to local authorities to finance. The alternative – care in hospital – may be more expensive in resources, but not in its cost to the local authority. Since the NHS is financed by central government, a local council will face a larger bill if people move out of hospital and into the community. The local council has very good reasons to oppose such moves, especially if its expenditure is capped.

In the mid-1970s the then Labour government recognised this perverse incentive and tried to reverse it by giving the NHS powers to give local authorities a grant to encourage them to develop community care services. This was called 'joint finance'. The sums of money involved were tiny, rising to only 5 per cent of social services departments' budgets in the mid-1980s. Moreover, the money was a *temporary* grant. Beyond a few years the local council had to take up the total cost of the new facility or service. As the screw tightened on local councils' funds after rate capping, they became reluctant to accept such long-term commitments. The 1990 National Health Service and Community Care Act was an attempt to resolve the problems. It created a new financial framework for community care, residential care and support for those who are mentally ill.

Specific grants for the mentally ill

The first part of the changes that came into effect in 1991 related to the mentally ill. It is a reflection of the level of public and political concern with this group that the government agreed to treat it as a special case and permit a specific grant. From 1991/2 a specific grant will be made to the social services departments of local authorities to develop social care services for people with mental illness including dementia, whatever its cause (see circular HC (90) 24/LAC (90) 10). Social services departments have to agree with their local district health authority what new social care services should be provided. Once formal agreement is reached, the regional health authority is informed, the Department of Health is told and the grant can be made. If no agreement is possible the region and/or the Social Services Inspectorate seeks to 'facilitate' agreement.

The grants will be annual, for up to three years initially, and will cover recurrent (that is, not capital) spending. In 1991/2 the grant amounted to £21 million towards a total cost of the schemes approved of £30 million. Local authorities meet the difference. The grant is allocated by adjusting the standard spending assessment (SSA) formula for local authorities (see page 84). Part is kept back to fund services for homeless mentally ill people in central London. Claims for the grant are made quarterly when the authority can show what it has spent to that point on these services.

Alcohol and drug misuse grants

In the same way, the government introduced another specific grant to cover payments made by local authorities to voluntary bodies providing services for alcohol and drug 'misusers'. The grant was to be available initially for 1991/2 and 1992/3. The total expenditure authorised was £2 million, 70 per cent of which would come from central government.

Other specific grants

Various other specific grants exist that relate to community care. Central government makes a small grant to cover the cost of training social services staff who work with elderly people, to private services for those with AIDS, and for management training for social services staff implementing the new policies.

No 'ring fencing'

When Sir Roy Griffiths proposed that social services departments should take charge of community care policy (DoH, 1988a) and take over the social security funds allocated to private residential care, he also said: 'central government should provide directly to social service authorities by a specific grant a substantial proportion of the total public funds it estimates are needed to meet national objectives' (para. 5.12–13). This would have included expenditure then financed from the social fund and joint finance. This recommendation was not followed. The only specific grants are listed above. He also suggested that NHS funds for community care should be separately identified or 'ring fenced'. This was not done either.

Transfer of social security funds

The practice of granting social security funds to pay fees at private residential homes is to be phased out in the period after 1993 and the same sums transferred from the social security budget to the local authority grant. That grant, as we saw in Chapter 5, is not tied to any particular service, though indicative amounts are included in the standard spending assessments by service area. Many interested in the care of the elderly feared that these extra sums would not find their way into additional services for the elderly. However, once one group can successfully claim this as a reason for a special grant or ring fencing, the same argument could be made for any other group. Over the 1980s local authorities spent more on personal social services than the targets central government set for them. With a sum fixed for them by central government this would not have been possible. Perhaps surprisingly, the local authority associations and most groups representing service users felt that Griffiths had been right (HC277, 1990).

The bulk of social service department funds come, like most other services, from the central government revenue support grant to local authorities, the local council tax and charges to users. In 1990/1 total gross current expenditure on the personal social services amounted to £4,630 million, with revenue from charges amounting to £544 million or 12 per cent.

An 'enabling' not a providing department

In line with the logic that lay behind the NHS reforms in the 1990 Health Service and Community Care Act, social services departments were to see themselves as *purchasers* of community care services (DoH, 1991). They were to be responsible for identifying the needs of their populations and publishing a plan for the provision of community care services in their area. In that plan, the government argued, departments should 'promote the mixed economy of welfare' (DoH, 1991, para. 2.1.4). They should, in meeting the needs for community care, do the following:

1. Invite tenders from private and voluntary bodies.
2. Stimulate the establishment of not-for-profit agencies.
3. Encourage new voluntary sector activity.
4. Create 'self-managed' units for services they continued to provide themselves.

The department stressed the advantages of splitting the assessment of individuals' needs and the purchase of services to meet them from direct service provision, as follows:

1. It would widen individual clients' and social workers' range of choice – for example, in the old people's homes or day-care facilities available.
2. It would help local authorities identify the true cost of service provision by making each provider unit in the local authority cover its costs and compete with external providers.
3. It would clarify budgetary responsibilities and encourage devolved management.

The government advice was also that the advantages of this approach would be greatest if 'the purchasing power is close to the client'. Care managers working with clients should have responsibility for purchasing care for their clients from a devolved budget. This follows the model evolved in Kent and evaluated and advocated by Davies and Challis (1986).

The Audit Commission (1989) similarly advocated such devolution of financial control. It argued that where the supply of services depended on central decisions in a social service department, allocations of services to clients became too concerned with fitting clients into existing premises or services rather than matching clients' needs to a flexible range of care. The Kent Community Care Scheme's answer, exemplified in the Audit Commission's advice, was that if you put cash in social workers' hands, they would have the power to buy a flexible mix of services from wherever they wished. The extent to which this will happen is unclear.

The United States has been taken as the model for such service contracting (Ketner and Martin, 1987). There is also much criticism of the results of the trend to a contract culture in personal care services there (Schlesinger *et al.*, 1986; Kramer and Grossman, 1987; Demone and Gibelman, 1989). The following arguments are put forward:

1. Setting and responding to such contracts is difficult, time-consuming and expensive. This tends to drive away the small and more informal organisations.
2. There are very few real competitors. Local statutory agencies

tend to build up close, 'sweetheart' relationships with local voluntary or private agencies.

3. Large organisations tend to move into areas where profits are to be made, undercut their rivals, drive them out and then raise their prices.
4. Getting contract compliance is very difficult to do well, as the measurement of standards and outcomes is technically difficult and expensive.
5. Contractors tend to dump the difficult cases to keep down their bids for the next round – 'adverse selection bias'.

Local authorities may find themselves in the worst of both worlds – abandoning existing direct managerial control of services without being able to achieve effective monitoring, and with no true market test because competition is limited. On the other hand, even limited choice may produce significant effects.

The non-statutory, non-profit sector

Non-statutory, non-profit providers are already more common in the personal social service sphere than in any other. There is already a mixed economy of care. Such organisations have long been funded by local authorities to provide specialist services on their behalf. Local authorities may have given a *general grant* in support of that organisation's activities. They may have made a *specific or reciprocal* grant on the understanding that the agency accepts families for intensive case work, for example. These quasi contracts will now become formalised. Nevertheless, the range of such organisations varies widely in different areas, suggesting this will become the dominant mode in the 1990s. In some areas they are numerous, in others not. In Birmingham, on one count there were at least 860 formal social service organisations (Newton, 1976). In two wards of Glasgow there were about 15 organisations per 10,000 population (Johnson, 1981). Hatch (1980) looked at the origins of such organisations in three towns, and found that though there was a considerable mortality rate amongst voluntary bodies (nearly 4 per cent per annum) new organisations were being formed faster than old ones were dying. The growth points appeared to be those concerned with the disabled, the playgroup movement, advice and counselling, and neighbourhood groups. Hatch and Mocroft (1983) surveyed the varied scale of support given by local authorities, looking in depth in two local areas. This variation persists.

After 1979, the Conservative government sought to increase the role of the non-statutory sector, leading up to the 1990 legislation I have discussed. Paradoxically, other policies pursued by the same government have made things harder for the non-statutory sector. Cuts in grants to local authorities, rate capping and even the abolition of the GLC and the metropolitan counties have harmed the sector. In any squeeze, councils tend to restrict cash grants to outside bodies.

The personal sector

The personal social services are unusual in another sense. Local authorities pay individuals and families to undertake a very important part of their functions. The most obvious example of this is the system of foster care, but the principle can be and is extended to other aspects of caring or 'tending' – neighbourly aid schemes or payments to local people to help certain elderly people in their street, for example. Over half of all children in local authority care are boarded out with foster parents, or are under the charge of a parent, guardian, relative or friend. Numbers in these categories have increased sharply in the last twenty years. However, the largest area of care is, as we saw in Chapter 9, unpaid caring by close kin.

The private for-profit sector

Running alongside the statutory and non-profit services, there are the private profit providers: homes for the elderly, day nurseries for the under 5s, child minders and many more. Because the groups that are being provided for are so vulnerable, there is a real danger of exploitation, and for that reason social services departments have considerable powers of inspection and regulation. Such facilities must be registered with the local authority and conform to minimum standards of staffing, building design and safety. During the 1980s the balance of provision for the elderly steadily shifted from local authority to private for-profit and non-

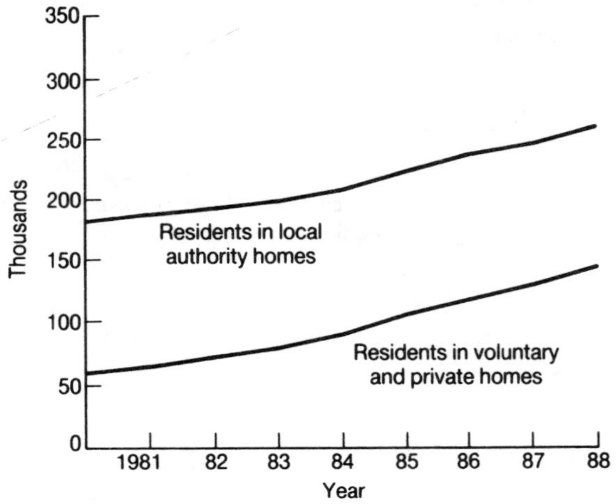

Figure 11.2 Elderly people in residential accommodation in the United Kingdom 1981–8 (Source: Central Statistical Office, 1991a)

profit organisations (see Figure 11.2) in response to government policy and especially to the social security changes.

Further reading

The best overall discussion of the history of charging is in Judge, K. and Matthews, J. (1980) *Charging for Social Care*, London: Allen & Unwin.

An account of changes in government policy on finance and spending since 1974 is to be found in Evandrou, M., Falkingham, J. and Glennerster, H. (1990), 'The personal social services: everyone's poor relation but nobody's baby', in J. Hills (ed.), *The State of Welfare*, Oxford: Clarendon Press.

The background to the most recent changes in the finance of the personal social services is to be found in: Audit Commission (1986b), *Making a Reality of Community Care*, London: HMSO; and DoH (1988a), *Community Care: Agenda for action*, London: HMSO. This was discussed by Hunter, D.J. and Judge, K. (1988), *Griffiths and Community Care: Meeting the challenge*, London: Kings Fund Institute.

For an American survey of contracting experience see Demone, H.W. and Gibelman, M. (1989) (eds.), *Services for Sale: Purchasing health and human services*, New Brunswick and London: Rutgers University Press.

CHAPTER 12

PAYING FOR EDUCATION

The history of education finance

Pre-1870

With the exception of very limited activities like regimental, workhouse and prison schools, the state in England was not involved in actually providing education until after the 1870 Education Act, and then only on a residual basis, filling in where the churches and private bodies had left gaps. State *provision* thus came later in England than in most other countries in Europe and North America. That did not mean, however, that the state played no part, in the United Kingdom. Ever since the seventeenth century in Scotland, grants from the local rates had been made to support parish schools, and in 1833, in the wake of the newly reformed Parliament, a very small grant was made to support the work of the National Society, which promoted Church of England schools, and the British and Foreign Schools Society, which promoted non-conformist ones. The grant amounted to only £20,000 and had to be matched by local voluntary donations. Parliament was in fact extremely reluctant to give assistance on a large scale, not merely because of the cost but because it was felt that if the state were to contribute generously this would merely reduce charitable or voluntary activity. As late as 1861 the Newcastle Commission argued that there was no case for state provision or compulsion to attend school. The commission's report argued that with more generous financial help the voluntary sector could meet the rising demand for education. Nevertheless, aid grew significantly from 1833 to 1870. Its purposes were extended from school building to the building of teacher training colleges and teachers' houses, the provision of furniture and equipment, and the costs of training teachers, their salaries and pensions.

The very complexity of this system, with its detailed checking of particular items of expenditure, put an intolerable burden on the Education Department of the Privy Council. In order to ease the problem, officials proposed that these grants should be replaced by a 'system of simply testing by examination and paying by results'. The Newcastle Commission broadly accepted this recommendation and the government consolidated the various specific grants into a single unit grant for each child who attended school regularly and passed the examinations set by Her Majesty's Inspector of Schools. The result was to concentrate the major part of the school's activities on the task of passing these exams. This became increasingly restrictive and unpopular and was abandoned in 1895.

Alongside this general system of finance for elementary education, there grew up a secondary source of state funds designed to encourage the creation of separate schools of science, art and design and to promote classes in such subjects in other schools, including elementary schools. This multiple system of finance lasted in a modified form to the end of the century, applying to both the voluntary and the new board schools. Payment by results was not finally abandoned until 1895.

This early history is important because it illustrates a basic lesson. State funding of private or voluntary provision does not necessarily bring greater freedom for those institutions. The extent of central control over the content of education was far greater in the voluntary schools of the last part of the nineteenth century than in the state-provided schools of today even with the National Curriculum.

The first major step to state provision of schooling came in 1870. The effective pressure came not from socialists or those who favoured state schools as such, but from non-conformists, better represented by the extended franchise, who resented their children being educated in Church of England schools because there were no non-conformist institutions in the area. Others argued that the old voluntary system was not capable of providing sufficient schools in the poorer urban areas. In short, it exemplified some of the classic problems of charitable provision that I discussed in Chapter 9.

1870–1918

Under the 1870 Act schools could be provided for the first time by locally elected school boards, but only where the voluntary societies were judged incapable of providing for all the children in an area. The boards funded the building of new schools out of the rates but they charged fees of up to 9d a week just like the church schools. Poor children could have their fees paid for them out of the education rate whether they attended church or Board schools. This was very unpopular with the non-conformists, who objected to 'church schools on the rates'. In 1876 the Poor Law Guardians took over this responsibility, but that caused more problems. Some local boards of education, and finally all, required children's attendance. Many parents said they could not pay the fees, while the Poor Law Guardians said they could. This led to interminable rows between the two statutory bodies, and the Conservative administration of Lord Salisbury in 1891 finally accepted the logic that compulsory attendance required free provision (Sutherland, 1973).

This period also illustrates another theoretical issue. West (1975) has argued that the evidence for the failings of the private system before 1870 were exaggerated by public sector bureaucrats anxious to see their power enhanced. Sutherland (1973), on the other hand, from a detailed study of the public records of the time, concludes that the initiatives that led first to compulsory and then to free education in 1891 came from external pressures transmitted by the politicians, not the civil servants. Yet West is surely correct in drawing attention to the way in which, once established, the state sector, drawing on its power to tax, gradually grew at the expense of the private sector. Such growth worried the Tories and the Church of England, and in 1902 the separate boards of education were abolished. Education powers were vested in the local education committees of the new county and county borough councils. Grants were paid to these education authorities, not directly to the schools. The unified grant was based partly on the poverty of the area and its population and partly on school attendance. Voluntary secondary (grammar) schools received a *per capita* grant if they recruited a minimum number of pupils from the public elementary schools. This 'direct grant' system was to last until 1976.

The period has another curiosity. The Technical Instruction Act of 1889 gave county authorities the power to provide technical education, and the 1890s Finance Act assigned the revenues raised from the new excise duties on wines and spirits to that purpose. Whatever amount that tax raised had to be passed on to the local authorities for technical education. It is one of the very few examples of assigned revenue we have had in public finance.

1918–58

From the outset, then, local authorities had received a specific education grant or grants. The origins of these grants lay in the period before there were education authorities or public provision, and the education lobby liked them. It is much easier to exert effective pressure if it is directed towards increasing a grant for a particular educational purpose, rather than towards urging central government to be generous to local government at large in the hope that that will benefit education. The Board of Education also liked the arrangement. But by the same token a specific education grant was unpopular with the Treasury. Even more unpopular with the Treasury was the percentage grant system introduced by the 1918 Education Act – one grant for elementary and one grant for higher (including secondary) education, which replaced the plethora of specific grants. The elementary grant was based on three elements: an authority's actual expenditure on teachers' salaries (60 per cent), special services like medical and school meals (50 per cent), and the rest, related to the number of children attending school. Poorer authorities gained more but the total grant never fell below half the expenditure of an education authority. The formula for secondary and higher education was simple; the government met half of whatever the authority spent. It was a clear and intended inducement to expand such education facilities, and it incurred the wrath of the Geddes Committee (1922), which was set up to find ways of reducing public expenditure. 'The vice of the percentage grant system is that the local authority which alone can really practise economy in these services loses much of its incentive to reduce expenditure' (Geddes Report, 1922, para. 4). It proved no easy task to wrest this highly advantageous grant from the hands of the Education Department – it was to take the Treasury forty years.

After the Conservative victory the previous year, the Chancellor, Churchill, sought to achieve major reductions in public spending in 1925. As a way of complying, Lord Eustace Percy, Minister of Education, produced his famous Circular 1371 proposing a block grant for all education spending fixed at a set level – 1 per cent below the previous spending level. This aroused so much opposition that it was finally dropped, and education escaped amalgamation with other grants in the 1929 block grant system. A revised percentage grant system for education and other services emerged after the Second World War, and it was not until 1958 that the Treasury, deploying arguments very similar to those in the Geddes Report, finally got its way. A single new grant – the forerunner of the revenue support grant – was for a wide range of local services, including education. The finance of local education, which had managed to stand apart for 125 years, finally succumbed.

Education spending

After nearly two decades of rapid growth, from the mid-1950s to the mid-1970s, public expenditure on education fell back. It did so as a share of the nation's gross domestic product from 1976 (see Table 12.1) and in absolute volume terms from 1979/80 until the late 1980s (Glennerster and Low, 1990).

The UK spending on education is in the middle range internationally, falling below that of several European countries (see Table 12.2).

Roughly half of all state spending on education is devoted to schools, with secondary schools taking the largest share. Universities, polytechnics and further education colleges take 15 per cent in not quite equal proportions (see Figure 12.1). The rest is spent on a variety of purposes including student maintenance.

Table 12.1 Public expenditure on education as a percentage of GDP in the United Kingdom 1950–90

Year	% GDP
1950	3.3
1955	3.3
1960	4.1
1965	5.1
1970	5.8
1975	6.4
1980	5.5
1985	4.8
1990	4.9

Source: CSO, 1991 (and appropriate years).

Table 12.2 International comparisons in education spending as a percentage of GDP 1987 or nearest year

Country	Public	Private	Total
Australia	5.25	0.38	5.63
Canada	6.53	0.59	7.12
Denmark	7.5	0.07	7.57
France	5.57	1.03	6.59
West Germany	4.24	0.17	4.41
Ireland	5.84	0.28	6.12
Italy	4.96	—	—
Netherlands	6.99	0.34	7.33
Norway	6.82	0.17	6.99
United States	4.77	1.68	6.44
United Kingdom	4.97	0.4*	5.37

* Glennerster and Low, 1991.

Source: OECD, 1990.

The present system of finance

The means by which schools, colleges and universities actually receive their funds is complex. There are several quite different systems of finance at work. I shall describe each in turn.

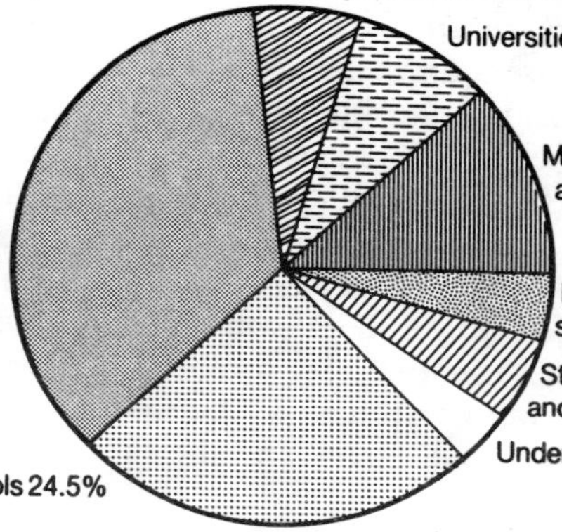

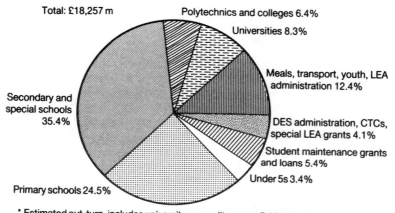

Figure 12.1 The distribution of the state education budget: current expenditure in England 1990–1* (Source: Cm 1511, 1991)

Specific grants

In the 1980s the DES managed to return to the principle of specific grants on a very small scale. It sliced off some £200 million from the LEAs' education element in the local authority grant allocation and used it to part-fund projects it approved. These have included computers in schools, training to implement LMS (see below), advisory teachers in maths and primary science, and education on drugs and health. This gives the Secretary of State some feeling that he or she has a lever on schools and some goodies to distribute, but the overall significance is tiny.

Central government repays 100 per cent of the fees and grants LEAs are required to give higher education students.

State schools

Most state schools get their money from their LEA (local education authority). The 1988 Education Reform Act significantly changed the way money reaches schools. Until that point LEA schools were allocated a certain number of teaching posts and the teachers were paid by the LEA. Schools were given sums of money to spend on equipment and books. Other facilities and services like careers centres and officers, educational psychologists, teaching advisers and teaching centres were provided by the LEA. Some local authorities had always delegated some financial independence to school heads. The Inner London Education Authority (ILEA) in the 1970s began to give more untied money and to allocate extra to schools in areas of disadvantage with more pupils facing particular difficulties. Cambridgeshire began a more radical experiment with a major devolution of budget responsibility. The 1988 Act took this further. Two quite distinct innovations were introduced, the first controversial, the second less so – 'opted-out' status and the local management of schools.

Opting out

A governing body of an LEA school can decide to ballot parents to ask whether they wish the school to opt out of LEA administrative control. On a simple majority vote, parents can take the school into what is called 'grant-maintained status' with the approval of the Secretary of State. The school is then run by an independent governing body which has on it five parent governors and up to two teachers plus the head; these are outnumbered by the other governors, drawn from the local area by the governing body. The property and staff are transferred from the LEA to this new body.

A grant-maintained school receives a regular current grant from central government, such capital grants as central government determines from year to year and some special grants on top. The capital grant covers the whole of approved capital expenditure. The size of the current annual grant – the maintenance grant – is calculated in the same way as the formula that the LEA in that area uses to allocate money to its own schools and the local management of schools (LMS). However, on top of this the government pays the grant-maintained schools a sum equal to the value of services the LEA provides centrally for its own schools. The opted-out school can use this money as it wishes. It may buy services from the LEA, buy them elsewhere, employ someone themselves (for example, to teach English as a second language), or not spend the money on these purposes at all. The higher the share of resources the LEA keeps back to allocate centrally, the more central government gives the opted-out schools on top of the formula-based grant. Central government meets 100 per cent of the approved capital expenditure of the schools. These provisions were designed to be attractive to schools.

By early 1991, sixty schools had opted for grant-maintained status. The total potential – all secondary and larger primary schools – amounted to well over 25,000.

Local management of schools

This scheme was introduced in April 1990 – later in London. It gives the school's governing body control of its own budget. LEAs decide first how much they will spend on their ordinary primary and secondary schools, excluding nursery schools and special schools for disabled children. This constitutes their general schools budget. They will spend part on minor capital works such as bicycle sheds, school transport and school meals. The remaining sum is called the potential schools budget or PSB (see Figure 12.2). From 1994 special schools will be part of LMS.

The Conservative government decreed that by 1993 at least 85 per cent of the PSB must go direct to schools. Items that the authority might want to hold back include the following:

1. Educational psychology service.
2. Teacher supply cover.
3. Peripatetic teachers – for example, music teachers.
4. Repairs and maintenance.
5. Provision for children with special needs.

There is much argument about whether the share kept centrally is too high or low. The remaining aggregate schools budget is allocated to schools. LEAs can choose their own formula but it must meet certain criteria laid down by the DES, as follows:

1. It must be based not on past allocations but on a principle of equity.
2. The 'central determinant of need' must be based on the number of pupils in the school, but this can be weighted to take account of various factors like age.
3. It must be simple.
4. It must reflect the costs of children with special needs.

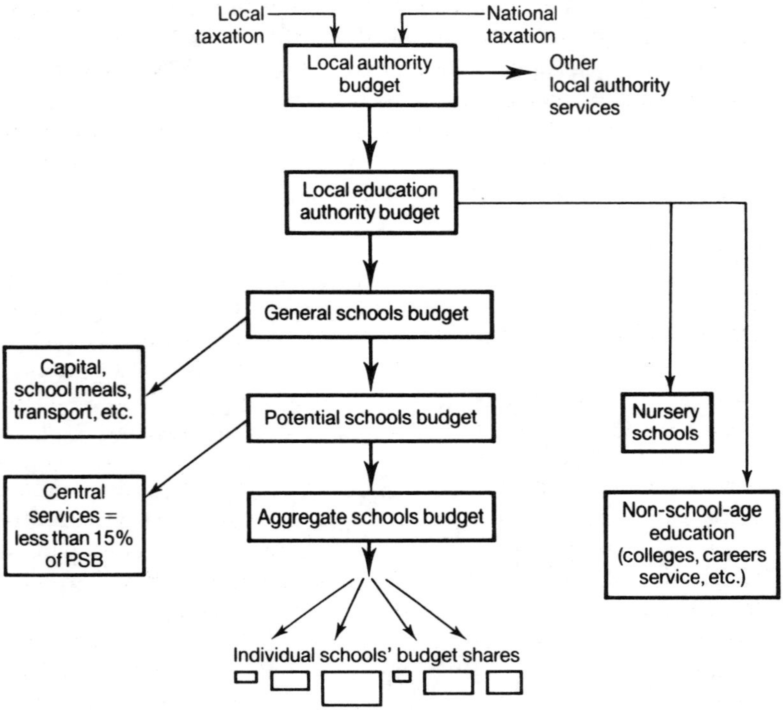

Figure 12.2 The operation of LMS (Source: Lee, 1990, adapted)

5. It may take account of social deprivation or numbers of specially gifted children.

LEAs have adopted rather different approaches to these formulae (Lee, 1990; Sammons, 1991).

From 1993 (1995 in London) the minimum that LEAs can allocate on the basis of pupil numbers will be 80 per cent. Once special needs are taken into account the room to include a weighting for social deprivation is not great.

The formula, based on average costs per pupil, worked to the disadvantage of schools that had a low turnover of staff and a high proportion of staff at the top of their salary scales. They had to cut their staff numbers to pay for the more costly teachers. These might be good, well-run schools or schools in relatively attractive middle-class suburbs which had done rather well under the old system. In the long run the system will be fairer, so long as full account can be taken of the pressures social deprivation brings: the fear in 1991 was that the government is giving too little scope for this. Once their money is allocated, the schools have much more freedom to spend it as they wish.

Free schooling?

Although local authority schools may not charge fees under the 1944 Education Act, that does not mean that schooling is free. David Bull's (1980) excellent study for the Child Poverty Action Group originally showed how many calls are made upon a parent's purse which are almost impossible to avoid without causing the child distress – essential clothing, uniform, sports kit, materials for domestic science lessons, and, increasingly, text books. Travel costs up to a statutory 'walking distance' fall on parents. There were some means-tested reliefs – school uniform grants, for example – but few know about them. In the 1980s, as schools sought to make up for cuts in allocations from the LEA, payments for certain extra lessons came to carry a charge. Parents took LEAs to court and won, but the 1988 Education Reform Act permits charges to be made for individual music tuition and for some education provided outside school hours. If these are part of the national curriculum, however, they must be free.

State support to private schools

Direct support

As we saw earlier, some secondary grammar schools that were non-profit institutions had received a direct grant from central government since the 1902 Education Act. In return they provided places for children nominated by local education authorities as well as taking fee-paying pupils. (For an account of these direct grant schools see DES, 1970; Glennerster and Wilson, 1970.) The Labour government abolished this category of school in 1976, giving them the option of becoming LEA schools or relying purely on fees. LEAs continued to have the power to pay fees at independent or private schools for particular categories of children for whom their own schools could not cater, like disabled children or those needing a boarding education. The Foreign Service and Defence Department also pay for places in boarding schools for staff serving overseas.

The Conservative government reversed the decision of the previous Labour government and introduced a scheme that replaced the direct grant system in a different form. This was called the assisted places scheme. It began in a small way in 1981 and built up to pay for 35,000 places in the late 1980s. Selected private schools could offer places to a certain number of children, and charge reduced fees related to the income of the parent. The difference was then recovered from the government. Roughly 40 per cent of pupils gained full remission. The total public expenditure was not great – £70 million planned in 1992 out of £25 billion public expenditure for education. Another £50 million was spent supporting city technology colleges (CTCs) – new independent schools which government had hoped industry would finance.

Indirect state support

Families can arrange their finances in such a way as to attract tax relief on money set aside to pay for their children's education. Private schools often have charitable status: all the major public schools do and less than half the smaller schools (Posnett and Chase, 1985). This entitles them to a range of tax reliefs – exemption from VAT on the fees charged, and from income tax, corporation tax and capital transfer tax, for example. Exemption from rates ceased to be an asset when rates ceased to exist, but might become important again if a full property tax were to return. The total size of these reliefs could be a little over 15 per cent of the school's income, or much less if the VAT element were excluded. (For a more extended account see Robson and Walford, 1989; Glennerster and Low, 1990.)

Private spending on private education

As state spending on education failed to keep pace with rising family income and rising expectations, families began to spend more themselves. Taking private and state school expenditure together in 1951/2, nearly a fifth was spent in private schools. As the state sector improved their share dropped – to below 10 per cent by 1979. During the 1980s, as the state sector was allowed to

Table 12.3 Private school current expenditure in England and Wales (£ million) 1951/2–1985/6

Year	Current spending	% of total spending on all schools
1951/2	51	18.6
1956/7	67	14.7
1962/3	91	12.5
1967/8	125	11.8
1976/7	100	8.9
1979/80	571	9.2
1982/3	1,228	12.9
1985/6	1,504	13.7

Source: Glennerster and Low, 1990.

stagnate, the share of the schools budget in the private sector rose (see Table 12.3). Total private education expenditure rose at more or less the same rate as incomes – an income elasticity of one – over the same period, and slightly faster in the 1980s (Glennerster and Low, 1990). Public expenditure on education was allowed to fall behind.

Financing further education

The Conservative government is proposing to remove further education, including sixth form colleges, from LEAs' administration too. Colleges, it is proposed, will become directly funded by a central government agency, as polytechnics in England are under the 1988 Education Reform Act. Created by the 1964–70 Labour government, polytechnics used to be administered by local authorities receiving funds from the local authorities that sent students to them. The Education Reform Act transferred the funding to the Polytechnics and Colleges Funding Council, which already funded higher-level courses taking place in LEA colleges. (In Wales the polytechnic was excluded from these arrangements and in Scotland the central institutions and colleges of education were already financed directly by the Secretary of State for Scotland.) The Funding Council was modelled on the way universities had been financed for many years. The Conservative government (DES,

1991) then proposed changing the system once again – this time amalgamating the Polytechnics and Colleges Funding Council with the Universities Funding Council.

Financing universities

Before the 1988 Education Reform Act's provisions, universities had been funded by the University Grants Committee (UGC). Prior to 1919, various specific grants were made directly by the Treasury to different universities. Then the Treasury amalgamated the grants into a single global sum and made this over to a committee, largely composed of senior academics, to judge the merits of different institutions and disperse the money. This system lasted until the mid-1960s, by which time higher education had become a major element in the education budget. The Department of Education became responsible for making the grant to the UGC, and assumed overall responsibility for planning. The UGC continued to perform its 'buffer' role, but became increasingly subject to government intervention (Kogan and Kogan, 1983).

Before the 1970s, little guidance came from the UGC on institutional or academic priorities. From then on, beginning with the 1972–7 quinquennium but most notably since 1979, the degree of 'guidance' grew. The 'UGC letter' which accompanied each year's grant became more specific about what priorities it expects from different institutions. It set student quotas for home students – a 6-per-cent cut in intake overall in 1980/1, for example. If the figures were breached the university was 'fined', losing grant next time. Until the mid-1970s universities charged low fees which did not discriminate between types of student or their origins. Then universities were told they must charge higher fees to overseas students (after 1976) and then the full cost (in 1980). For home students, universities received what was effectively a grant for each student, varying according to subject and level, and assuming that a given fee was charged.

The 1988 Act took this process of increasing central control to its logical conclusion. It transformed the academic buffer of the UGC into an explicitly intervening successor – the Universities Funding Council (UFC). This body was, in the original bill, to make contracts with universities. Protests and revolts in the House of Lords watered the wording down but the intention was not greatly altered (Glennerster *et al.*, 1991). Section 131 (6) stated: '[The Council] shall have power to make grants (to universities) subject to such terms and conditions as they think fit.' Late in 1991, new legislation was to give the combined funding council even wider powers of intervention.

A new framework?

The Conservative government's proposals (DES, 1991) changed the grant-giving structure and resumed the move to greater central control of higher education. The separate funding of polytechnics and universities – the binary divide – disappears. There will be funding councils for all higher education institutions in England, in Scotland and in Wales. The second break with the past will be the separate funding of teaching and research. The UGC paid universities and their staff to do a mixture of teaching and research. These staff could get extra funds to mount particular research projects, but the generality of research was financed as a joint product with teaching. This had the disadvantage, from the government's point of view, that if it wanted to fund universities to take more history students, it also had to buy more research by history dons. Given its wish to expand higher education more cheaply, the government decided to separate the finance of teaching and research. The new funding council will pay universities and the old polytechnics to teach all students on the same basis. The colleges/universities will also be able to charge higher fees to home students. These may be paid by LEAs, or by students themselves. The fee plus the funding council grant will cover only the teaching costs, including costs of libraries and laboratories. This could be not much more than half the previous average grant per student at universities.

The Higher Education Funding Council will also give some money for general research, based on a rating of institutions' research performance. This is likely to be concentrated in a small number of institutions. The research councils will finance specific research projects. Overseas students will pay the full cost of their education as before. There will be fierce competition to get

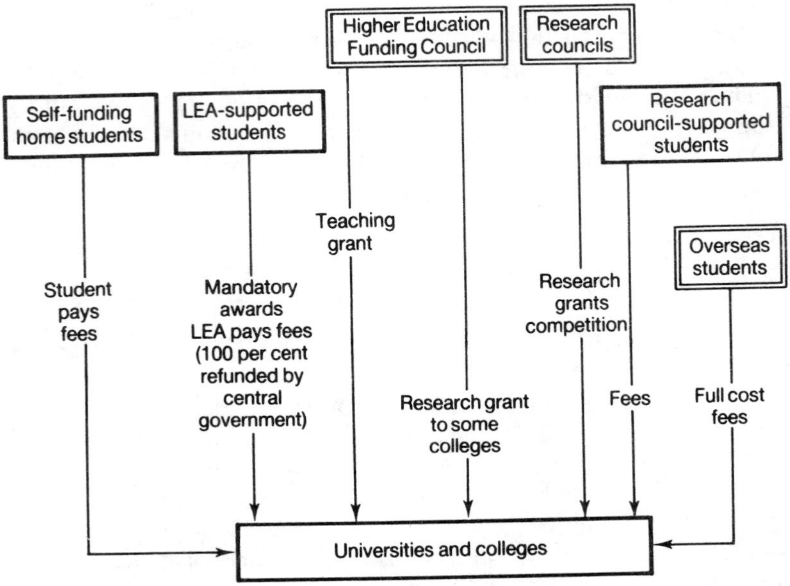

Figure 12.3 The sources of funds for higher education in the United Kingdom in the 1990s

students who bring resources with them. However, universities and colleges who expand their 'fees only' student numbers will be given preferential treatment in the basic grant too, rewarding those who offer a cheap education. For the whole pattern see Figure 12.3.

Financing students

From the 1944 Education Act onwards, undergraduate students at universities could be given awards by local education authorities, which both paid their fees and gave them a subsistence allowance to cover their living expenses and residential costs. More generous grants and rights to them dated from 1962. The actual sums given depended on the income of students' parents, unless they were older ('mature') students. In the 1970s these grants were not maintained in line with inflation, and the means test level of income was lowered so that more and more families and students came within the band of reduced maintenance allowances. The reduction in the real level of grant was sharpest between 1980 and 1986 (DES, 1988). Then, in the social security changes of the mid-1980s, housing benefit was withdrawn for students (see Chapter 14). All these changes made it much more costly to be a student.

Loans

Government argued that since public expenditure was inevitably going to be constrained, it should be spent on teaching and research in higher education and not on maintaining students. Hence grants should continue to be phased out and 'topped up' by loans to students, which they would have to repay when their incomes were higher. Those on very low incomes in any year could claim exemption from repaying (see below). Gradually loans would replace grants as the means by which students' living expenses would be supported by government. The level of repayment would rise as inflation rose.

This system has proved very costly in administrative terms. The take-up has been low. The scheme also seems unfair to many. Lower income earners do not lose their liability to repay, it is merely deferred by up to 25 years. This 'mortgage-type' loan scheme differs from a 'graduate tax', which makes graduates subject to a higher rate of tax in return for the extra use they have made of the higher education system and the higher earnings they may get as a result, and under which low earners or non-earners do not have a given repayment sum hanging over them. (The top up loans scheme is evaluated and alternatives proposed by Barr, 1989.)

'Manpower' and training

Employers – or enterprises, as we have called them – are the major funders of training. They provide training for their own employees and they pay for them to attend courses, often in local authority further education colleges.

The Manpower Services Commission (MSC) was set up in 1974 as one of a whole series of attempts to promote and organise industrial and other training. It was not financed from the education budget. The responsible minister was the Secretary of

State for Employment in England, and the respective Secretaries of State in Scotland and Wales. The MSC gained its funds from central government and in turn dispensed funds to employers and other agencies to finance training and youth employment schemes. Its relatively small scale of activity was, however, rapidly expanded in response to growth in youth unemployment. Building on previous schemes in 1983, it introduced the Youth Training Scheme to provide a one-year traineeship for all unemployed 16-year-old school leavers. Employers taking part in the scheme received a grant for each trainee, covering the trainee's 'allowance' and contributing to the cost of 'training'. This and other programmes, financed through the MSC and its successor the Training Commission, grew until the late 1980s, when funds were once again trimmed back. The Conservative government then experimented with a training voucher, giving young people a claim to training and a government subsidy they could take to an employer who had hired them. The early results were not encouraging: take-up was low.

Into the 1990s

A specific grant for education?

The education world and some Secretaries of State for Education look nostalgically back to the time when education had its own specific grant. It gave ministers the opportunity to ensure that money won in the PES round for a particular purpose actually brought results in local authority spending. As it is, money gained for education in the block grant may be spent on old people's homes. Shirley Williams, when Secretary of State for Education in the mid-1970s, expressed her frustration when she won money for the rate support grant to pay for nursery education and post-experience courses for teachers, only to find many local authorities ignoring those purposes.

In its Green Paper, *Alternatives to Domestic Rates* (Cmnd 8449, 1981), the Conservative government included an appendix outlining some ways in which the funding of the education service could be changed to reduce the burden on the rates. They were as follows:

1. Financial responsibility could be removed from local authorities altogether.
2. Central government could take over complete responsibility for teachers' salaries.
3. Central government could pay an education block grant, rather like the education element in the present revenue support grant but going to education authorities only.

The case against change turns largely on the fear of central political control over the education service.

Abolish LEAs?

Some argue that opting out and LMS should be taken to their logical conclusion. Why not fund all state schools direct from central government, like the old direct grant schools? The LEA would then be redundant (see, for example, ***Independent***, 1991). The arguments for and against are a direct reflection of the issues we reviewed in Chapter 3.

Efficiency

Advocates of full competition between schools have always argued that the case for state involvement in education extends only to its responsibility to empower parents to buy education. Schools are no different from other service providers (Friedman, 1962; West, 1965; Maynard, 1975). Under the UK school market now emerging, the government will ensure that an acceptable standard of common education is provided by means of the National Curriculum, assessment tests and local inspections regulated by Her Majesty's Inspectors of Schools. With information on school performance, parents and pupils will be able to judge in an informed way between the services offered by competing schools. The most efficient will gain pupils and resources, the others will decline. This is the traditional form of efficiency competition of a free market, but as we saw in Chapter 3 it is not the only competition in which schools will engage.

Selectivity

Just as it is critically important for any health care provider to exclude high-cost, high-risk patients, so the equivalent is true for schools. Work by Rutter *et al.* (1979) produced elaborate and effective measures of what constituted 'good' secondary schools. Yet it was still true that, when taken in conjunction with information on pupils' basic abilities and parental background, what went on in the school only explained about 5 per cent of the variance in pupil achievements. An even more detailed longitudinal study of the differential effectiveness of primary schools in London was able to explain 9 per cent of the variance in pupils' reading achievements and 11 per cent of the variance in maths attainments by reference to schools' effects (Mortimore *et al.*, 1988). Any school entrepreneur acting rationally would seek to exclude pupils who would drag down the overall performance score of the school. Any non-selective system of schooling would then be in unstable equilibrium. A process of adjustment would follow, moving towards an equilibrium in which schools would cater for children in different bands of ability, and from different social backgrounds. Some would welcome that result, others would not. What economic theory suggests is that a pure internal market between schools based on unadjusted scores would not produce a neutral outcome.

In so far as LEAs did succeed in obtaining a mixed entry to the schools in their area, parents would be able to judge the relative merits of schools' performance starting from a level, as opposed to a staggered, start. It would be necessary, in any system offering choice, for the LEA to produce studies of the relative performance of schools in value-added terms, taking account of the social and other characteristics of individual schools, as the Inner London Education Authority (ILEA) did before it was abolished. The Audit Commission (1991) argued that crude league tables of exam results would be misleading, but that measures of one year's exam results compared with previous years in the same school would give a value-added measure. It would do so only if the results of the same children were compared or if the social and ability mix did not change.

The case so far has been that schooling can be reconciled with an element of market discipline only with a number of safeguards. These require the local education authority to play a significant role, which would be as follows:

1. To choose a pattern of education provision, selective or non-selective, in line with local parents' collective choice.

2. To plan a structure of schools in the area. This would take account of expected demographic change and the preferences being revealed in parents' choice of school.
3. To support schools with a good inspection and advisory service, which could diagnose those in trouble and give them special and early support to prevent a long terminal illness before closure.
4. To provide other services on demand at a market price.

Finance parents not schools?

These proposals would extend state support to private schools as well. State cash would go direct to parents. In Britain, most of the advocates of vouchers are on the political right. That is not the case in other countries, most notably the United States, where vouchers are seen as a way of enabling minority groups to opt out of traditional state school education. The arguments for the changes are as follows:

1. Minimum state involvement in the provision of education is desirable to reduce the risks of political indoctrination of children, to create diversity of practice and view, and to reduce the number of state employees. Private provision is necessary to sustain political freedom (Friedman, 1962).
2. Parents are the best judges of their children's educational needs. The case is forcefully argued by Sugarman (1980) and at greater length by Coons and Sugarman (1978). There is no consensus, they argue, over what are the proper goals and means of education. Some parents want strict discipline, others lax; some more play, others none; some want a classical 'three Rs' syllabus, others a more creative one; some want denominational teaching, others none. Thus parental choice must be paramount. 'The family is the best decision maker. Typical families listen to the child, care about the child and know more about aspects of the child's personality than any possible official choosers' (Sugarman, 1980).
3. Education and schools are like any other market. Inefficient schools will be avoided by parents. Under a voucher scheme, inefficient schools would improve or go bankrupt (see the previous section).

4. There are inevitably some households or tax payers who have high preferences for education spending. Others have low or medium preferences. Electoral bartering produces a compromise level of spending, too high for some, too low for others. If parents were given the present value of state spending on the average child (through a voucher), they could add their own marginal extras and pay fees at a school matching their higher preference (Stubblebine, 1965). This would go some way to equating preferences with educational provision, and result in a higher overall level of education spending.

Different kinds of *voucher scheme* are advocated by those who lay different emphasis on the above arguments. Friedman stresses the importance of expanding the private sector of education and the case for encouraging parents who wish to spend more. Coons and Sugarman (1978) want more choice but they also want equality of opportunity. Jencks (1971) wants better provision for the poor and to foster choice within the state sector. These differences give rise to three fundamentally different kinds of voucher schemes, as follows:

1. Vouchers limited to state schools versus vouchers 'cashable' at any school, public or private.
2. Vouchers that cannot be 'topped up' from parental means versus vouchers that can be added to pay fees.
3. A flat-rate voucher, the same for every child, versus one that was higher for poor children and lower for children of rich parents.

These three possibilities can be combined in different ways to produce a wide range of options.

Those who oppose this move argue as follows:

1. State interference by a totalitarian government in the curriculum will not be inhibited by financial or accounting methods. As we saw at the beginning of the chapter, the extent of central government control of the curriculum was greatest in the period when schools were privately run and state financed.
2. The practical problems of ensuring minimum educational standards in thousands of private schools are enormous. We are

not dealing with an ordinary market. Parents are being compelled to purchase a service by law with the tax payer's money. The dangers of exploitation and profiteering at the tax payer's expense must be great.

3. Given the wide variation in parental experience of education, the rapid changes in educational practice in the past twenty years, and children's own rights and feelings on the matter, parents may not be the best judges. Choices between subjects are more important to children than choice between schools, and the two objectives conflict with each other for geographical reasons. To ensure viable classes in a wide range of subjects at GCSE and A-level, a school must be quite large. In most areas outside big towns, choice involves travelling long distances. The smaller the schools the larger the choice *between* schools, but the *narrower* the choice between subjects in any one of them.
4. Schools are not like the corner grocer's shop. They cannot readily go bankrupt and be replaced by new entrants to the market. The consequences of run-down and closure for children are serious.
5. The argument that total education spending will be increased is based on a set of assumptions that are questionable. It presumes that the electorate would be prepared to vote education as much money with a voucher scheme as under the present system. That cannot be proved and can be doubted (Glennerster and Wilson, 1970). Where many if not most parents were in the private sector, richer voters might well prefer to vote for lower taxes and lower vouchers.

Abolish private education?

The counter-case is that advanced by those who would either make the private provision of education illegal or severely restrict it. They argue that if the ideal goal is to achieve equal opportunity or an equal start in life for all children then it cannot be right to permit some children to acquire a superior education to others. Not only do private schools permit this, they also have links with colleges at Oxford and Cambridge and sustain a network of social contacts that give those whose parents can afford private education a striking advantage in career terms and in entry to elite positions. Moreover, they foster the social segregation of children of different classes (Crosland, 1956, 1962).

Opponents argue that the right to send your child to a school that holds your beliefs as a parent, and provides what you think is an appropriate education, is a fundamental human liberty. Even if equality of opportunity is a good objective, liberty must take priority. A monopoly of education by the state, with no power to withdraw your child from its instruction, is a dangerous step to totalitarianism.

Some argue that at least the state should not subsidise private education directly or indirectly unless the schools provide for all classes without privilege (DES, 1968).

Extend or abolish loans to students?

Students should, some argue, repay the *whole* cost of their education and not just the maintenance element.

The case for loans

In 1990/1, maintenance grant expenditure was about £700 million. This could be used more effectively. At present, full-time, young, first-degree students are relatively generously treated, but others – sixth formers, technicians, non-degree students and adults – are poorly treated. If some of the cost of maintenance grants were reallocated to these other groups and kept merely for the very poorest university students, it would be a fairer distribution of limited funds.

On general efficiency grounds, economists argue that students should be faced with the true costs of the resources they are using. This argues for going further and charging students a full cost fee, and getting them to repay it when they begin earning. On equity grounds the present system is unfair. It largely benefits children of higher-income group parents, who then go on to earn high income themselves (see Farmer and Barrell, 1982). Thus on average five times as much public money is spent on the higher education of children from the highest income groups than of the low (Le Grand, 1982). Loans or a graduate tax would help counteract that 'perverse' distribution of income effect.

The case against loans

In practice, loans bring no immediate gains to the Exchequer. They can do the reverse in the short run. This is evident in the present limited scheme, which will cost the government £350 million by 1993 if it continues with almost no income. No scheme in this or other countries actually exacts a full market rate of interest. To avoid the criticisms, often levelled at such schemes, that they are unfair on those graduates who do not earn high salaries or do not earn at all, our and other countries have fairly generous exclusions, which again reduces the potential revenue.

Far from seeing loans as fairer to lower income groups, many, like the Robbins Committee (1963), believe that the prospect of a large loan debt would only put off more working-class young people whose parents could not cushion them. This would have efficiency consequences for the economy as well as equity. Even income contingent loans or a graduate tax, it is argued, could have such an effect. Woodhall (1982) suggests the evidence of other countries does not support this.

A graduate tax

To ease the problem of a loan being a disincentive to poorer students with little family experience of higher education or a mortgage, a graduate tax alternative was proposed many years ago (Prest, 1966; Glennerster *et al.*, 1968). A version was introduced in Australia in 1989 under the title 'Higher Education Contribution Scheme'. Graduates who receive full higher education also undertake to pay a subsequently higher rate of tax. This links repayment to ability to pay and means that those with low incomes or no incomes do not have to pay at all and *do not* retain the obligation to pay if their incomes *remain* low. Barr (1989) modified the proposal, suggesting that a higher national insurance contribution would be a good way to collect the tax.

A lifetime entitlement

At the other extreme, a way of achieving equity in post-school education would be to give everyone the right to receive a certain financial entitlement to post-school education or training at some time in their life – a kind of educational bank account (Schuller and Walker, 1990). This can be combined with ideas about educational leave from work. Many European countries have partial elements of such schemes (Glennerster, 1981a). A limited scheme of this kind was proposed in Britain by the Advisory Council for Adult and Continuing Education (1982).

Further reading

For a discussion of LMS see Lee, T. (1992), *Local Management of Schools*, Milton Keynes: Open University Press.

Voucher schemes are compared and the case for experiment expounded in Maynard, A. (1975), *Experiment with Choice in Education*, London: Institute of Economic Affairs, and propounded powerfully by two American liberals, Coons, J. and Sugarman, S. (1978), *Education by Choice: The case for family control*, Berkeley, Calif.: University of California Press.

The difficulties with markets for schooling are discussed in Glennerster, H. (1991), 'Quasi-markets for education?', *Economic Journal*, **101**, pp. 1,256–67.

The pros and cons of different forms of student finance are reviewed in Woodhall, M. (1989), *Financial Support for Students: Grants, loans or graduate tax?*, London: Kogan Page.

A critique of the top-up loan introduced in the United Kingdom in 1990 is given and an alternative proposed in Barr, N.A. (1989), *Student Loans: The next steps*, David Hume Paper no. 15, Aberdeen: Aberdeen University.

CHAPTER 13

PAYING FOR HOUSING

Nowhere is it more important to distinguish the provision of a service from its finance, and the effect of direct public spending from tax expenditures, than in housing. Much of the chaos into which housing finance has fallen is a direct result of failing to distinguish or appreciate the inter-related consequences of each form of state intervention. We can only understand the present confusion by looking at its historical origins. Over the past century the state has come to be involved in the housing market in at least six distinct ways, as follows:

1. Regulating the standard of houses built and permitted to remain in occupation.
2. Controlling the level of rents charged by private landlords and giving security of tenure to certain tenants.
3. Building, owning and managing houses itself.
4. Subsidising the housing costs of its own tenants and tenants of private landlords and housing associations.
5. Subsidising the improvement of property by public and private owners.
6. Subsidising house purchase through the tax system.

I shall try to trace briefly the sequence of events that led the state down this long and confusing route.

The history of housing finance

State regulation, provision and subsidy

In the nineteenth century the private, speculative builder and landlord responded to the rapidly changing housing demands created by industrialisation. In many ways they did so remarkably effectively, providing houses that were better than most in Europe at a price affordable by many of the new industrial working class. However, even they could not provide tolerable accommodation for the poorest classes. The costs of building even the meanest housing with an adequate rate of return on capital were too high for the lowest income groups. Overcrowding grew worse throughout the century. Housing and health standards declined in the poorest parts of the large cities and came to pose several kinds of threat to the wider society – contagious disease, and a threat to public order and accepted social values. 'Slums' presented such a disturbing element that Victorians sought drastic remedies (Steadman-Jones, 1971; Gauldie, 1974). The early efforts either made things worse or made little difference. Public health legislation, notably in 1848 and 1875, enforced sanitation and set minimum standards for housing – ventilation, light, water, space. It also gave powers to local authorities to close and demolish slums and to prohibit overcrowding. This both increased the minimum cost of housing and reduced its supply, hence pushing it further out of the reach of poor families.

Left to itself the housing market will clear; there will be supply of a sort for the poorest, even if it is the self-built corrugated iron shacks on the outskirts of large cities that one can see in some parts of the world today, or the extreme slum conditions or 'rookeries' of Victorian London. However, if society is not prepared to accept that outcome, then government must find a way of creating a supply of a minimum standard of housing at a price low-income families can afford, or it must subsidise the incomes of poor households to ensure they meet these housing costs. The Victorian response was to use the voluntary sector to supply low-cost housing. They hoped that with efficient building at low interest and stern housing management, the market could still work, though on a philanthropic rather than pure capitalist model. To some extent this did work with a limited social group, but it did not solve the real problem. (Only 100,000 such dwellings were built in London up to 1914.) In other countries, however, this response was much more effective, since government or employers stepped in to subsidise such provision either directly or through low-interest-rate loans (Power, 1992) .

Local authorities, under the 1890 Housing the Working Classes Act, had the power to build but did not receive subsidies. Hence they also were unable to provide housing at minimum standards for the poorest without some dubious accounting that only a few authorities indulged in. On the other hand, paying money to poor families direct to help them pay rent for better accommodation conflicted with sound Poor Law principles. Increasingly, reformers turned to the only solution they could identify as politically feasible – Exchequer subsidies to local authorities.

The First World War produced the first major precedent for the later pattern of finance that was to be reinforced by the experience of the Second World War (Bowley, 1945; Wilding, 1972; Merrett, 1979). The war worsened the housing shortage. The new prime minister, Lloyd George, had committed the post-war government to a massive building programme, and in response to unrest and rent strikes the government controlled rents. In those circumstances the only agencies that could deliver such a programme seemed to be the local authorities, but early returns showed they were most reluctant to do so if the costs fell on the rates. Thus the 1919 Housing Town Planning Act (the Addision Act) gave local authorities the power to build and charge low rents. If there were a deficit they had to spend up to a 1d rate subsidising it, but the whole of the remaining deficit would be borne by the Exchequer. This form of financial carrot, and the presumptions of low rents for council tenants, remained, at least until recently. The complex but interesting early history of Exchequer housing subsidies can be read in Nevitt (1966), Merrett (1979), Donnison and Ungerson (1982), Holmans (1987) and Malpass (1990).

In the aftermath of the Second World War and an even greater housing shortage, councils were given the primary role in meeting the shortage fast. They were given priority in the allocation of scarce building materials – they built three-quarters of all new houses in the 1940s. Subsequently their role reverted to redevelopment on a massive scale in the 1960s, to specialist housing and to granting subsidies on improvements to older housing. Each change of policy produced a new subsidy, so much per year for the life of the loan raised to build each new house. The result was a peculiar museum of bits and pieces of central government subsidy accumulated over the decades by councils. They were increasingly pressed by central government to concentrate that subsidy on poorer tenants by charging differential or income-related rents (Parker, 1967).

The 1972 Housing Finance Act swept these old subsidies away and introduced a new system. Government grants to support councils' housing costs were to be based on each council's *current* financial and housing needs. More important, low-income tenants, both public *and* private, who were wage earners could apply to the local authority for help. Local authority tenants received a rent rebate, private tenants a rent allowance. This was the basis of the modern system of housing benefit (see below).

In the aftermath of the economic crisis in 1976, local authority house building was cut drastically. The Conservative government in the 1980s switched its priority to funding housing associations as the main new providers of low-cost housing to rent.

Penalties on the private landlord

As we saw, the private landlord had been the dominant provider of housing in the nineteenth century and at the end of it over 90 per cent of houses were rented to tenants by private owners. Throughout the present century, however, a number of factors have combined to erode this position steadily, so that in 1990 only 7 per cent of households in the United Kingdom were tenants of private landlords. The First World War began their decline. Rent control, introduced in 1915, was gradually relaxed, then reintroduced in the Second World War, and relaxed again in stages. Rent control on new lettings was ended by the 1988 Housing Act. It is often condemned as the main reason for the demise of the private sector by limiting the profitability of the landlord's housing stock. Undoubtedly it played its part, but, as the experience of the 1957 Rent Act showed, even when rent controls were removed from a large part of the market for a period, its decline continued. Nevitt's (1966) analysis shows why. The tax laws continued to treat a new house as a permanent asset, not as a piece of investment that depreciates and can be set against tax to reduce the investor's tax liability. If a business invests in new machinery, it can offset the costs against tax. Thus, Nevitt argued, private housing was badly treated by the tax laws. Far more important, the tax treatment of owner occupiers was so generous as to make owning your own house always preferable to renting in sheer financial terms, reducing the demand for private tenancies. The modern tax situation is set out by Hills (1991a). It is, indeed, this tax treatment of owner occupiers that has become the decisive factor in housing finance, yet it also came about as something of an accident.

Bonus for the owner occupier

Owner occupation began to expand in the nineteenth century because of the invention of building societies. They were originally self-help groups of artisans who formed a club and contributed regularly to a fund out of which they would buy or build houses for themselves. Its job done, the society was wound up. Then people realised the society could continue on a longer-term basis as a 'permanent society', borrowing from local savers and lending to local people to buy houses. Strictly hedged with legislation after various scandals, the local building society became the normal means of collecting small savings and financing house purchase. In the low-interest-rate, low-housing-cost period between the wars, owner occupation boomed in the better-off areas of the South and the Midlands. The societies were given relatively favourable tax treatment compared to other financial institutions, but the real tax bonus did not begin until the 1960s.

Originally, owner occupiers were of marginal importance and the tax system simply applied the existing rules. They were treated as if they were their own private landlord. They were assumed to be paying themselves a rent – the level of rent other people living in a similar house would pay – and they were taxed on that notional rent, just as a private landlord would be. It made good economic sense, and was a system followed in many other countries. The owner occupier's real income *was* higher since he or she paid no rent, while his or her neighbour paid the rent each week. Both the owner occupier and the private landlord could offset interest and other costs against gross income, just like any business. Thus the owner occupier received tax relief on the interest he or she paid to buy the house – just as a private landlord or other business would, on the necessary cost of investment. This system lasted until 1963, but it was gradually being eroded. Not having the benefit of weekly economics classes, owner occupiers could not see the logic of paying income tax on income they never saw. This notional income was set in 1936 values and never changed after the war, so its real value fell, and therefore so did the real value of the revenue the Treasury received. As the number of owner occupiers grew, the pressure to abolish the tax grew. In 1963 the Conservative Chancellor did abolish it. Because there had been no revaluations of houses, the revenue was small, administratively cumbersome to collect and unpopular to boot. The Labour Party did not object.

So far so good, but what about the other side of the equity balance – the right to set off the interest paid on mortgage against tax? That remained in place. At that time all interest payments could be set against tax even for consumption purposes. When that relief was finally abolished in 1974/5, loans for house purchase were again exempt. The combined effect of these incremental moves has been a growing tax subsidy to owner occupation, the economic case for which has totally disappeared and which does in fact have wide and serious economic consequences I shall discuss later (Atkinson and King, 1982).

Another major subsidy also arose by accident. The Labour government introduced a capital gains tax in 1965. It was a tax on the difference between the purchase price of a capital asset and its selling price. Owner-occupied housing was exempt. There was some justification for this. If house prices are rising, and you need to buy a new house when you sell your old one, you need to use the money you gained from your sale. However, it has also encouraged people to 'trade up' – to buy as expensive a house as they can, then sell, and buy larger and more expensive houses as their incomes rise. This both reduces their tax burden and enables them to reap a capital gain, often on retirement, when they move into a smaller house or into other forms of tenure.

House purchase thus became a combined form of pension, life assurance and tax avoidance – the higher the income, the greater the gains: the more expensive the house bought and the interest set off against tax, the greater the benefits. Moreover, the higher the marginal rate of tax, the greater was the tax relief. Those on very high marginal rates of tax were effectively getting almost interest-free loans. The Labour government in 1976 took the first steps to put some limits to the system. Tax relief was only available on mortgages up to £25,000. The next Conservative government raised the limit to £30,000 in 1983, but it was not increased for the rest of the decade and its real value steadily declined. Then in the first post-Thatcher Budget in 1991 the extra relief for higher-rate tax payers was withdrawn.

Aid from social security

Since the days of the Poor Law, assistance payments covered rent, at least in part, and then came to include payment of the interest on owner occupiers' mortgages. The Supplementary Benefits Commission was in effect one of the largest providers of cash help towards housing costs, about £900 million compared to the total housing subsidy and tax allowance bill of £2,600 million in 1979 (Kilroy, 1982). This form of support to poor householders overlapped with rent rebate schemes run by local authorities for their tenants, and with the rent allowance scheme for those not on supplementary benefit. Poor tenants were caught in the midst of this tangle and the Supplementary Benefits Commission wanted to rid itself of involvement in determining 'reasonable' rents. In 1983 the government introduced the housing benefit scheme that was intended to concentrate all cash assistance to poor families in one scheme administered by local authorities. It was this scheme that was overhauled during the Social Security Review of the mid-1980s (see Chapter 14 and below).

Comprehensive reform fails

A major review of the whole system of housing finance was carried out by the Labour government in the mid-1970s. The result – *Housing Policy* (DoE, 1977) – produced a mass of valuable information and analysis but no significant political action. It was the Conservative administrations of the 1980s that produced some decisive changes in housing finance.

Expenditure on housing

Figure 13.1 shows how the state's involvement in housing finance has changed since the economic crisis of 1976 and over twelve years of Conservative government. In 1976/7 net capital expenditure by local councils and housing associations (that is, excluding building financed from sales of property) amounted to £8 billion in 1989 prices. By 1989/90 the level of net capital spending permitted by both local authorities and housing associations had fallen to about £1 billion. That total was shared almost equally by local authorities and housing associations. On top of that, local authorities were presumed to be able to spend nearly as much again on self-financed capital from their sales.

The next big change was in the form of Exchequer support for local authorities' current spending and the extent to which tenants' rents were subsidised. In 1976 a large sum, over £3 billion in 1989 prices, was given as a general subsidy to local authorities' housing revenue accounts. This went to lower the general level of rents that had to be charged to make those accounts balance. Then there

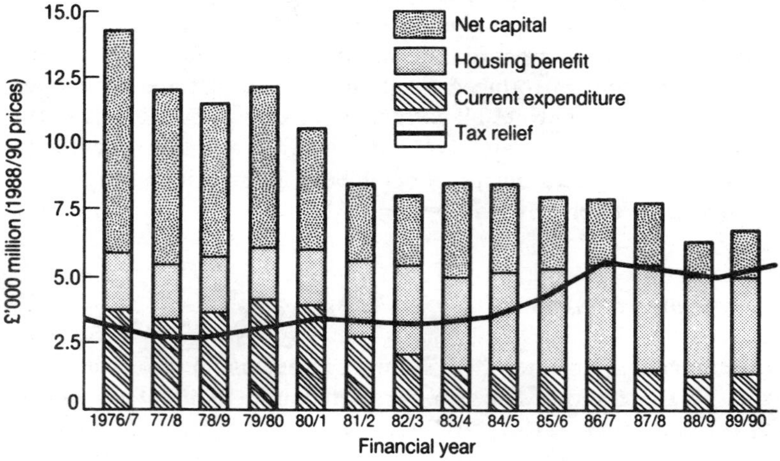

Figure 13.1 Public expenditure on housing in Britain 1976/7–1989/90 (Source: Hills, 1991b)

were the cash benefits to particular tenants to relieve the burden of rent. In 1976 the total level of spending on means-tested housing benefits to both council and private tenants was less than half the cost of the general subsidy to councils' housing costs. By 1989/90 the whole balance had shifted. General subsidies to local authorities' housing revenue accounts had all but disappeared. The great bulk of public expenditure was by then in the form of housing benefit to poor households of any tenure, though in practice a great many council tenants received benefit as the largest group of poor tenants. Overall, as we can see from Figure 13.1, the level of real public expenditure on housing of all kinds fell by half between the mid-1970s and 1990.

Coincident with these changes was an increase in the support given to owner occupiers. It nearly doubled in the same period, as Figure 13.1 also shows.

Forms of finance in the 1990s

Local housing authorities

Unlike the case with the rest of their finances, local authorities must keep a separate housing revenue account (HRA) into which goes all the income and expenditure that relates to their own housing stock. Other aspects of their housing service, like house improvement grants or bed and breakfast for homeless people, comes out of the council's general funds like all other services. The exact contents of the HRA are carefully defined. The latest version of the definition is in the 1989 Local Government and Housing Act. In brief it comprises: gross income from rent; charges for services like heating; central government subsidy; and interest on capital sums gained from the sale of its property to council tenants (capital which remains in the bank because the government has not given permission for it to be spent). Expenditure includes: repairs; maintenance and management of the stock; small-scale capital expenditure from income; rent rebates paid to tenants to help them pay their rents; and loan charges on borrowing to build or repair the stock. The same Act introduced the latest in the line of subsidies to local housing authorities. The key step was to 'ring fence' the HRA. In the past it had been possible for local authorities to use their general funds to subsidise the HRA and hence reduce rents overall. From 1990/1 this has not been permitted.

The old general housing subsidy from the central government has disappeared, and with it the practice of paying the housing benefit to which council tenants were entitled. Central government had forced local authorities to raise rents and was consequently being forced to pay higher housing benefit to council tenants, who then paid the council. It was a rising indirect subsidy from social security funds to local councils. Under the 1989 Act, councils are forced to go on raising their rents each year in line with rents in the private and housing association sectors.

The subsidy from the central government to the HRA is calculated as follows:

a) management and maintenance allowance (£*x* × number of dwellings)	£4 million
b) the interest on past loans	£5 million
c) cost of rent rebates	£6 million
	£15 million
Less	
d) gross rent guideline (recommended rent levels *R* × number of dwellings, where *R* is a guideline set annually by central government)	£14 million
Subsidy	£1 million

Clearly, the higher the government sets the rent guideline the lower will be the subsidy local authorities receive. In the above example, if the guideline rent were raised, the expected income could rise to £15 million. Assuming nothing else changed, that would eliminate the government subsidy. It would leave the cost of supporting the rents of poorer tenants to be borne by the income raised from the rents of other tenants. In practice, rent rebates would rise too.

The guideline rent is fixed in relation to the valuation put on council houses that tenants have bought in that area. If they have had to pay twice the national average value of council houses, the target rent will be twice the national guideline. To ease in the new system, the government calculated a dampening factor to move rents over a period to the levels implied by the target guidelines. The system is fully elaborated in Hills (1991a).

A future Labour government might wish to base its guidelines on different principles. It would want to encourage local authorities to build more houses, which would increase the expenditure side of the HRA as the much higher costs of loan repayment began to fall on the account. This would begin to require rents to rise. Central government would then have to decide whether to increase its subsidy and whether to 'un-ring fence' the HRAs by allowing councils to subsidise tenants' rents from general council revenue. The pattern evolved in the 1980s does, however, have advantages that are likely to remain. One is that clear target sums are indicated for spending on management and maintenance of property, which local authorities have at times in the past neglected. It remains necessary to ensure those sums are well spent.

Transferring the stock

The 1980 Housing Act gave council tenants the right to buy the property they inhabited from the council at a discount; that is, below the valuation made by the local valuer of the property. The extent of the discount depended on the length of time the applicant had been a tenant. The reduction in the value at which the tenant could buy was another form of capital subsidy to owner occupiers. Poorer tenants would also lose their right to housing benefit. Better-off tenants would not have received such benefits. For them the net gains were considerable. Between 1979 and 1990 about a million and a half council dwellings were sold to tenants and the number of council dwellings as a proportion of all dwellings fell from about a third to less than a quarter.

As the number of tenants able to buy even at a discount began to dry up, the Conservative government devised another way of reducing the stock of council-owned properties. In 1988 the Housing Act gave private landlords or housing associations the right to acquire blocks of council houses or whole estates, so long as tenants approved in a rather odd voting system. Tenants already had the power to choose to form a housing association or tenant co-operative. Few compulsory transfers had taken place by 1992, but an increasing number of voluntary ones had. In addition, the government took powers to create housing action trusts. These can be used to take bad estates compulsorily out of the hands of local authorities and place them in the hands of a trust, which will improve the estates and hand them on to private or housing association owners. After a slow start and much modification, several schemes were in progress by 1992.

A longer period of Conservative government will almost certainly see most of the housing stock of local authorities sold to or taken over by housing associations or other non-governmental agencies. A trend towards more tenant ownership of estates and devolved responsibility for them is probable under any administration.

Housing associations

Both the 1974 Labour government that set up the Housing Corporation and extended the system of support for housing associations, and the Conservative government of the 1980s, were anxious to diversify the range of landlords available to poorer tenants. If the private market had virtually ceased to exist for this group of tenants, some variety, choice and means of exit was needed rather than reliance on a vast single public landlord. In 1967 the Labour government extended to housing associations the right to receive government subsidies, like local authorities. However, the local authority had to act as the channel and many were reluctant to do so, thus spending resources they would have preferred to use themselves. In 1974 a separate housing association grant was introduced, based on an entirely new principle. It involved giving associations at the beginning of a new scheme a *capital* sum, sufficient to reduce the loan repayment charges to such a point that poorer tenants could pay the rent. The local rent officer would set a 'fair' rent for that new property. The newly created Housing Corporation would set a sum it expected to be spent on management and maintenance of the property. It also set cost limits to the building or renovation of the property. The total capital cost was, therefore, tightly controlled. So, too, were the other regular expenditures. It was possible to work out how high rents would have to be to cover the interest payments and the other regular expenditure. A capital sum was then given to the association sufficient to reduce its debt, and therefore its interest payments, to a point where the weekly costs of the association equalled the rent set by the rent officer. The grant was called the housing association grant (HAG).

As it turned out, the system had a fatal flaw. It assumed that the fair rent fixed at the outset would hold for the life of the project, or at least would only be raised sufficiently to meet rising management and maintenance costs. In the long run this meant that housing associations' rents would fall behind fair rents generally. If rents were raised in line with other prices and rents in the economy, the housing association would be making a surplus on that property. This led to various attempts to recover the surplus or redirect it. Other experiments in attracting private capital were tried in the 1980s.

The next major change to the system came in the Housing Act 1988. It applied to new schemes after 1989, and reversed the old procedure. Grants are fixed as a proportion of the total capital cost, and private loans are meant to cover the rest. Rents are fixed not by a local rent officer but by the housing association itself, taking into account the costs it has to face. Associations are grouped into three kinds: tariff associations, which agree a programme of development with the Housing Corporation; non-tariff associations, which are smaller and more specialist, and need support from the Housing Corporation for some risks; and very small or new associations.

Tariff associations

The Housing Corporation sets total cost indicators which are cost limits for building or renovation work. They vary by type of dwelling and purpose; for example, sheltered housing. A programme of work is agreed with the Housing Corporation, and a total spending figure for the programme is agreed. A proportion of that; such as 80 per cent, is then given as a grant. The rest of the capital cost has to be raised on the private market. If the costs of the scheme overshoot there is no more government help. Rents are fixed to cover the costs of the loan charges and management and maintenance.

Non-tariff associations

These receive a separately negotiated 'appropriate' percentage of the actual capital cost in grant plus overruns up to 130 per cent of the total cost indicator or 110 per cent of the original scheme's estimated costs.

Other associations
These might find it difficult to raise private capital, and so can be given loans to make up the difference between grant and capital cost, from the Corporation.

Rents fixed by housing associations have to cover loan repayments plus a recommended level of management and maintenance spending. The Housing Corporation advises local associations that 'the overriding requirement is that rents remain within the reach of people in low paid employment'. As Hills (1991a) points out, the problem is that the Housing Corporation and the government gave no advice on what constituted 'within the reach of', 'low paid' or 'affordable'.

The grants I have just described apply to new developments in the 1990s. Old grants on old property continue. Thus housing association finance is in a somewhat comparable situation to local authority housing finance in the period before 1972. It is equally ripe for reform.

Private landlords

The reasons for the decline in private landlords have been described. Rent control and the 1988 Housing Act enabled landlords to charge a market rent for new lettings. For more detail see Hills (1991a).

Improvement grants

Dating from the period after the Second World War, government has given grants to private landlords, owner occupiers and other owners of property to improve the standards of the accommodation. This could mean installing basic amenities, or turning an old property into new dwellings. Later grants were associated with a local strategy to improve a whole area. The economic logic behind this approach is that, while it may not be in the interests of any one owner to improve a property in a run-down area, if every owner is encouraged to do so the area as a whole would increase in value and attractiveness. An externality is being created.

Again, a change in the system was introduced in the late 1980s. A single grant replaces the old complexity. Grants will be mandatory; that is, the council must give one if a property is thereby brought up to a given standard. Discretionary grants can be given for a higher standard. Local authorities will be expected to concentrate their efforts in 'renewal areas'. Grants can be given up to 100 per cent of costs, depending – and this was new – on the landlord's or tenant's income. The income used is that in the year of the grant, yet the value of the enhanced property continues. The grant may go up if the cost of the improvement rises. These aspects are open to abuse and the scheme may well be modified in the 1990s.

Cash aid to tenants

We saw earlier that the emphasis of government funding has moved from subsidising rents generally to giving cash aid to poor tenants. The Housing Benefit system underwent a series of changes in the 1980s. Following the social security review which we discuss in the next chapter, a new pattern of benefit was introduced in 1988. Under it, tenants on income support received 100 per cent of their rent. For others, housing benefit was scaled in relation to income. The higher a household's income above an 'applicable amount', the less the benefit. Benefit was reduced by 0.65p in the pound of any income above that point. Coming on top of other means-tested benefits, housing benefit has produced a continuing major poverty trap (see next chapter).

Into the 1990s

The fundamental reform of housing finance has been on the political agenda since the early 1970s. The reasons should already be clear. To many in all political parties the present 'system' seems both inefficient and inequitable. On the other hand, to tamper with it would both upset a great many voters and cause unfairness of a different kind to people who have invested their life's savings in a particular form of ownership on the expectation that its advantages were guaranteed.

The efficiency case against general subsidies

The case is as follows:

1. The case for full cost pricing, outlined in Chapter 8, applies with particular force to housing. It is a matter of individual taste best accommodated by the matching of price to consumer preference. Beyond the minimum public health standards there are few convincing public good or externality arguments against the market. Individuals can judge between houses. Competitive markets in technical advice are available.
2. General public subsidies spread the limited amount of public money thinly over households that do and do not need help to purchase an adequate standard of accommodation. There is less available to help the poorest.
3. Collective subsidised *provision* for the poor has been associated with creating social class ghettos, and council housing estates that are unduly expensive, badly built and poorly managed (Gray, 1968; Webster, 1981; Dunleavy, 1983; Power, 1987a).
4. The heavy subsidy to those who borrow money for housing encourages a high demand for building society loans. It means that a disproportionate share of the limited supply of savings in the economy is attracted to house purchase. The result, it is argued, has been to lower industrial investment (Atkinson and King, 1982).
5. General subsidies to both these sectors undermine forms of private rented provision and are an inefficient form of help to tenants, because many who do not need help get it to the detriment of other poorer tenants – in the private or public sectors.
6. Indirect subsidies to private tenants through rent control reduce housing supply and are unfair to landlords, many of whom are not wealthy themselves.
7. To argue against general subsidies does not deny the need to make it possible for poorer households to pay for the minimum standards of housing that the state insists are necessary on public health, citizenship or other grounds.

Proposed reforms

Nevitt's (1966) 'fundamental objectives' for housing reform remain the basis of many later proposals. They are as follows:

1. Families with average and above average incomes should pay

for their own accommodation without subsidy. Those with below average incomes should receive a carefully scaled subsidy relating to their housing need.
2. A single system of subsidies that did not distinguish between types of tenure should be introduced.
3. A system of taxation that did not distinguish types of owner should be introduced.
4. The total flow of capital for housing investment, irrespective of sector, should be controlled.

Others have argued against income-related housing allowances because of the effect they have on the accumulation of means-tested benefits that together form the poverty trap. They argue for a universal housing allowance. I mention some of the proposals beginning with the most radical. Interested students are advised to pursue the original versions. A useful overview is given by Hills (1991a).

A universal flat-rate housing allowance
Lansley (1982) proposes a flat-rate allowance paid to all householders depending on housing need – size of family – and housing costs, which would vary, for example, by region. This could take the form of a tax credit – an absolute sum which the Inland Revenue would reduce tax payment by or give as a cash payment. It would be crude and would cause difficulties for those on supplementary and housing benefit who now receive their whole rent. The other main difficulty is that housing costs vary a lot from one area to another, which would make a single level of benefit inadequate in many areas. It would also be very costly and go to owner occupiers who have paid for their house. These objections could be met in theory but would pose administrative problems.

A comprehensive means-tested housing benefit
This would effectively extend the present housing benefit system to owner occupiers and remove other forms of support. It would avoid some of the problems a universal flat-scheme would entail (Grey *et al.*, 1981; Donnison and Ungerson, 1982).

Abolition of tax relief on mortgage interest payments
Sudden abolition overnight would affect the capital value of owner-occupied houses. It could be argued that this does not

matter because all house prices will fall together, but people who have used house purchase as a means of saving for retirement would suffer. However, most people who want change argue that it must be phased. The Major government began that process by abolishing relief gained by top-rate tax payers and holding the value of a mortgage that can be set against tax to £30,000.

The case for subsidised owner occupation

The case against any of these strategies comes from both the political left and right, but above all from those who currently benefit. They argue as follows:

1. Tax relief is not a subsidy. This was argued by the building societies in their evidence to the Housing Policy Review (DoE, 1977), but is difficult to sustain in economic theory without rejecting the whole concept of tax expenditures. In any case, the argument for treating all rental income and capital gains equivalently remains.
2. Changes in the tax laws would be unfair to present owners. People have made major financial decisions on the basis of the present tax law. The present value of houses reflects that part of the present tax subsidies which have been 'capitalised'. To remove them would produce a rapid fall in property values and destroy many people's lifetime savings. (This ignores the fact that house prices are affected by other changes in economic and tax policy on a regular basis.)
3. Owner occupation has major public benefits beyond the fact that most people prefer it as a form of tenure. It makes people feel they have a stake in the society. It also gives people an inducement to ensure a high level of maintenance and repair and to invest their own time and money in their homes. This sustains the standard of housing for later generations. It is thus of general 'public' benefit, and should in principle be subsidised.
4. Large-scale public ownership is a bad thing in itself, giving too much power to local councils and preventing the market working. Housing should therefore be sold off to those who want to buy.

The right policy to follow, the argument goes, is to remove all forms of subsidy and let market prices and market rents apply. Minford *et al.* (1987) propound such a policy. This would be accompanied by some form of support for the very poorest in any tenure. It would entail removing all remaining rent controls on existing tenancies, raising local authority and housing association rents to market levels, and giving housing benefit at 100 per cent of rent to all those who were on benefits other than unemployment and sickness benefit. Those temporarily out of the labour market would have their benefit cut off when it reached 70 per cent of their previous salary.

The case for public provision

One argument is that housing is a joint product – an appreciating asset and a consumption good. Where ownership is split between tenant and owner, their interests diverge. A private landlord especially has an interest in selling for gain, while the tenant wants security. This contractual relationship of landlord and tenant cannot be properly monitored. Thus either owner occupation, or public or non-profit ownership of rented property with social duties laid on the public or non-profit landlord, are the only fair forms of tenure that overcome this problem (Whitehead, 1984). (This argument may justify public provision but not general subsidies.)

A second is that if society wishes to see people occupy minimum standard accommodation, for the reasons discussed, over and above what some could afford, it should pay this cost.

Those who defend public provision of housing do so on grounds of efficiency. A local authority is able to acquire and develop large sites, and reap economies of scale in improvement schemes. Many elderly owner occupiers cannot cope with repairs and maintenance and let their properties decay. The public sector has the least under-occupation. The way we finance owner occupation ensures that older owner occupiers whose families have grown up are often no longer paying for their mortgage, or paying only a low figure, and have little inducement to move to a smaller house and free the accommodation for a family. Lower-income families and many other social groups will never be able to afford a home of their own, and many do not want one.

The case for diverse social provision

Many accept the case above, in part, but argue that monopoly landlords are especially bad for poor tenants who have little power, and that a diversity of tenures for the least advantaged is essential. It is possible to improve the management of housing estates by devolving management responsibilities to an estate level with some success (Power, 1987b, 1991), but ideally full control and choice by tenants depends on their owning their own estates or blocks of flats co-operatively, or being tenants of small-scale housing associations with tenant representation. Some kinds of need can only be met by private landlords, and a small market of this kind should be encouraged (Glennerster *et al.*, 1991).

All in all, housing finance is probably the most unsatisfactory of all the systems we have discussed, but it is the most difficult to reform.

Further reading

The fullest account of housing finance and taxation is to be found in Hills, J. (1991a), *Unravelling Housing Finance: Subsidies, benefit and taxation*, Oxford: Clarendon Press.

Another set of proposals is to be found in Malpass, P. (1990), *Reshaping Housing Policy: Subsidies, rents and residualisation*, London: Routledge.

A good comparative text on housing more generally, including finance, is still Donnison, D.V. and Ungerson, C. (1982) *Housing Policy*, Harmondsworth: Penguin. See also: Lansley, S. (1979), *Housing and Public Policy*, London: Croom Helm; and Merrett, S. (1979), *State Housing in Britain*, London: Routledge.

An influential report of a committee chaired by the Duke of Edinburgh was first published in 1985 by the National Federation of Housing Associations. New edition 1991.

CHAPTER 14

PAYING FOR SOCIAL SECURITY

The history of social security finance

The state has become involved in maintaining, supplementing or varying the income of its citizens in six distinct ways, as follows:

1. Providing last resort assistance to those in extreme financial distress.
2. Sustaining, if at a reduced level, the incomes of those who are, or have been, part of the labour force, but whose earnings have been temporarily interrupted by sickness or unemployment, or who have retired.
3. Supplementing family income during the period when there are dependent children to look after – a period when family income is reduced but outgoings are high.
4. Varying tax liabilities to encourage people to provide for their own retirement, sickness or widowhood.
5. Enforcing benefit provisions on employers for their employees' sickness or redundancy.
6. Regulating occupational pension schemes.

Each one of these distinct systems of income maintenance has developed its own form of finance.

Public assistance

This was the earliest form of state-provided relief. In Tudor times parishes were given powers to supplement private alms-giving by imposing a tax to relieve the poor. A series of Acts was consolidated in 1601. Public assistance was to remain locally administered and financed until the depression of the 1930s, despite growing central regulation. For more than three centuries, poor relief was financed by a tax on local property values – the poor rate or its successors. The tax base gradually moved from the boundaries of the local parish, to combinations of parishes or 'unions' in 1834, and to larger local authorities after 1929.

Two factors brought the end of this system in the 1930s. The first was the heavy concentration of unemployment in certain areas of the country. The central government had to step in to finance means-tested benefits for the longer-term unemployed whose right to unemployment benefit had lapsed. The second was that central government feared that generous benefits would have a potential disincentive effect on workers. This led to clashes first with Labour-controlled Boards of Guardians, and then with some local authorities who were administering poor relief after 1929. Both factors came together in the 1930s (Thane, 1982), and unemployment assistance became an Exchequer-funded and centrally administered system under the Unemployment Act of 1934.

The relief of poor old people was taken over by a reconstituted Assistance Board in 1942. They were to be treated in a less stigmatising way than by the local public assistance committees, and the Exchequer was to meet the bill. In 1948 all public assistance became the responsibility of the National Assistance Board, as Beveridge had recommended (Cmd 6404, 1942), and Parliament set the national minimum scales that determined what benefits should be paid by local offices and voted the funds out of general taxation. This system of support was renamed 'the supplementary benefit system' in the mid-1960s and became 'income support' in the 1986 Social Security Act. Though the pattern of benefits has changed over this long period and more people have been drawn into the means-tested net, the essence of the scheme, and above all its Exchequer-funded nature, have not changed. For an account of the detailed changes to the social security system in the 1980s and the drift towards income related payments as the basis of social security, see Hill (1990).

In a relatively small and homogeneous *economy* with much geographical mobility, different standards of basic benefit are difficult to sustain. Higher than average benefits attract those out of work and their dependants to those areas providing generous benefits. In a largely urbanised society with labour mobility between jobs and similar costs of living, where a national sense of citizenship can be *politically* articulated, different local standards of income maintenance become difficult to sustain. As Europe's economy moves towards greater interdependence and labour mobility, the same pressures for a common basic level of income support will grow. That is already evident in the European Social Charter and the debate upon it which will develop into the 1990s.

Social insurance

Forms of mutual support, or group insurance, by working people to keep them and their families off poor relief spread in the nineteenth century. When the state was looking for a way of ensuring that some form of income support was provided, it was attracted to build on this form of activity for two reasons. First, the trade unions, friendly societies and private insurance companies had come to be powerful vested interest groups capable of exerting considerable political pressure. Secondly, the idea of mutual aid by workers earning future benefit rights seemed consistent with the dominant values of thrift and the work ethic in Britain and American society. The idea appealed to paternalistic and socialist value systems alike (Rimlinger, 1971). On the continent of Europe different institutional legacies, the influence of the Catholic church, labour unions, social democratic parties and the fascist movements of the 1930s, have all left their mark (Esping-Andersen, 1990).

There was, however, a third motive, which the early history in Britain illustrates well (Thane, 1982). The poverty of the elderly posed a financial problem, not least as a growing burden on the poor rate in the late nineteenth century. The trade union and labour movement, radical liberals and social scientists like Booth, were pressing for some form of state pension. Some favoured finance from a regular weekly payment by workers, others funding out of general taxation. The unions opposed contributions from already low-paid workers, and so did the Treasury, on the grounds that it would mean a complicated and expensive machinery to collect it, duplicating the ordinary tax system. Added to these,

Asquith, as a traditional Liberal, did not see state pensions as a long-term necessity, merely as a temporary expedient reflecting the particular difficulties that that generation had faced. He argued against a duplicate and complex contributory system. Hence when state pensions were introduced in 1908, they were financed out of ordinary taxation.

Yet that, too, had its problems, as Lloyd George found out during the passage of the legislation and afterwards. Universal pensions at 65 were very costly. The Treasury opposed spending anything like the sum required, and to get the scheme at all the Cabinet had to agree to a limited and restricted scheme beginning at 70 for those below a certain income. The pressure not to undermine the existing voluntary contributory schemes, and the fear of adding to the income tax paid by the middle class, led Lloyd George to turn to weekly contributions as the means of financing the new sickness and unemployment scheme of 1911. The effect was to limit contributions to those who were in the schemes – workers earning less than a set income (£160 a year in 1911). The lower-paid workers and their employers would largely pay for the scheme. When pressure grew, in the 1920s, to lower the age of entitlement for old age pensions to 65, that extension was limited to and financed by those in the existing national health insurance scheme. The Beveridge proposals legislated after the Second World War extended membership of the national insurance scheme to the whole working population and created a single national scheme administered by central government rather than a vast array of local societies, but the contribution principle remained. A flat-rate sum would be levied from all employees and employers, which would buy a stamp actually stuck on to a card that was to be held by the employer, then passed on to a person's next employer. These contributions earned the right to benefits from the national scheme. The money was to go into quite separate national insurance funds, held by the central government and supplemented by the Exchequer from ordinary tax revenue to a limited extent.

Beveridge had originally argued that every member should pay the same contribution and receive the same benefit. This put severe constraints on the scheme. Benefit levels were tied to the contributions the poorest could afford. Other countries had not adopted this model: they had linked both contributions and benefits to earnings. From 1959 onwards, governments of both parties moved further in that direction. Contributions were raised and became a percentage of earnings. However, the old Beveridge notion that they were entitlements to benefit and not just a tax remained. Thus contributions rose with earnings but only up to a certain point – one and a half times average earnings. Beyond that point people pay no more. The Labour Party proposed to abolish that limit. Social security contributions would rise with income. They thus become a social security tax in all but name.

In the 1960s and 1970s benefits were split into two. On top of the Beveridge basic flat-rate pension, for example, was built the state earnings related pension scheme (SERPS) in 1975. The Conservatives proposed abolishing it in the review of social security in the mid-1980s but, in a less generous form, it survived.

Beveridge (Cmd 6404, 1942) had argued that a clear link between contributions paid in and benefits 'earned' was necessary to distinguish insurance-based benefits received as a 'right' from Exchequer-based, means-tested assistance that would continue to carry some stigma, and rightly so in his view. 'National assistance must be felt to be something less desirable than insurance benefit. Otherwise insured persons get nothing for their contributions' (Cmd 6404, 1942, para. 369). This distinction has always been a fiction to economists, and the changes of the 1980s have blurred the distinction even more.

Child benefits

Probably the first proponent of cash allowances to families was Tom Paine, author of *The Rights of Man* (1791: Paine, 1969). Poverty among the working poor was, he argued, the result of the fact that their wages were not enough to support their children. Families with children should be excused the payment of taxes and paid £4 a year to bring up their children and send them to school. He was the true originator of the modern negative income tax as well as the education voucher! Much later, but just as lucidly, Eleanor Rathbone (1924, 1940) made essentially the same case. Early in the life cycle, and when children were grown up, a family's minimum needs might well be met even on a low wage, especially if there were two earners, but when children were born the spending needs of the family rose sharply, and usually the family's income fell as the wife left work. A negotiated or statutory minimum wage, which the trade unions advocated, could never be set high enough to meet the needs of the largest families. There was no such thing as a static average family. Minimum needs varied with the number and age of children in a family. Incomes must reflect the extra needs of children. The only way to do that, she argued, was to link incomes to the number of children in the family. But who should pay? In Australia and New Zealand, where family allowances had been introduced after pressure for a minimum wage on precisely these grounds in the 1920s, the cost was met out of General Exchequer funds. (The allowances were income-related, tapering off as income rose.)

In Europe, family allowances had grown up first in France before the First World War as a form of occupational welfare – paid by firms as part of the wage. After the war the practice spread, but to counteract the obvious incentive for employers not to take on employees with families, allowances were paid out of 'equalisation funds'. A levy on local employers who belonged to the scheme was paid into a common fund and then drawn upon by individual firms to pay the child allowance. In other countries the new schemes were financed out of contributions from employees, employers and the state. In Britain, during the Second World War, servicemen's incomes included a children's allowance; thus the state began to pay family-related incomes to a large part of its 'workforce' almost by accident (Hall *et al.*, 1975).

What proved decisive in Britain, however, was the desire to limit wage increases at the beginning of the Second World War and the introduction of a comprehensive system of national insurance benefits for those not in work. These benefits were related to the number of dependants a worker had – a wife and children. If these were to be reasonably generous, there was a severe danger that many workers would be better off out of work than in work. Beveridge (Cmd 6404, 1942, paras 4.11, 4.12) argued that this would be unfair and economically perverse. Thus, the state must ensure that incomes for those with larger families were supported when they were *in* work and out of it. This view carried the day in Cabinet and with the Treasury (Macnicol, 1980). It is very interesting to observe the same logic beginning to dawn even on American neo-conservatives (Glazer, 1988). The cost was to be met out of general taxation, which has applied ever since. Internationally, family allowances or child benefits continue to be financed in a variety of ways. The best review of the diverse ways in which families are supported internationally is still to be found in the study by Bradshaw and Piachaud (1980): see also Kamerman and Kahn (1983); Rainwater *et al.* (1986).

Supplementing family income

Just because universal cash benefits paid out of taxation are so expensive, it has been difficult for governments to increase child benefit to a level that would raise all families above the poverty line. In 1971, after an election campaign in which family poverty had featured as a significant issue, the Conservative government introduced an additional means-tested benefit for poor families where a member of the household was in work but earning so little that they fell below the poverty line. It was called 'family income supplement' (FIS). Under this scheme, families on low incomes could apply to the DHSS to have their incomes supplemented. The scheme was financed out of general taxation. It applied to very few people, had a low take-up and hence cost relatively little. The family was paid half the difference between their assessed income and a target figure set in relation to the family's size. In the 1986 Fowler reforms, the scheme was renamed 'family credit' and the definition of income changed. It was to be calculated after deducting taxes and insurance contributions. This eased the harshness of the poverty trap on these families a little (see below). It was still paid out of general taxation.

Fiscal support

Tax relief on private pension schemes and various life assurance arrangements dates back a long way (Titmuss, 1962). Relief on life assurance premiums is as old as income tax itself: it is to be found in Pitt's 1789 Tax Act. It later disappeared, to be reintroduced by Gladstone in 1853 to enable people who were dependent on earned income to save for their retirement. This was, of course, half a century before the state provided any cash benefits to retired people. As higher tax rates were introduced, this form of saving became increasingly attractive to higher-income groups. However, it lost the Exchequer large sums of money and tipped the balance in favour of this particular form of saving. These reliefs were gradually withdrawn in the 1980s. A wide range of other reliefs and encouragements to save, especially through share ownership, were introduced in Conservative budgets up to 1991. Tax relief on private pensions of various kinds still exists (see below).

Regulated and statutory employer benefits

In the 1970s and 1980s, the state took over a new and important role in social security provision. It essentially made employers responsible for administering benefits to a standard set by the state. The 1975 Social Security Pensions Act provided for a new wage-related pension on top of the basic national insurance pension. If employers wished to contract out of this scheme, they could, as long as they provided at least an equivalent pension. The principle was taken even further by the 1979 Conservative government in their statutory sick pay scheme. From April 1983, employers have been obliged to pay a set level of sickness benefit. The costs are recovered from the government by the employers, who subtract their expenditure on such benefits from the national insurance contributions the firm pays to government. The 1986 Social Security Act applied the same principle to statutory maternity pay. Statutory and occupational welfare have become closely intertwined.

Expenditure today

Social security spending in 1990 was equivalent to 11.4 per cent of GDP, or £56 billion. The share of GDP rose during the unemployment crisis of the early 1980s but the 1990 figure was not very different from that in 1980. It is substantially lower than the EEC average and below that for the OECD as a whole; that is to say, below that of most of the advanced industrial world (see Table 14.1).

About half of the UK total is spent on benefits for the elderly – pensions, housing benefit and income support combined (see

Table 14.1 Social security benefits internationally as a percentage of GDP 1960–89

Country	1960	1970	1980	1989*
Netherlands	—	17.4	25.9	25.3
France	13.6	17.0	19.2	21.4
Sweden	8.0	11.1	17.6	19.5
Denmark	7.4	11.6	16.6	18.1
Italy	9.8	12.4	14.1	17.7
West Germany	12.5	13.1	16.5	15.6
Norway	—	12.3	14.4	18.1
United Kingdom	6.9	8.7	11.7	11.9
United States	5.3	7.9	10.9	10.8
Japan	3.8	4.6	10.1	11.8
Canada	8.0	8.1	9.9	11.8
EEC average	10.6	13.1	15.9	17.1
OECD average	6.9	9.1	12.7	13.5

* Or nearest year.

Source: *OECD Economic Outlook: Historical Statistics 1960–89*, Paris: OECD 1991; and previous issues.

Table 14.2). The next largest element is the cost of benefits received by the sick and long-term disabled – about a fifth of the total. Benefits to the unemployed constituted less than 10 per cent, and a combination of benefits going to other families roughly twice that.

The scale of social security spending relative to GDP grew more rapidly than any other major category of government spending in the 1960s and 1970s, as the level of benefits rose to keep pace with real incomes in the rest of the economy. The elderly population grew and the scale of unemployment did too. What has been remarkable about the 1980s is that that rise has been checked, despite the much higher levels of unemployment. The reasons are two-fold. The increase in the size of the elderly population over 65 has levelled off; more importantly, the Conservative government broke the link between the annual benefit increase and the rise in the earnings of the employed labour force. Benefits were only raised in line with prices, and not even that for child benefit. Benefits thus fell behind average earnings, becoming a smaller and smaller percentage of previous or average earnings year by year. From 1977 to 1987 the basic supplementary benefit rate fell from

Table 14.2 Total social security benefit expenditure in Britain 1990–1

Beneficiary group	£ million
Elderly people	28,590
Sick and disabled people:	
Long-term	10,120
Short-term	1,220
Family benefits*	9,940
Unemployed people	4,850
Widows and orphans	1,190
Total	55,910

* Child benefit, one-parent family benefit, family credit, maternity benefit, maternity pay, income support to families, housing benefit.

Source: Cm 1514, 1991.

just over 17 per cent of average earnings to 13.5 per cent For a detailed analysis of social security expenditure and outcomes in the 1970s and 1980s, see Barr and Coulter (1990).

Financing social security today

The national insurance fund

Prior to 1948 there were no fewer than fifteen separate social insurance funds administering different benefits. To sustain the notion that the new benefits would be 'earned as of right', Beveridge proposed unification into a single scheme. Three funds – a basic fund, a reserve fund and an industrial injuries fund – were created, into which national insurance contributions were paid and from which benefits were paid out. In 1975 the separate funds were amalgamated. To quote from the Comptroller and Auditor General's prelude to his report on the Accounts for 1989/90:

> The national insurance scheme is financed on a pay-as-you-go basis from contributions, which are mainly earnings-related, and income from the investments of the National Insurance Fund. The rates of contributions for any year are fixed at a level which will enable the

Table 14.3 National insurance fund 1989/90*

Receipts and payments	£'000	£'000
Receipts		
Contributions	30,756,362	
less Employers' recoveries in respect of statutory sickness payments	1,044,000	
less Employers' recoveries in respect of statutory maternity payments	307,000	
		29,405,362
Consolidated fund supplement		—
Income from investments		1,040,377
Other receipts		1,018
		30,446,757
Less		
Payments		
Benefits		27,000,207
Personal pensions		2,434,461
Transfers to Northern Ireland		210,000
Administration		856,536
Other payments		7,222
Total payments		30,508,426
Excess of payments over receipts		61,669
Statement of balances		
Balance at beginning of year		10,368,808
less Excess of payments over receipts		61,669
add Excess of receipts over payments		—
Balance at end of year		10,307,139

* Account for the year ended 31 March 1990, prepared in accordance with Section 133 of the Social Security Act 1975.

Source: HC, 617, 1989/90.

> Fund to meet the expected expenditure in that year on benefits and administration and retain a working balance. (National Insurance Fund Account 1989/90, HC 617 1989/90)

The balance sheet of the combined national insurance fund for 1989/90 is summarised in Table 14.3. From that we can see that the fund expended over £30,000 million in that year and received almost as much, running a deficit of £61 million, thus reducing its balance in hand to about £10,000 million. This was a much larger surplus than the fund used to run but only equivalent to about a third of a year's expenditure. Another major difference from the past is the blank in the line for consolidated fund supplement. That means a sum paid by the Treasury from general taxation. Beveridge had assumed this would be a large element, and for many years it amounted to about 18 per cent of the income of the fund. Then the Conservative government began reducing it. It formed only 13.4 per cent of the total receipts in 1982/3. It gradually fell until it was formally abolished in 1988/9. Social security benefits were to be entirely financed by contributions and the ordinary tax payer relieved of the burden. That was one reason why the government in the 1980s was able to reduce the standard rate of income tax but had to raise the social security contribution to match it. It was also able to generate a surplus to help offset borrowing elsewhere by the government.

Employees' contributions

These depend on earnings and whether you are opted into the state earnings-related pension scheme. In 1991/2 you paid 2 per cent of your earnings up to £52 a week, the lower earnings limit, and 9 per cent on earnings between that and £390 a week. These lower and upper limits are changed every year. The Labour Party is pledged to abolish the upper limit. That would mean that individuals would pay 9 per cent of all their incomes over £52 a week. The extra revenue would pay for higher pensions. For those contracted out of SERPS the sum paid is 7 per cent, not 9 per cent, above the lower earnings limit.

Members of personal pension schemes run by private insurance companies pay the same sum as any contracted-out member of an employer's scheme, but the government pays the private pension scheme a sum equal to the 2-per-cent difference between the opted-out and the opted-in rates – a form of subsidy to the private scheme.

Self-employed earners pay at a lower rate on the assumption they are responsible for their own pensions.

Employers' contributions

The employer has to pay a contribution for each of his or her employees and the amount depends on the wages or salaries of the

Table 14.4 Employers' contributions for workers in SERPS 1991/2

Weekly earnings (£/week)	Rate of contribution (%)
52.00– 84.99	4.60
85.00–129.99	6.60
130.00–189.99	8.60
185 and above	10.40

worker. For an employer in 1991/2 whose employees were in SERPS the rates were as shown in Table 14.4. There is, in short, no upper limit on what an employer has to pay. For employees contracted out of SERPS, employers pay 3.8 per cent less. The United Kingdom raises less in the form of a separate social security tax than most European countries. In particular it levies less on employers.

Economists doubt the validity of these distinctions. They argue that if the market sets the labour cost per employee, the combined employee and employer social security tax merely forms part of the labour cost faced by the employer. Thus the higher it is set, the smaller the market wage actually paid to the employee in wages. The extent to which the tax is passed on in lower wages rather than absorbed in lower profit levels or passed on in higher prices will reflect the price elasticities and market power of employers and workers. International comparisons do suggest that social security contributions are levied at the expense of lower wages – they are shifted on to wage earners (Brittain, 1972). In that sense all contributions are paid by employees.

Funding

As we saw in Table 14.3, the national insurance fund does not carry a huge surplus invested in government securities or company shares. Private schemes run a balance sufficient to pay out the promised pension or benefit even if no more income came in tomorrow. These schemes are fully 'funded' – or supposed to be so. The pension is secured by the investments, the security and value of which vary with economic fortune. With national insurance, if the government decides to cut the income to the fund and thus cut the benefits, or simply to wipe out a benefit, it can do so. The Conservative government did indeed do just that in 1980 when the earnings-related sickness and unemployment benefits were abolished. Why is the state scheme not funded in the same way? The reasons are partly political and partly economic, as follows:

1. If a large surplus accumulates, political pressure mounts to use the surplus to increase benefits to current pensions.
2. Conservatives in general and City institutions in particular fear the huge sums that government would be able to build up and the power this would give it in the market. For the opposite reasons socialists have argued for at least the partial funding of a national superannuation scheme (Labour Party, 1958).
3. 'Pay-as-you-go' schemes enable governments to pay out pensions now. A fully funded scheme would mean either waiting many years for the fund to build up, or imposing very high contributions to build up a surplus quickly, or a bit of both.
4. The major economic problem has been that inflation has rapidly eroded the value of pension funds, whether public or private. With pay-as-you-go schemes, both benefits and contributions can rise in line with inflation each year.
5. Since the state can enforce sufficient contributions to ensure payment of benefits it does not need a large investment fund to guarantee its income.

Tax expenditures

Subsidies to individual tax payers who invest in their own retirement constitute a major cost to the Exchequer. Just how large a cost is a technical argument which rests essentially on one's view as to what form of tax ought to be levied (Board of Inland Revenue, 1983). The situation at present is as follows:

1. Employees do not pay tax on that part of their income they pay as contributions to pension funds, on the grounds that the pensions themselves are taxed. Total value 1989/90 = £31,800 million.

2. Employers' contributions are treated as an expense and are not taxed. Total value 1989/90 = £3,100 million.
3. Investment income of superannuation funds is not liable for tax, as the pensions that they pay are taxed. Total value 1989/90 = £4,100 million.
4. Lump sum payments up to certain limits at retirement are not liable for tax. Total value 1989/90 = £1,000 million.

There is some disagreement about whether pensions should be treated as deferred pay and not taxed twice, and if so whether original income should be fully taxed and pensions not at all, or vice versa. Another view says that pensions are not deferred pay but an investment. If I choose to invest in shares or capital, I get no relief. I pay tax on my original income and on the interest my savings earn. For consistency, the same should happen if I invest in a pension scheme. If we want to encourage any form of savings, for example, through an expenditure tax that is another matter (see Chapter 7).

Occupational pension schemes

Running alongside but regulated by government are the occupational pension schemes. An employee must be a member of the state scheme or an employer's occupational scheme or, under the 1986 Social Security Act, a personal private pension scheme with a private insurance company. Moreover, the minimum level of contribution an employee must pay is also set by the state. It does not want to permit people to free-ride and make no provision for their old age, thus requiring the state to provide income support rather than let the person starve. Thus in the United Kingdom a person can effectively choose only whether to be taxed directly by the state or indirectly by his or her employer, or pay into his or her own pension scheme up to a given sum set by government. Most private schemes used to have no inflation proofing at all and others have only partial proofing. After twenty years of inflation even an apparently generous pension will be tiny in real terms. A not-with-profits pension of £20 a week in 1964 – very generous – would only have been worth about £2.30 in 1984. State pensions have at least kept their real value in that period, despite failing to be linked to rising *earnings*. To try to rectify this weakness of private schemes, the Conservative government in 1986 required all new pensions in the private sector to promise to pay inflation proofed pensions of up to *3 per cent* a year inflation. Such a low level of inflation has not been reached for many years.

Into the 1990s

It is difficult to discuss alternative ways of financing social security without discussing major changes to the whole system of social benefits. To do this in detail is beyond the scope of this chapter, but it is possible to sketch the broad outlines of very different financing strategies that have been under discussion and will be part of the agenda for the 1990s. One thing is certain: social security policy will not stand still fifty years after Beveridge.

The compulsory private model

The Conservative government's 1986 reforms are a move in this direction. The state would provide a basic flat-rate pension, but there would be no guarantee that its value would be preserved. By not uprating it in line with inflation, the state pension could be phased out. Every one would have to be a member of a private occupational or a personal private pension scheme. Income support would remain for existing pensioners, but in order to ensure that people did not simply rely on it, membership of an occupation pension scheme or personal private pension scheme would become compulsory.

The logic of these trends will lead eventually to the following system: the state sets minimum levels of pensions and sickness benefits which employers must provide. These are fixed at, or above, the level of income support. The pensions are financed by contributions paid by the employee and the employer, aided by government tax reliefs. Pension rights would be transferable. The only state benefits would be income support or a negative income tax payment financed out of general taxation. Such a system of nationally regulated occupational and private pensions is much nearer the practice of many European countries. There representatives of employers and trade unions bargain on basic features of occupational schemes until a common national minimum emerges, which is then legislated as a requirement in all schemes by the national government. It also secures the schemes and guarantees the value of the pension with inflation proofing. Pensions policy thus involves trade unions and employers much more than in the United Kingdom. The trade-offs between wages, employer and employee contributions, and taxes are made more explicit and subject to direct negotiation (Walker *et al.*, 1984).

The *advantages* claimed for such schemes are as follows:

1. Their low cost in terms of direct public spending and taxation.
2. The choice that workers would be able to exercise in negotiating more or less generous or flexible pension arrangements.
3. The creation of large pension funds that would finance economic growth.

The main *disadvantages* of such schemes in the past – failure to inflation-proof or transfer pension rights – can be overcome, it is claimed, though the government did not feel able to insist on full inflation proofing in 1986. Other disadvantages or objections levelled at such proposals are as follows:

1. The lower tax burden argument is spurious. Enforced membership of a pension scheme and a compulsory contribution up to a given level are merely systems of taxation under another name.
2. In practice, workers' representatives have little or no choice in the form of their pension scheme.
3. Sums levied compulsorily by private pension schemes are invested with major economic and distributive effects by socially 'irresponsible' or unaccountable insurance firms (Titmuss, 1958, 1976).
4. The argument that private pension schemes encourage savings in an economy and hence investment and growth has much exercised economists (Feldstein, 1980; Aaron, 1982). The evidence seems inconclusive.
5. Without very stringent national regulation, occupational pensions tend to perpetuate or even exaggerate the inequalities of working life. Those who have been healthy and had a fortunate employment history, as well as getting better pay, get much better retirement terms.

6. Such arrangements may suit paid lifetime employees. They are of little help for many women and others out of the labour market.
7. Implicit are many unacknowledged transfers, between early leavers, married and divorced or widowed couples, for example.

The libertarian free-choice residual model

Those who see the state's compulsion as pernicious, whether operated through employers or through its own agencies, prefer a more libertarian approach. They would permit individuals to make their own pension arrangements, for example, with private companies. The state could provide a minimum basic standard pension or confine its activity to emergency last resort help for those not able to make such provision.

The *advantages* are seen to be those of the previous model, but without the element of compulsion embodied in it.

The *disadvantages* are as follows:

1. If the state supplementary pension or benefit scheme is relatively generous or humane, this constitutes, for most people, a strong disincentive to taking out a private pension. People get little benefit from their private pensions, which merely reduces entitlement to their state means-tested pension. If the basic pension scheme is very inadequate, then the encouraging of private provision will lead to suffering on the part of those who have to rely on the state.
2. Private pension funds could borrow inflation-proofed bonds from government, enabling them to inflation-proof pensions to some extent, but that is in effect to give private pension schemes a large, open-ended grant from the Exchequer. They already receive major tax reliefs. These are effectively paid for by all the population but disproportionately benefit the better-off, who gain the highest pensions.

Back to Beveridge

Some writers simply advocate that the principle of the Beveridge Report should be implemented, something that was never fully done because benefits were never generous enough to live on. Contributors should receive an *adequate* benefit or pension so that they do not need supplementary benefit. The basic principles would be as follows:

1. Payment of flat-rate social security benefits to all those not in work at a level set at the minimum needs of a single person or married couple, as appropriate. These needs could be set relative to average earnings. Benefits would be taxed.
2. Unconditional child benefit set at a level sufficient to meet the minimum needs of children of different ages.
3. Means-tested benefits only as a last resort; thus the benefit levels would be set sufficiently generously to eliminate most means-tested extras.
4. A tax structure that began to tax above these minimum levels.

The *advantages* of the system would be as follows:

1. It removes the disincentives of the poverty trap, and the indignities and low take-up that result from means testing.
2. It is simple to understand and administer.
3. It leaves individuals free to add their own private arrangements on top of the basic provision, and gives them an incentive to do so because they know the income they gain from a private scheme cannot reduce the value of their state pension of benefit.

The *disadvantages* would be as follows:

1. The Beveridge contribution principle gives rights to benefit to those who have the most fortunate employment histories, and discriminates against the disabled, the marginal worker and women, especially divorced and separated women. This can be overcome only by an extensive and generous system of crediting such groups with 'contributions' paid by the Exchequer. The more this is done the more notional becomes the contribution principle.
2. Employers' contributions are passed on in reduced wages or higher prices, or result in reduced employment. It would be much more democratic to make the costs clear to those who are

paying. National insurance contributions are taxes: we may as well be honest about them.

One alternative is to continue to give contingent-based benefits – for old age, sickness, etc. – but to finance the benefits out of general taxation or a social security tax that carries no link with benefits and is proportional to income. The 'back-to-Beveridge' strategy was best discussed in the Meade Report (Meade, 1978).

Abolish tax allowances on pension funds

Any of the above proposals could be combined with the removal of tax concessions to pension schemes, or to those who contribute to them, for reasons similar to those in the case of housing. Tax laws encourage this particular form of saving because the returns are greater and divert funds from other types of investment. This distortion of the market is inefficient, and since higher-income groups benefit most it is also inequitable.

A two-tier national social security scheme

This model largely accepts the objections to both the occupational benefit and back-to-Beveridge schemes, but does not wish to break with the contribution principle entirely. It argues for both a generous flat-rate benefit for all categories of need, regardless of whether contributions have ever been paid, and on top of that for an earnings-related state benefit corresponding to previous earnings and hence previous contributions. The first part would be financed from taxation, the second by earnings-related employee and employer contributions.

The *advantages* claimed for such a scheme are as follows:

1. It provides adequate benefits for the disabled, late entrants to the labour market, and those who have spent most of their lives bringing up children or looking after dependants without recourse to means testing. The benefits are at the same level as the flat-rate benefit received by those who have not been in work.
2. The second level provides benefits for all categories of worker,

not merely those whose employers can afford an occupational scheme. If no cash or tax subsidies are offered to private schemes, the state scheme would offer better benefits for most of its members than private schemes. It would therefore reduce inequality in old age compared with the present system.

Such a scheme would be an extension of the 1975 Castle legislation, which was undermined by the 1986 Conservative legislation. It bears some resemblance to the US Federal Social Security provisions, and it is subject to the same kinds of criticism. Its *disadvantages* are as follows:

1. A state scheme on a pay-as-you-go basis is unfair competition for private schemes, tends to produce a monopoly and restricts choice and variety in pensions and other benefits.
2. The Castle scheme substantially increased pensions for a couple on average earnings, but did little for the couple on, say, two-thirds of average earnings. What extra money can be raised should be added to the basic pension (Kay, 1984).

A social dividend scheme

Such a scheme (Pigou, 1920; Rhys-Williams, 1943; Jordan, 1987; Parker, 1990) would give each man, woman and child a sum enough to live on by him or herself by virtue of citizenship rather than past contributions or capacity to work. It should be paid out of general taxation. Those who worked would earn and pay (rather high!) taxes. All other cash benefits could be abolished. The negative income tax alternative gives cash benefits to citizens through the tax system, which reduce in value the higher the income of the recipient. This still leaves unresolved the problems of defining the tax unit or household (Green, 1967; Dilnot *et al.*, 1984).

Further reading

For the case for a unified system of national insurance, read the Beveridge Report, the first part of which is still the most lucid exposition of his case (Cmd 6404, 1942).

An up-to-date history of social security policy is Hill, M. (1990), *Social Security Policy in Britain*, Aldershot: Edward Elgar.

The economics of social security are best found in: Barr (1993) *The Economics of the Welfare State*, (second edn) London: Weidenfeld; Dilnot, A. and Walker, I. (1989), *The Economics of Social Security*, Oxford: Clarendon Press; Atkinson, A.B. (1989), *Poverty and Social Security*, Hemel Hempstead: Harvester Wheatsheaf.

A good alternative to all versions of the Beveridge model is to be found in Dilnot, A.W., Kay, J.A. and Morris, C.N. (1984), *The Reform of Social Security*, Oxford: Clarendon Press. Regular updating of the benefits and contributions in the United Kingdom are to be found in the Child Poverty Action Group (1991), *Rights Guide to Non-Means Tested Benefits* and *The National Welfare Benefits Handbook*, both London: Child Poverty Action Group.

The gender issues raised at the end of the chapter are discussed in Lewis, J. (1983), *Women's Welfare, Women's Rights*, London: Croom Helm.

PART V

The future: into the 1990s

CHAPTER 15

CAN WE AFFORD THE WELFARE STATE?

In the first chapter of this book I began by emphasising that welfare, as I defined it, could be financed and provided in a variety of ways. In the chapters that followed I showed that the ways in which people in the United Kingdom pay for their welfare state has changed significantly in the past decade. Direct income taxation on the highest-income groups has been reduced but other forms of taxation have risen. The average earner and the poorer households have had to bear a larger part of the burden. Central government determination of both taxes and spending has increased at the expense of local determination. Social spending stabilised as a share of the economic activity in the United Kingdom and other countries in the aftermath of the crises of the mid-1970s. The scale of welfare spending by governments in the largest OECD nations reached a plateau after the rapid increases of the 1960s and early 1970s. The slower growth, or actual decline, in national incomes in the 1970s, and the growing burden of financing unemployment, shook the complacent view that such growth in publicly financed services was inevitable or even desirable. Some writers swung to the opposite extreme, claiming that welfare states were in crisis and that major changes in their finance were necessary and unavoidable (Gough, 1979; OECD, 1981; Mishra, 1983; Offe, 1984). This crisis view was shared by those with very different political values – free-market Conservatives and Marxists. Both believed that a mixed economy with a largely publicly provided element was inherently incompatible with a capitalist economic structure. The radical right argued that the balance must shift decisively towards individual purchases in a private market and that voters would support such a move. Marxists argued that either a *financial* crisis would result from trying to pay for the welfare sector out of taxation, or a *legitimacy* crisis would result from trying to dismantle it.

Neither of these predictions was borne out by the experience of the 1980s, a decade in which radical right ideas were influential with Conservative governments, and others in such diverse countries as Chile and Israel (Glennerster and Midgley, 1991). Yet overall, as we have seen earlier, there has been neither a collapse of welfare spending with a major move to the market nor a revolutionary crisis as a result of restraining growth in social spending. Instead, there has been an adjustment to the slower growth of the western economies and a stabilisation of state spending.

The forms of provision have changed, however. There has been more emphasis on mixed forms of provision and on market-type forms of organisation within the state sector. There has been an attempt to increase the efficiency of the social welfare systems and to get more value for tax payers' money. The political system responded incrementally to a range of pressures. All in all, the political market model of welfare finance outlined in the first edition of this book has stood up to the past decade of change rather well.

The market for welfare

It is possible to think of the political market for welfare services as an extension of the traditional market for other goods and services (see Figure 15.1). On the horizontal axis we measure the quantity of service provided. On the vertical axis we measure the price the public has to pay for the services it receives – the tax price or the level of taxation that has to be set in order to pay for a given level of service or a given policy. This might be the expansion of higher education or a higher level of old age pension.

The supply

It will be clear that the more units of tax-based social services are provided, the higher the total cost. It is also probable that unit

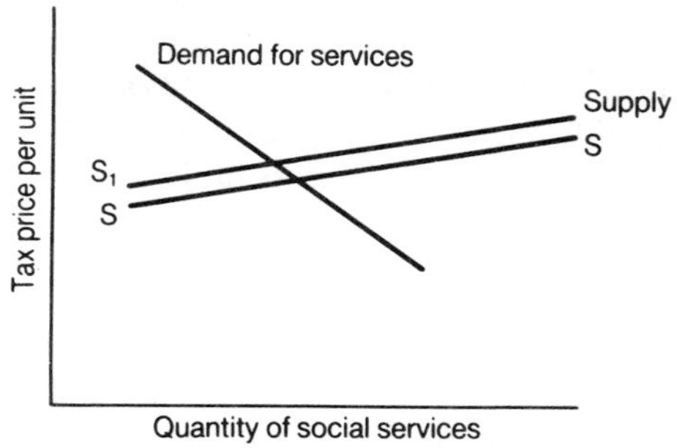

Figure 15.1 The political market for social services

costs tend to rise the larger the sector grows. The most expensive resource is the staff employed, and the more highly qualified the staff the more difficult it is to recruit them. The more physics teachers you need the more you are likely to have to pay to employ the same quality of staff. The supply curve therefore *slopes* upwards to the right. The cost per unit of service provided rises the more you seek to provide.

The price of a service like education or health is also likely to rise as wages in the rest of the economy rise. It is a very labour-intensive activity. As the workers in the Ford Motor car plants raise their productivity and earn more, so it becomes necessary to pay public sector workers more to retain the services of staff who are as well qualified. This has the effect of *shifting* the supply curve upwards, frcm S to S^1. It increases the price of supplying a given policy: setting a maximum class size of 25 for all secondary science pupils, for example. The price of medical treatments and procedures tends to rise faster than general costs in the economy too. These costs are pulled up by advances in medical science in other countries where prices and wages are higher.

Other factors can have the same price effect. A change in the population structure is a case in point. The policy of giving an adequate pension to all over 65 becomes more expensive if the number of over 65s increases.

The cost of producing social services has risen for all these reasons and has an inherent tendency to do so. In short, S^1 has kept shifting upwards. The tax price people must pay to buy the same quantity of care or service has risen. In a traditional supply-and-demand model we would expect the demand to fall off. The quantity of services supplied through the political market-place will tend to fall as voter resistance to tax increases builds up. At the same time, however, demand may increase.

The demand

Pressure groups representing either service users, their carers or those who work in the services will articulate demands on the political system. They will press for higher standards in education or better old age pensions or shorter waiting times for hospital. Politicians will have to respond if they want votes, but they will also know that many voters want lower taxes or at least taxes not to be increased. Hence the downward-sloping demand curve. The demand falls more as the price of responding to these demands for better services grows higher. Different parties compete by offering different mixes of high benefits and high taxes, and low benefits and low taxes. It may not be that clear in their manifestos, but the public are pretty quick to see what the issues are. The debate may not simply centre on the tax price of an improved service but on other supposed effects. It may be possible to persuade the electorate that an increase in social welfare spending is bad for the economy because it takes people away from really 'productive work'. Others may try to persuade the voters that more education is necessary for the health of the economy. There are also other extraneous things in the electoral basket, like feelings towards the Falklands War or Europe, that cloud the clear choice on that one issue. But in a competitive electoral situation parties will make adjustments to the contents of their baskets to appeal more closely to the revealed preferences of the electorate. Over time the preferences may change too, shifting between tax cuts with low benefits to higher taxes with higher benefits. There is evidence that major shifts have occurred in such attitudes the past twenty years in the United Kingdom.

The balance between supply and demand factors will vary through time with no predictable resting place. The outcome in the 1990s may prove very different from that in the 1980s.

Supply-side factors into the 1990s

Population changes

It is in the early and late years of life that we are heavy users of the social services. This U-shaped curve of spending by age is evident in the expenditure on health care (see Figure 10.1). The costs of schooling and further and higher education are also heavily age based. Even if the size of a population remains constant, the fact that it has a higher number of elderly people in it will affect the costs of providing the same level of services. Over the last half century this has been one of the most important factors increasing the cost of social policy. It is not just that more has to be paid out in terms of pensions or care, but that the size of the working population relative to the 'economically inactive' one has declined. This means that the tax cost per worker is higher because the number of workers paying taxes is relatively low. The traditional way to think about this problem is in terms of a dependency ratio – the number of people in the age groups that do not work, expressed as a percentage of those that do. This is done in Figure 15.2.

It should be said that these figures ignore critical features of the labour market, above all the percentage of women who are working and the unemployed. The decline in the number of men in the labour force was made up for by the larger number of women who joined it. What Figure 15.2 does show is the sharp rise in the size of the age group that has not, for statutory and other reasons, been available for work. They are either in compulsory schooling or retired. The sharpest long-term rise occurred between 1941 and 1972 when the school leaving age was raised. From 1972 through to the mid-1980s there was a sharp fall in the number of children passing through the schools. This saved the Exchequer large sums of money and helped the Conservative government hold down education spending. The number of elderly people over retirement age ceased to rise in the 1970s compared with the whole population, and the numbers in working-age groups rose in the 1980s. Thus the demographic pressures on the cost of pensions were relieved. At the same time the numbers of the very elderly grew so that the cost consequences of caring for them did rise.

In the late 1980s and the 1990s the total size of the dependent

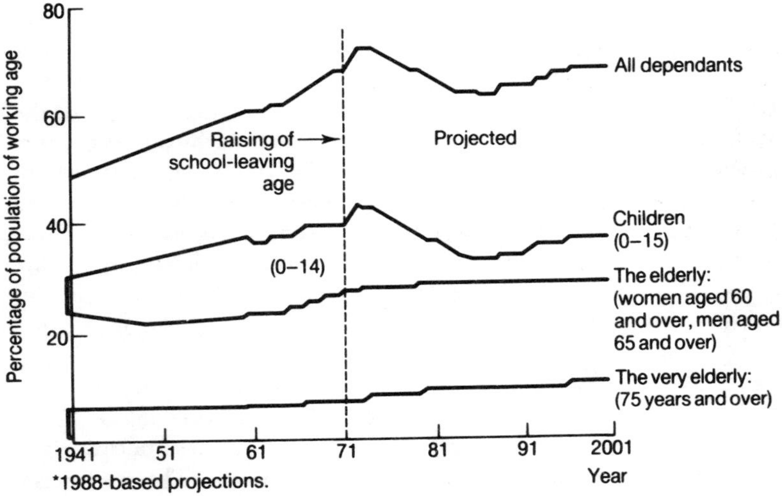

Figure 15.2 The dependent population in the United Kingdom 1941–2001* (Source: Central Statistical Office, *Social Trends*, various editions, London: HMSO)

Table 15.1 Number of pensioners in various countries relative to numbers in 1980

Country	2000	2025
France	122	150
Germany (FR)	134	170
Italy	122	144
Japan	172	215
United States	136	215
United Kingdom	103	130

Source: Disney, 1990.

age groups have begun to rise again (see Table 15.1). Compared with other western countries this change will be quite small in the United Kingdom (OECD, 1988). In the year 2000 what was West Germany would have had 34 per cent more pensioners than in 1980. Japan will have *72 per cent* more elderly people in the year

2000, and more than twice the number of elderly people by the year 2025. The United Kingdom will have only 3 per cent more people of pensionable age by the year 2000, though 30 per cent more by 2025. The United Kingdom should be in a stronger position to support its welfare spending for *demographic* reasons in the 1990s than it was in the 1940s, 1950s and 1960s, or than other countries in Europe, the United States or Japan. It faced their problems in those earlier decades. However, the size of the elderly population will begin to rise again quite sharply in the 2020s in the United Kingdom.

Specific service demands

Health

Robinson (1991) estimates that increases in demand for hospital and community health services in the 1990s, for both demographic and technical reasons, are likely to require an annual growth rate of between 1.3 per cent and 2.1 per cent a year in the NHS budget. The demands on the family doctor service may be greater. Even if GDP were to grow at 3 per cent a year and governments in the 1990s were no more generous than Thatcher's with the growth dividend, they would only allocate 0.6 per cent more a year to the NHS. Since so many 'efficiency' savings have already been squeezed from the NHS, such a rate of growth would have a very damaging, perhaps fatal, effect on it. The NHS probably needs a growth of 2 per cent per annum in the volume of resources it receives in the 1990s to survive.

Social security

Spending demands here are more than usually difficult to forecast because unemployment plays such a large part. During the 1980s we saw that spending had been held down by reducing the levels of benefit relative to earnings. Bradshaw (1991) has estimated that if that assumption were broken in the 1990s and we assume a modest 1.5 per cent a year growth in real earnings and benefits, social security spending would need to increase by £8.3 billion even if there were no new policy developments. Given a modest growth in GDP, however, this should not present a major problem unless unemployment levels rise significantly. In fact, though, policy is unlikely to stand still. Membership of the European Community may force Britain to improve its social security provisions but a Conservative goverment will look to this budget for potential savings.

Personal social services

Hulme (1991) concludes that the demands on these services will be at least as great in the 1990s as they were in the 1980s; indeed, more so, because they will have to bear the consequences of the end to social security support (see Chapter 11). He concludes that a growth rate of 2.5 per cent a year is the least we can expect, and that the top end might reach 4 per cent. If the whole of the social security element that pays for care is transferred and there is inflation at no more than 4 per cent per annum, he estimates that by 1999 we shall be paying at least £4 each a week for personal social services. That compares with about £1.50 in 1990.

Education

We saw that private preferences suggest that spending should increase at least as fast as incomes. To regain the share education took of GDP in the late 1970s would mean raising it from 4.9 per cent in 1990 to 5.5 per cent, and then keeping it there. Even that would mean spending less than most of our European competitors. The main additional demands come from the increasing trend to stay on into higher education. The Conservatives' White Paper of 1991 (Cm 1541) predicted that by the year 2000 a third of all 18–19 year olds would be entering higher education. In 1987 the figure was nearer a fifth. This implied an increase of from 700,000 to 1,200,000 students. The government's subsequent spending policy statements suggested that much of this increase was to be achieved by pushing more students through the same facilities. Alternative ways of financing this expansion were discussed in Chapter 12.

Housing

Current spending here depends entirely on the government's subsidy policy and on capital spending plans. Policy as it was at the beginning of the 1990s meant that spending could fall. A change of policy and government would suggest an increase in social housing, and therefore the need to keep those rents within the range poor people can afford. Hence we could expect a rise in the subsidy bill.

Recession-related spending

The tragedy was that in the 1980s the demographic dividend was spent, not on improving services or cutting taxes, but on unemployment benefits and youth training schemes that were really disguised dole payments. As unemployment rose above 3 million, about one fifth of all benefit expenditure went on payments to the unemployed in 1984, despite the reduction in the levels of benefit the unemployed received. In 1970 the fraction had been only one *fourteenth* of the total budget. Other service spending, including increases in police expenditure and health expenditure, can be related to the costs of unemployment (Hakim, 1982). The 1990s are beginning with another slide into recession and 3 million unemployed. If that number were to be reduced, if we could learn to run the UK economy with lower levels of unemployment, there would be a chance to reap the gains a larger workforce could bring.

The relative price effect

Another way in which the government in the 1980s sought to contain spending was to keep down the rate of increase in public sector pay relative to that in the private sector. At the beginning of the 1980s there were a number of catching-up pay awards that were a hang over from pay inquiries set up by the departing Labour government. Over the 1980s, however, real wage increases in the public sector have been low and in some years negative; that is, pay rose less than prices (see Table 15.2). Such a policy has its costs. If relative wages and salaries are lowered, so, other things being equal, will be the quality of the labour employed. There will be worse teachers, social workers, nurses and doctors, because the competing labour market will have taken away the bright new recruits and those willing to move. If demands for quality services in the 1990s persist, they will only be met by making the salaries in the public sector competitive. That may not necessarily mean across-the-board increases. It could mean some reductions in staff at some levels and increases for teachers in some subjects, like maths, but not so much in others. Overall, though, higher quality will require higher public sector pay. The relative price effect will reassert its logic.

The economy

The ultimate supply-side factor is the health of the economy. The

Table 15.2 Real pay increases in the public sector in the United Kingdom 1981/2–1990/1

Year	Increase (in per cent per annum)
1981/2	−1.6
1982/3	−1.0
1983/4	1.0
1984/5	0.5
1985/6	0.4
1986/7	4.3
1987/8	6.0
1988/9	2.0
1989/90	−0.6
1990/1	−0.7

Source: Trinder, 1990.

faster the economy grows the more revenue the government can raise while still keeping the tax *rates* the same. If we buy more goods with our higher incomes, VAT receipts rise automatically, and the Chancellor does not have to come to the dispatch box in the House of Commons and announce a tax increase to pay for better schools.

In the decades immediately after the Second World War, the UK growth rate was, on average, half that of its major industrial rivals in Europe. That meant that politicians had a smaller growth dividend to allocate in those years for service improvements than their continental counterparts. In the 1980s – indeed since the United Kingdom became an oil state – its rate of growth recovered to its long-run average since the war of over 2 per cent per annum. Countries in Europe have fallen nearer to the same kind of rate of growth. Productivity gains are more difficult to make in already advanced service societies. The poor growth of the US economy in the past two decades is a warning. Modest long-term growth seems the best prospect we can look forward to in the 1990s. It means a modest growth in individual and family income and in the absolute levels of personal prosperity. That is likely to constrain politicians' capacity to raise taxes and increase the standard of social services merely by spending a lot more.

Growth brings costs as well as benefits. The main costs may be environmental, and to counter environmental damage is going to be both expensive and higher on the political agenda.

Welfare spending: burden or boost?

In the 1970s, social welfare spending was widely blamed for the economic crisis of the time. Bacon and Eltis (1976) were two of the most influential critics, but similar critiques appeared in other countries. Social services took resources that could be better used to build up the productive, growth-related sectors of the economy. They crowded out capital expenditure by laying first claim on the savings of the population, thus denying them to industry. They took labour from the rest of the economy, thus increasing the shortages faced by industry and forcing up wages. These arguments convinced many people in all political parties.

In fact, the massive reduction in public sector investment in the late 1970s and 1980s has not produced an equivalently massive increase in manufacturing investment. The notion that there is an overall shortage of labour, when unemployment levels are so much higher than in the decades after the war, is implausible. There are shortages of skilled people and it has begun to dawn, even on politicians, that maybe this is the consequence of too little, rather than too much, spending on education and training. Professor Moser's (1990) address to the British Association on the subject making this point drew a quite unprecedentedly favourable response. In 1992 parties promising higher social spending won most votes but lost the election – a failure of the political market.

In Chapter 2 we saw that modern economics has developed an increasing understanding of why some forms of social provision may be more efficient than the private market. Not to allocate resources publicly in those circumstances reduces the efficiency of the economy and wastes resources that could be available elsewhere. If the UK National Health Service can deliver the same or a similar standard of health with 6 per cent of the total national income as a country like the United States can with 12 per cent, that means that United Kingdom citizens have that 6 per cent more income to spend on other things. (It may be that the United Kingdom can only actually reach a comparable standard by devoting nearer 7 per cent of its national income to health, but the essential point is the same!)

The peace dividend
Unlike other decades, the present one has begun with some hope that the need to compete in a massive arms build-up between the east and the west is a thing of the past. As the taxes we paid for that purpose decline, so some fiscal dividend should be available, whether for reduced taxes or for better services. The choice will be ours.

The demand-side effects into the 1990s

How much are people prepared to support political parties that raise taxes *and* service standards? Again, the story of the 1990s may be different from that of the 1980s. Public opinion polls in the period between 1960 and the mid-1970s suggested that support for social spending was steadily declining. By 1974 (Whiteley, 1981) support for *increasing* taxes and service levels had disappeared. Most people favoured the existing levels of spending and taxation to support social services, but about 30 per cent thought service spending and social benefits were too generous. By the time of the 1979 general election, this view had gained more support. Thatcher, therefore, had identified a real underlying shift in public priorities. The economic crisis of the mid-1970s had reduced the growth in incomes; the higher levels of taxation had reduced the real levels of take-home pay for the average family; and their private standard of living had fallen. It was not surprising that so many welcomed the chance to keep more of their pay and enjoy a reduction in taxation, especially if they were told that this could all be done by cutting out inefficiency and waste and not by reducing service standards.

It soon became evident, however, that things were not that simple. Very soon some reductions in service levels became apparent. Even where they did not, and services grew in scale, so did the demands upon them. The level of service per person at risk sometimes fell. This more complex story is set out in some detail in Hills (1990). Thus the government were right to claim that more money was being devoted to social policy, but social needs and expectations were outpacing it. Evidence for this last point is of two kinds.

The first kind of evidence is that private spending on services like education went on rising at the same rate or rather faster than incomes (see Chapter 12, and Glennerster and Low, 1990). In short, people were prepared to spend more on education out of their own pockets as their incomes rose, but the state was not. In local authority areas that had cut education spending most in the 1980s, the rise in private school spending was greatest, standardising for relevant factors. The rising expectations of families for their children's education were not being matched by the state, and people voted with their feet, or their children's feet.

The second kind of evidence is to be found in surveys of social attitudes. Over the 1980s the British Social Attitudes Survey (Jowell *et al.*, 1983–91) has asked the same set of questions to a national sample of the British population about these issues. They have also asked the same questions of people in other countries (Jowell *et al.*, 1989). The results are striking.

British attitudes to spending and taxing

Despite the Thatcher years, the British population's support for the view that the government has prime responsibility for certain aspects of social life remains strong, and stronger than in many other countries. Nearly the whole sample in 1990 responded by saying that they felt it was the government's responsibility to provide health care for the sick, and the percentage saying so had not changed since 1985. The same was true of its obligation to provide a decent standard of living for the elderly. The view that government should, or perhaps could, provide an economic climate in which every one had a job had declined from 68 per cent to 60 per cent in the same five years. The idea that society has a collective responsibility for health, education, support for the elderly and income support and redistribution more generally is very strong in the United Kingdom. Just how strong can be seen by comparing the responses to the same set of questions addressed to people in other countries (see Table 15.3).

In 1988 in Britain, 86 per cent of people believed it was *definitely* the state's job to provide health care, but only 36 per cent of those in the United States thought that. Only Italians felt more strongly than the British. In every society, providing a decent standard of living for the unemployed is given a much lower priority. Even so,

Table 15.3 Attitudes to the state in different countries 1988

Question	Percentage of respondents replying positively				
	Britain	United States	Australia	West Germany	Italy
Is it definitely the government's responsibility to:					
provide health care for the sick?	86	36	60	54	87
provide a decent standard of living for elderly people?	79	43	62	56	82
provide a decent standard of living for unemployed people?	45	16	15	24	40
reduce income differences between rich and poor people?	48	17	24	28	48

Source: Jowell *et al.*, 1989.

45 per cent of British respondents felt this was definitely the government's job, but only 16 per cent of those in the United States and only 24 per cent in West Germany. When it comes to wanting to see more spent on these services by the state, again the British are way ahead (see Table 15.4). Even before the easing of east–west relations and the end of the Berlin Wall, increased defence expenditure came low on most people's priorities. Only 17 per cent of Britons and 6 per cent of West Germans put it on their shopping list. (Culture and the arts came even lower, it is fair to say, in all countries except West Germany and Italy!)

How did these preferences stand up to the tougher question, 'Would you be prepared to pay higher taxes to get these better services?', and how did the Thatcher years change things? These questions have been reviewed by Taylor-Gooby (1991) using the historical run of results. The number of British people saying they wanted government to reduce taxes and spend less was never great – 9 per cent in 1983 – but it had fallen to only 3 per cent in 1990 (see Table 15.5). By contrast the number who said they wanted to

Table 15.4 Those wanting more state spending on various services in different countries 1988

Service	Percentage wanting more/ much more state spending				
	Britain	United States	Australia	West Germany	Italy
Health	88	60	62	52	81
Old age pensions	75	44	55	46	76
Education	75	66	64	40	63
Unemployment benefit	41	25	13	35	57
Police and law enforcement	40	51	67	30	48
The environment	37	43	32	83	61
Military and defence	17	20	46	6	12
Culture and the arts	10	16	10	14	33

Source: Jowell *et al.*, 1989.

Table 15.5 Attitudes to raising taxes in Britain 1983–90

Question	Percentage of respondents replying positively		
	1983	1986	1990
If the government had to choose, it should:			
reduce taxes and spend less on health, education and social benefits?	9	5	3
keep the taxes and spending at the same level as now?	54	44	37
increase taxes and spend more?	32	46	54

Source: Taylor-Gooby, 1991.

increase taxes and spend more rose in the same period from 32 per cent to 54 per cent.

Health was the top priority, with more people wanting to spend more on pensions and education as the decade passed. A class analysis of these results is interesting. The desire to *reduce* taxes and service levels is greatest amongst the working class and least amongst the 'salaried'. Support for high-quality services like health and education is strong amongst the new middle class, and they are the fastest growing part of the population.

Levels of dissatisfaction with state social services rose in the 1980s, but this led not to more support for privatisation but to a view that more resources and more taxes were necessary to improve them (Taylor-Gooby, 1991). The shift in attitudes, at least as expressed in these surveys, does seem to be more favourable to paying for welfare than it was in the late 1970s. At the same time, if public services do not keep pace with the rising standards and expectations that families have for their children or their own health, they will hesitate much less before they have recourse to the private market than their parents did. More families will have the money to do so. The shadow of the war and collective feelings of communality have long since waned. Frustrated by state schools or the local hospital, they will do what they can afford to get the services they want.

Forty-five years ago, in a ravaged economy, when real incomes were less than half what they are today, people voted for what came to be called the welfare state, and paid the price, and voted to continue affording it. Will their grandchildren in the 1990s?

Further reading

Read the latest edition of the *British Social Attitudes Survey*, published annually, on views about social service spending and taxation.

A special feature in the journal *Public Money and Management*, **11**, no. 4, Winter 1991, contains a discussion of spending prospect for the 1990s.

BIBLIOGRAPHY

Aaron, H. and Swartz, B. (1984), *The Painful Prescription*, Washington, D.C.: Brookings Institution.

Aaron, H.J. (1982), *The Economic Effects of Social Security*, Washington, D.C.: Brookings Institution.

Abel-Smith, B. (1958), 'Whose welfare state?', in N. ManKenzie (ed.), *Conviction*, London: McGibbon & Kee.

Abel-Smith, B. (1964), *The Hospitals 1800–1948*, London: Heinemann.

Abel-Smith, B. (1976), *Value for Money in Health Services*, London: Heinemann.

Abel-Smith, B. (1984), *Cost Containment in Health Care*, Occasional Papers on Social Administration no. 73, London: Bedford Square Press.

Abel-Smith, B. and Townsend, P. (1984), *Social Security: The real agenda*, London: Fabian Society.

Advisory Council for Adult and Continuing Education (1982), *Continuing Education: From policies to practice*, London: ACACE.

Alt, J.E. (1971), 'Some social and political correlates of county borough expenditures', *British Journal of Political Science*, **1**, part 1, pp. 49–62.

Armstrong Committee (1980), *Budgetary Reform in the United Kingdom*, Oxford: Oxford University Press.

Arrow, K. (1963), 'The welfare economics of medical care', *American Economic Review*, **53**, pp. 941–73.

Ashford, A.E., Berne, R. and Schramm, R. (1976), 'The expenditure-financing decision in British local government', *Policy and Politics*, **5**, no. 1, pp. 5–24.

Atkinson, A.B. (1969), *Poverty in Britain and the Reform of Social Security*, Cambridge: Cambridge University Press.

Atkinson, A.B. (1975), 'Income distribution and social change revisited', *Journal of Social Policy*, **4**, part 1, pp. 57–68.

Atkinson, A.B. (1981), *On the Switch to Indirect Taxation*, Taxation and Disincentives Research Project Paper no. 24, London: SSRC/LSE.

Atkinson, A.B. (1989), *Poverty and Social Security*, Hemel Hempstead: Harvester Wheatsheaf.

Atkinson, A.B. and King, M.A. (1982), 'Housing policy, taxation and reform', *Midland Bank Review*, Spring, pp. 7–15.

Atkinson, A.B. and Stiglitz, J.E. (1980), *Lectures in Public Economics*, London and New York: McGraw-Hill.

Audit Commission (1984), *The Impact on Local Authorities' Economy, Efficiency and Effectiveness of the Block Grant System*, London: HMSO.

Audit Commission (1986a), *Managing the Crisis in Council Housing*, London: HMSO.

Audit Commission (1986b), *Making a Reality of Community Care*, London: HMSO.

Audit Commission (1989), *Better Financial Management*, Management Paper no. 3, London: HMSO.

Audit Commission (1991), *Two B's or Not?: Schools' and Colleges' 'A' level performance*, London: HMSO.

Bacon, R. and Eltis, W. (1976), *Britain's Economic Problems: Too few producers*, London: Macmillan.

Bains Committee (1972), *The New Local Authorities: Management and structure*, London: HMSO.

Banks, T. (1979), 'DHSS programme budgeting', in T. Booth (ed.), *Planning for Welfare*, Oxford: Martin Robertson and Basil Blackwell.

Barclay Committee (1982), *Social Workers: Their roles and tasks*, London: Bedford Square Press.

Barnes, J. and Barr, N. (1988), *Strategies for Higher Education: The alternative White Paper*, David Hume Paper no. 10, Aberdeen: Aberdeen University.

Barr, N.A. (1981), 'Empirical definitions of the poverty line', *Policy and Politics*, **9**, no. 1, Jan, pp. 1–21.

Barr, N.A. (1989), *Student Loans: The next steps*, David Hume Paper no. 15, Aberdeen: Aberdeen University.

Barr, N.A. (1992), 'Economic theory and the welfare state: a survey and interpretation', *Journal of Economic Literature*, forthcoming.

Barr, N.A. (1993), *The Economics of the Welfare State*, 2nd edn, London: Weidenfeld.

Barr, N.A. and Carrier, J., 'Women's aid groups: the economic case for state assistance to battered wives', *Policy and Politics*, **6**, no. 3, pp. 333–50.

Barr, N.A. and Coulter, F. (1990), 'Social security: solution or problem?', in J. Hills (ed.), *The State of Welfare*, Oxford: Clarendon Press.

Barr, N.A., Glennerster, H. and Le Grand, J. (1988), *Reform and the National Health Service*, Welfare State Discussion Paper no. 32, Suntory Toyota International Centre for Economics and Related Disciplines, London: London School of Economics.

Barr, N.A., Glennerster, H. and Le Grand, J. (1989), 'Working for patients: the right approach?', *Social Policy and Administration*, **23**, no. 2, pp. 117–27.

Bartlett, W. (1991), 'Quasi-markets and contracts: a markets and hierarchies perspective on NHS reform', *Public Money*, **11**, no. 3.

Baumol, W. (1967), 'Macroeconomics of unbalanced growth: anatomy of urban crisis', *American Economic Review*, **57**, no. 3, pp. 415–26.

Becker, G.S. (1976), *The Economic Approach to Human Behaviour*, Chicago: University of Chicago Press.

Bennett, R. (1990) (ed.), *Decentralisation, Local Governments and Markets: Towards a post-welfare agenda*, Oxford: Clarendon Press.

Beveridge, W. (1948), *Voluntary Action*, London: Allen & Unwin.

Billis, D. (1989), *A Story of the Voluntary Sector: Implications of policy and practice*, Centre for Voluntary Organisation, London: London School of Economics.

Blackstone, T. (1971), *A Fair Start*, London: Allen Lane.

Blackstone, T. and Plowden, W. (1988), *Inside the Think Tank: Advising the Cabinet 1971–1983*, London: Heinemann.

Blair, P. (1991), 'Fees and charges: an underdeveloped local authority resource', *Local Government Studies*, **17**, no. 2.

Blake, D. and Ormerod, P. (1980), *The Economics of Prosperity*, London: Grant McIntyre.

Blau, P. (1964), *Power and Exchange in Social Life*, New York: Wiley.

Boaden, N. (1971), *Urban Policy Making*, Cambridge: Cambridge University Press.

Board of Inland Revenue (1983), *Cost of Tax Reliefs for Pension Schemes: Appropriate statistical approaches*, London: Inland Revenue.

Booth, T. (1979), *Planning for Welfare: Social policy and the expenditure process*, Oxford, Martin Robertson and Basil Blackwell.

Borcherding, T.E. (1977), *Budgets and Bureaucrats: The sources of government growth*, Durham: N.C.: Duke University Press.

Bosanquet, N. (1984), *Extending Choice for Mentally Handicapped People: The case for service credits*, London: MIND.

Bowley, M. (1945), *Housing and the State 1919–44*, London: Allen & Unwin.

Bradford, D.F., Malt, R.A., Oates, W.E. (1969), 'The rising cost of local public services: some evidence and reflections', *National Tax Journal*, June.

Bradshaw, J. (1991), 'Social security expenditure in the 1990s', *Public Money and Management*, **11**, no. 4, pp. 25–9.

Bradshaw, J. and Piachaud, D. (1980), *Child Support in the European Community*, Occasional Paper on Social Administration, London: Bedford Square Press.

Bramley, G., Evans, A., Leather, P. and Lambert, C. (1983), *Grant Related Expenditure: A review of the system*, Working Paper no. 29, Bristol: School of Advanced Urban Studies.

Brannan, J. and Wilson, G. (1987) (eds.), *Give and Take in Families*, London: Allen & Unwin.

Brennan, G. and Buchanan, J.M. (1980), *The Power to Tax: Analytical foundations of a fiscal constitution*, Cambridge: Cambridge University Press.

Breton, A. (1974), *The Economic Theory of Representative Government*, London: Macmillan.

British Medical Association (1970), *Health Service Financing*, London: BMA.

Brittain, J.A. (1972), *The Pay Roll Tax for Social Security*, Washington, D.C.: Brookings Institution.

Brown, C.V. (1983), *Taxation and the Incentive to Work*, Oxford: Oxford University Press.

Brown, C.V. and Levin, E. (1974), 'The effects of income tax on overtime: the results of a national survey', *Economic Journal*, **84**, no. 336, pp. 833–48.

Bull, D. (1980), *What Price 'Free' Education?*, Poverty Pamphlet no. 48, London: Child Poverty Action Group.

Burtless, G. and Housman (1978), 'The effect of taxation on labour supply: evaluating the Gary negative income tax experiment', *Journal of Political Economy*, pp. 1103–30.

Buxton, M.J. and Klein, R. (1975), 'Distribution of hospital provision: policy themes', *British Medical Journal*, **8**, Feb.

Buxton, M.J. and Klein, R. (1978), *Allocating Health Services: A commentary on the report of the Resource Allocation Working Party*, Royal Commission on the National Health Service, Research Paper no. 3, London: HMSO.

Byrne, T. (1986), *Local Government in Britain: Everyone's guide to how it all works*, Harmondsworth: Penguin.

Carr-Hill, R. (1990), 'RAWP is dead: long live RAWP', in A.J. Culyer, A.K. Maynard and S.W. Posnett (eds.), *Competition in Healthcare: Reforming the NHS*, London: Macmillan.

Central Statistical Office (1990), *Social Trends 1990*, London: HMSO.

Central Statistical Office (1991a), *Social Trends 1991*, London: HMSO.

Central Statistical Office (1991b), *United Kingdom National Accounts*, London: HMSO.

Centre for Policy Studies (1983), *Personal and Portable Pensions – For All*, London: CPS.

Charity Trends 1990, Tonbridge: Charities Aid Foundation.

Chartered Institute of Public Finance and Accountancy (CIPFA) (1984), *Health Care UK 1984*, London: CIPFA.

Child Poverty Action Group (1991a), *Rights Guide to Non-Means Tested Benefits*, London: Child Poverty Action Group.

Child Poverty Action Group (1991b), *The National Welfare Benefits Handbook*, London: Child Poverty Action Group.

Chubb, J.E. and Moe, T.E. (1990), *Politics Markets and America's Schools*, Washington, D.C.: Brookings Institution.

Clotfelter, C. (1985), *Tax Incentives and Charitable Giving*, Chicago: University of Chicago Press.

Cmd 1581 (1922), *Report of the Committee on National Expenditure*, London: HMSO.

Cmd 6404 (1942), *Social Insurance and Allied Services*, London: HMSO.

Cmd 6730 (1946), *Report by the Government Actuary on the Financial Provisions of the National Insurance Bill*, London: HMSO.

Cmnd 1432 (1961), *Control of Public Expenditure*, London: HMSO.

Cmnd 4755 (1971), *Strategy for Pensions*, London: HMSO.

Cmnd 7615 (1979), *Royal Commission on the National Health Service: Report*, London: HMSO.

Cmnd 7746 (1979), *The Government's Expenditure Plans 1980–81*, London: HMSO.

Cmnd 7866 (1980), *The Government's Public Expenditure Plans 1980/81 to 1983/84*, London: HMSO.

Cmnd 8449 (1981), *Alternatives to Domestic Rates*, London: HMSO.

Cmnd 8789 (1983), *The Government's Public Expenditure Plans 1983/4 to 1985/6*, London: HMSO.

Cmnd 9058 (1983), *Financial Management in Government Departments*, London: HMSO.

Cmnd 9008 (1983), *Rates*, London: HMSO.

Cmnd 9135 (1984), *Training for Jobs*, London: HMSO.

Cmnd 9143 (1984), *The Government's Expenditure Plans 1984/5 to 1986/7*, London: HMSO.

Cmnd 9189 (1984), *The Next Ten Years: Public expenditure and taxation into the 1990s*, London: HMSO.

Cmnd 9428 (1985), *The Government's Expenditure Plans 1985/86 to 1987/88*, London: HMSO.

Cmnd 9714 (1986), *Paying for Local Government*, London: HMSO.

Cm 555 (1989), *Working for Patients*, London: HMSO.
Cm 1021 (1990), *The Government's Expenditure Plans 1990/91 to 1992/93*, London: HMSO.
Cm 1511 (1991), DES Departmental Report: The Government Expenditure Plans 1991–2 to 1993–4, London: HMSO.
Cm 1513 (1991), *The Government's Expenditure Plans 1991/92 to 1993/94*, Department of Health and Office of Population Censuses and Surveys, Departmental Report, London: HMSO.
Cm 1514 (1991), *The Government's Expenditure Plans 1991/92 to 1993/94: Social security*, London: HMSO.
Cm 1541 (1991), *Higher Education: A new framework*, London: HMSO.
Cockburn, C. (1977), *The Local State*, London: Pluto Press.
Collard, D. (1978), *Altruism and Economy: A study in non-selfish economics*, Oxford: Martin Robertson.
Coons, J. and Sugarman, S. (1978), *Education by Choice: The case for family control*, Berkeley, C.A.: University of California Press.
Coughlin, R.M. (1980), *Ideology, Public Opinion and Welfare Policy*, Institute of International Studies, Berkeley, C.A.: University of California.
CPRS (1975), *A Joint Framework for Social Policies*, London: HMSO.
CPRS (1980), *Education, Training and Industrial Performance*, London: HMSO.
Crew, M. and Young, A. (1977), *Vouchers for Students*, London: Institute of Economic Affairs.
Crosland, C. (1956), *The Future of Socialism*, London: Jonathan Cape.
Crosland, C. (1962), *The Conservative Enemy*, London: Jonathan Cape.
Culyer, A.J. (1976), *Need and the National Health Service*, Oxford: Martin Robertson.
Culyer, A.J. (1980), *The Political Economy of Social Policy*, Oxford: Martin Robertson.
Culyer, A.J. (1990), *The Internal Market: An acceptable means to a desirable end*, Discussion Paper no. 67, York: York University, Centre for Health Economics.
Danziger J.N. (1978), *Making Budgets: Public resource allocation*, London: Sage.
Davies, B.P. (1968), *Social Needs and Resources in Local Services*, London: Michael Joseph.
Davies, B.P. (1978), *Universality, Selectivity and Effectiveness in Social Policy*, London: Heinemann.
Davies, B.P. and Bebbington, A.C. (1980), 'Territorial need indicators: a new approach. Parts I and II', *Journal of Social Policy*, **9**, parts 2 and 4, pp. 145–68 and 433–62.

Davies, B. and Challis, D. (1986), *Matching Resources to Needs in Community Care*, Aldershot: Gower.

Davies, B.P., Barton, A.S., McMullan, I.S. and Williamson, V.K. (1971), *Variations in Services for the Aged*, London: Bell.

Davies, B.P. (1972), *Variations in Children's Services Among British Urban Authorities*, London: Bell.

Davies, B.P. (1983), *Kent Community Care Project: Final report*, Canterbury: University of Kent, Personal Social Services Research Unit.

Davies, G. and Piachaud, D. (1983), 'Social policy and the economy', in H. Glennerster (ed.), *The Future of the Welfare State*, London: Heinemann.

Day, P. and Klein, R. (1990), *Inspecting the Inspectorates*, Bath: Bath University, Centre for the Analysis of Social Policy.

Deakin, N. (1983), *The Voluntary Sector and the Future of London Government*, London: London Voluntary Services Council.

Demone, H.W. and Gibelman, M. (1989) (eds.), *Services for Sale: Purchasing health and human services*, New Brunswick and London: Rutgers University Press.

DES (1967), *Children and their Primary Schools*, The Plowden Report, London: HMSO.

DES (1968), *Public Schools Commission: First report*, London: HMSO.

DES (1970), *Public Schools Commission: Second report*, London: HMSO.

DES (1983), *Statistics of Finance and Awards 1981–2*, London: DES.

DES (1988), *Top Up Loans for Students*, Cm 520, London: HMSO.

DES (1991), *Higher Education: A new framework*, Cmnd 1541, London: HMSO.

de Sweinitz, K. (1947), *England's Road to Social Security*, Philadelphia: Philadelphia University Press.

DHSS (1976a), *Priorities for Health and Personal Services in England*, London: HMSO.

DHSS (1976b), *Sharing Resources for Health in England*, London: HMSO.

DHSS (1976c), *The National Health Service Planning System*, London: DHSS.

DHSS (1976d), *Sharing Resources for Health in England*, Report of the Resource Allocation Working Party, London: HMSO.

DHSS (1977), *The Way Forward*, London: HMSO.

DHSS (1980), *Inequalities in Health: Report of a research working group*, The Black Report, London: HMSO.

DHSS (1981), *Care in Action*, London: HMSO.

DHSS (1983), *Health Care and its Costs*, London: HMSO.

DHSS (1984), *Population, Pension Costs and Pensioners' Incomes*, London: HMSO.

DHSS (1989), *Review of the RAWP Formula*, London: DHSS.

DHSS and the Thames Region (1979), *Assessing Target Allocations within the Thames Region*, London: DHSS.

Dilnot, A. and Walker, I. (1989), *The Economics of Social Security*, Oxford: Clarendon Press.

Dilnot, A.W., Kay J.A. and Morris C.N. (1984), *The Reform of Social Security*, Oxford: Clarendon Press.

Disney, P. (1990), *Proceedings on Medium Term Prospects for Public Expenditure*, London: Public Finance Foundation.

DoE (1977), *Housing Policy: A consultative document*, Cmnd 6851, London: HMSO.

DoE (1981), *Alternatives to Domestic Rates*, Cmnd 8449, London: HMSO.

DoE (1982a), *Housing Subsidies and Accounting Manual*, London: HMSO.

DoE (1982b), *Housing Statistics*, London: HMSO.

DoE (1986), *Paying for Local Government*, London: HMSO.

DoE (1991), *A New Tax for Local Government*, London, Edinburgh and Cardiff: Department of the Environment, Scottish and Welsh Offices.

DoH (1988a), *Community Care: Agenda for action*, London: HMSO.

DoH (1988b), *Inspection of Cleveland Social Services Department's Arrangements for Handling Child Sexual Abuse*, London: HMSO.

DoH (1988c), *Inspection of Child Protection Services, London Borough of Southwark*, London: HMSO.

DoH (1989), *Caring for People: Community care in the next decade and beyond*, Cm 844, London: HMSO.

DoH (1991), (Social Services Inspectorate), *Purchase of Service*, London: HMSO.

Donnison, D.V. (1983), *Urban Policies: A new approach*, London: Fabian Society.

Donnison, D.V. and Ungerson, C. (1982), *Housing Policy*, Harmondsworth: Penguin.

Douglas, J. (1983), *Why Charity? The case for a third sector*, London: Sage.

Downs, A. (1957), *An Economic Theory of Democracy*, New York: Harper & Row.

Downs, A. (1967), *Inside Bureaucracy*, Boston: Little Brown.

Dunleavy, P. (1983), *The Politics of Mass Housing in Britain 1945–75*, Oxford: Clarendon Press.

Dunleavy, P. (1991), *Democracy, Bureaucracy and Public Choice*, Hemel Hempstead: Harvester Wheatsheaf.

Easam, P. and Oppenheim C. (1989), *A Charge on the Community*, London: Child Poverty Action Group.

Eckstein, H. (1964), *The English Health Service*, Cambridge, Mass.: Harvard University Press.

Else, P.K. and Marshall, G.P. (1981), 'The unplanning of public expenditure', *Public Administration*, **59**, Autumn, pp. 253–78.

Enthoven, A.C. (1985), *Reflections on the Management of the National Health Service*, London: Nuffield Provincial Hospitals Trust.

Enthoven, A.C. (1991), 'NHS market reform', *Health Affairs*, **10**, no. 3, pp. 60–70.

Equal Opportunities Commission (1980), *The Experience of Caring for Elderly and Handicapped Dependants*, Manchester: EOC.

Ermisch, J. (1983), *The Political Economy of Demographic Change*, London: Heinemann.

Esping-Andersen, G. (1990), *The Three Worlds of Welfare Capitalism*, Oxford: Polity Press and Basil Blackwell.

Etzioni, A. (1976), 'What to do about the nursing homes', *Juris Doctor*, **6**.

Evandrou, M. (1990), *Challenging the Invisibility of Carers: Mapping informal care nationally*, Welfare State Programme Discussion Paper no. 49, London: London School of Economics.

Evandrou, M., Falkingham, J. and Glennerster, H. (1990), 'The personal social services: everyone's poor relation but nobody's baby', in J. Hills (ed.), *The State of Welfare*, Oxford: Clarendon Press.

Evandrou, M., Falkingham J., Hills J. and Le Grand, J. (1991), *The Distribution of Welfare Benefits in Kind*, London: London School of Economics Welfare State Programme.

Farmer, N. and Barrell, R. (1982), 'Why student loans are fairer than grants', *Public Money*, **2**. no. 1, pp. 19–24.

Feldstein, M. (1974), 'Social security, induced retirement and aggregate capital accumulation', *Journal of Political Economy*, **82**, no. 5, pp. 905–26.

Feldstein, M. (1975), 'The income tax and charitable contributions', *National Tax Journals*, **xxviii**, pp. 209–26.

Feldstein, M. (1980), 'International differences in social security spending', *Journal of Public Economics*, **14**, pp. 225–44.

Feldstein, M. and Boskin, S. (1975), 'Effects of charitable deductions on contributions by low and middle income households', Harvard Institute of Economic Research Discussion Paper 427, Cambridge, Mass.: Harvard University Press.

Feldstein, M. and Clotfelter, C. (1974), 'Tax incentives and charitable contributions in the US', Harvard Institute of Economic Research Discussion Paper 381, Cambridge, Mass.: Harvard University Press.

Ferlic, E. and Judge, K. (1981), 'Retrenchment and rationality in the personal social services', *Policy and Politics*, **9**, no. 3, pp. 333–50.

Finch, J. (1987), 'Family obligations and the life course', in B. Bryman, B. Blytheway, P. Alliat and T. Keil (eds.), *Rethinking the Life Cycle*, London: Macmillan.

Finer Committee (1974), *Report to the Committee on One-Parent Families*, Cmnd 5629, London: HMSO.

Flora, P. and Heidenheimer, A. (1981), *The Development of Welfare States in Europe and America*, London: Transaction Books.

Flynn, R. (1988), 'Political acquiescence, privatisation and residualisation in British housing policy', *Journal of Social Policy*, **17**, p. 3.

Fogarty, M. (1982), *Retirement Policy: The next fifty years*, London: Heinemann.

Foot, M. (1973), *Aneurin Bevan*, **2**, London: Davis Pointer.

Foster, C.D., *et al.* (1980), *Local Government Finance in a Unitary State*, London: Allen & Unwin.

Friedman, M. (1962), *Capitalism and Freedom*, Chicago: University of Chicago Press.

Friedman, M. and Friedman, R. (1979), *Free to Choose*, Harmondsworth: Penguin Books.

Gauldie, E. (1974), *Cruel Habitations: A history of working-class housing 1780–1918*, London: Allen & Unwin.

Geddes Report (1922), *Reports of the Committee on National Expenditure*, Cmd 1581, London: HMSO.

Gerard, D. (1983), *Charities in Britain: Conservatism or change*, London: Bedford Square Press.

Gibson, J. (1990), *The Politics and Economics of the Poll Tax: Mrs Thatcher's downfall*, Worley: EMAS.

Gilbert, B.B. (1966), *The Evolution of National Insurance in Great Britain*, London: Michael Joseph.

Gilbert, N. (1983), *Capitalism and the Welfare State*, New Haven and London: Yale University Press.

Glazer, N. (1988), *The Limits of Social Policy*, Cambridge, Mass.: Harvard University Press.

Glennerster, H. (1971), *The Finance of Education*, Milton Keynes: Open University Press.

Glennerster, H. (1975), *Social Service Budgets and Social Policy*, London: Allen & Unwin.

Glennerster, H. (1979), 'The determinants of public expenditure' in T. Booth (ed.), *Planning for Welfare*, Oxford: Martin Robertson.

Glennerster, H. (1980) 'Prime cuts: public expenditure and social service planning in an hostile environment', *Policy and Politics*, **8**, pp. 367–82.

Glennerster, H. (1981a), 'The role of the state in financing recurrent education', *Public Choice*, **36**, 3, pp. 551–71.

Glennerster, H. (1981b), 'From containment to conflict? social planning in the seventies', *Journal of Social Policy*, **10**, part 1, pp. 31–51.

Glennerster, H. (1983) (ed.), *The Future of the Welfare State*, London: Heinemann.

Glennerster, H. (1991), 'Quasi-markets and education', *Economic Journal*, **101**, pp. 1,256–67.

Glennerster, H. and Low, W. (1990), 'Education and the welfare state: does it add up?' in J. Hills (ed.), *The State of Welfare*, Oxford: Clarendon Press.

Glennerster, H. and Midgley, J. (1991), *The Radical Right and the Welfare State: An international assessment*, Hemel Hempstead: Harvester Wheatsheaf.

Glennerster, H. and Wilson, G. (1970), *Paying for Private Schools*, London: Allen & Unwin.

Glennerster, H., Korman, N. and Marslen-Wilson, F. (1982), *Social Planning: A local study*, London: Department of Social Science and Administration, London School of Economics.

Glennerster, H., Korman, N. and Marslen-Wilson, F. (1983), *Planning for Priority Groups*, Oxford: Martin Robertson.

Glennerster, H., Matsaganis, M. and Owens, P. (1992), *A Foothold for Fund Holding*, London: Kings Fund Institute.

Glennerster, H., Power, A. and Travers, T. (1991), 'A new era for social policy: a new enlightenment or a new leviathan?', *Journa' of Social Policy*, **20**, no. 3, pp. 389–414.

Glennerster, H., Wilson, G. and Merrett, S. (1968), 'A graduate tax', *Higher Education*, **1**, no. 1, pp. 26–38.

Goldberg, E.M., Warburton, R.W., McGuinness, B. and Rowlands, S.H. (1977), 'Towards accountability in social work: one year's intake into an area office', *British Journal of Social Work*, **7**, Autumn, pp. 257–83.

Goldberg, E.M. and Hatch, S. (1981), *A New Look at the Personal Social Services*, Research Paper no. 4, London: Policy Studies Institute.

Goldberg, E.M. and Warburton, R.W. (1979), *Ends and Means in Social Work*, London: Allen & Unwin.

Golding, P. and Middleton, S. (1982), *Images of Welfare: Press and public attitudes to poverty*, Oxford: Martin Robertson.

Goldman, S. (1973), *The Developing System of Public Expenditure Management and Control*, Civil Service College Studies no. 2, London: HMSO.

Goodin, R. and Le Grand, J. (1987), *Not Only the Poor: The middle classes and the welfare state*, London: Allen & Unwin.

Gordon, A. (1982), *Economics and Social Policy*, Oxford: Martin Robertson.

Gough, I. (1979), *The Political Economy of the Welfare State*, London: Macmillan.

Gould, F. (1983), 'The development of public expenditures in Western industrialised countries', *Public Finance*, **xxxviii**, no. 1, pp. 38–69.

Goss, S. and Lansley, S. (1982), *What Price Housing?* London: SHAC, London Housing Centre.

Gray, H. (1968), *The Cost of Council Housing*, London: Institute of Economic Affairs.

Green, C. (1967), *Negative Income Taxes and the Poverty Problem*, Washington, D.C.: Brookings Institution.

Green, D. (1990), *The NHS Reforms: Whatever happened to consumer choice?*, London: Institute of Economic Affairs.

Green, H. (1988), *General Household Survey 1985: Informal carers*, London: HMSO.

Greenwood, R. (1979), 'Local Authority Budgetary Process', in T. Booth (ed.), *Planning for Welfare*, Oxford: Martin Robertson.

Greenwood, R., Hinings, C.R., Ranson, S. and Walsh, K. (1980a), 'Incremental budgets and the assumption of growth', in M. Wright (ed.), *Public Spending Decisions, Growth and Restraints in the 1970s*, London: Allen & Unwin.

Greenwood, R., Hinings, C.R., Ranson, S. and Walsh, K. (1980b), *Patterns of Management in Local Government*, Oxford: Martin Robertson.

Gretton, J. and Posnett, J. (1983), 'Academic salaries: how to distinguish payment for teaching and research in universities', *Public Money*, **2**, no. 4, March, pp. 29–34

Grey, A., Hepworth, N. and Olding-Smee, J. (1981), *Housing Rents Costs and Subsidies: A discussion document*, London: CIPFA.

Griffith, J.A.G. (1965), *Central Departments and Local Authorities*, London: Allen & Unwin.

Gupta, S.P. (1968), 'Public expenditure and economic development – a cross section analysis', *Finanzarchiv*, Oct.

Hadley, R. (1981), 'Social service departments and the community', in E.M. Goldberg and S. Hatch (eds.), *A New Look at the Personal Social Services*, London: Policy Studies Institute.

Hakim, C. (1982), 'The social consequences of high unemployment', *Journal of Social Policy*, **11**, part 4, Oct, pp. 433–67.

Halfpenny, P. (1990), 'Volunteering in Britain', *Charity Trends, 13th edn*, Tonbridge: Charities Aid Foundation.

Hall, A. (1974), *The Point of Entry*, London: Allen & Unwin.

Hall, P., Land, H., Parker, R. and Webb, A. (1975), *Change, Choice and Conflict in Social Policy*, London: Heinemann.

Hall, R. E. (1973), 'Wages income and hours of work in the US labour force', in G. Cain and H. Watts, *Income Maintenance and Labour Supply Econometric Studies*, Chicago: Markham.

Hambleton, R. (1978), *Policy Planning and Local Government*, London: Hutchinson.

Hanuscheck, E.A. (1986), 'The economics of schooling', *Journal of Economic Literature*, **23**, no. 3, pp. 1,141–77.

Harrison, A.S. (1989), *The Control of Public Expenditure 1979–89*, Policy Journals, New Brunswick and Oxford: Transaction Books.

Harwin, J. (1990), 'Parental responsibilities in the Children Act 1990', *Social Policy Review 1989–90*, London: Longman.

Hatch, S. (1980), *Outside the State*, London: Croom Helm.

Hatch, S. and Mocroft, I. (1979), 'The relative costs of services provided by voluntary and statutory organisations', *Public Administration*, Winter.

Hatch, S. and Mocroft, I. (1983), *Components of Welfare*, London: Bedford Square Press.

Heald, D. (1983), *Public Expenditure*, Oxford: Martin Robertson.

Heclo, H. and Wildavsky, A. (1981), *The Private Government of Public Money*, 2nd edn, London: Macmillan.

Heigham, D. (1982), 'Grant related expenditures: an invisible push towards efficiency in local government', *Public Money*, **2**, no. 1, June, pp. 39–42.

Hemming, R. and Kay, J. (1982), 'The future of occupational pension provision in Britain', in M. Fogarty (ed.), *Retirement Policy: The Next Fifty Years*, London: Heinemann.

Hewitt, P. (1989), 'A way to cope with the world as it is', *Samizdat*, no. 6, pp. 3–4.

Hill, M. (1990), *Social Security Policy in Britain*, Aldershot: Edward Elgar.

Hills, J. (1988), *Changing Tax: How the tax system works and how to change it*, London: Child Poverty Action group.

Hills, J. (1990) (ed.), *The State of Welfare: The welfare state in Britain since 1974*, Oxford: Clarendon Press.

Hills, J. (1991a), *Unravelling Housing Finance: Subsidies, benefit and taxation*, Oxford: Clarendon Press.

Hills, J. (1991b), *Thirty Nine Steps to Housing Finance Reform*, York: Rowntree Trust.

Hills, J. and Sutherland, H. (1991), *Banding, Tilting, Gearing, Gaining and Losing: An anatomy of the proposed council tax*, LSE Welfare State

Programme Discussion Paper no. 63, London: London School of Economics.

Hirsch, F. (1977), *Social Limits to Growth*, London: Routledge.

Hirschman, A.O. (1970), *Exit, Voice and Loyalty: Responses to decline in firms, organisations and states*, Cambridge, Mass.: Harvard University Press.

Hirst, M. (1984), *Moving On: Transfer from child to adult services for young people with disabilities*, York: University of York, Social Policy Research Unit.

HM Treasury (1981), *Economic Progress Report*, London: HMSO.

HM Treasury (1984), *The Next Ten Years: Public expenditure and taxation into the 1990s*, Cmnd 9189, London: HMSO.

Hochman, H.M. and Rodgers, J.D. (1969), 'Pareto optimal redistribution', *American Economic Review*, **59**, pp. 542–7.

Hogwood, B.W. (1989), 'The hidden face of public expenditure: trends in tax expenditures in Britain', *Policy and Politics*, **17**, no. 2.

Holmans, A.E. (1987), *Housing Policy in Great Britain*, London: Croom Helm.

Honnigsbaum, F. (1979), *The Division of British Medicine*, London: Kogan Page.

Honnigsbaum, F. (1983), 'The interwar health insurance scheme: a rejoinder', *Journal of Social Policy*, **12**, part 4, pp. 515–23.

Hood, C. and Wright, M. (1981), *Big Government in Hard Times*, Oxford: Martin Robertson.

Houseman, J.A. (1981), 'Labour supply', in H. Aaron and J.A. Peckman, *How Taxes Affect Economic Behavior*, Washington, D.C.: Brookings Institution.

House of Commons (1980), *The Funding and Organisation of Courses in Higher Education*, Fifth Report from the Science and Arts Committee, HC 787, 1979/80, London: HMSO.

House of Commons General Sub-Committee of the Expenditure Committee (1976), *Report*, HC 718, 1975–76, London: HMSO.

House of Commons (1990), *National Insurance Fund Account 1989/90*, HL 617, London: HMSO.

House of Commons Select Committee on Estimates (1958), *Treasury Control*, House of Commons Paper No. 294, London: HMSO.

House of Commons Social Services Committee (1990), *Third Report Community care funding for local authorities*, HC 277, 1989/90, London: HMSO.

House of Commons Treasury and Civil Service Sub-Committee (1983), *The Structure of Personal Income Taxation and Income Support*, HC 386, Session 1982/3, The Meacher Report, London: HMSO.

Housing Corporation (1989), *Rent Policy and Principles*, Circular HC/89, London: Housing Corporation.

Howson, J. (1982), 'Variations in local authority provision of education', *Oxford Review of Education*, **8**, no. 2.

Hulme, G. (1991), 'Expenditure on personal social services in the 1980s and 1990s', *Public Money and Management*, **11**, no. 4, pp. 31–4.

Hunter, D.J. and Judge, K. (1988), *Griffiths and Community Care: Meeting the challenge*, London: Kings Fund Institute.

Independent (1991), *Schools Charter*, London: *Independent* newspaper.

Independent Schools Information Service (ISIS) (1984), *How Grandparents can Help with School Fees*, London: ISIS.

International Labour Office (1984), *Into the Twenty-First Century: The development of social security*, Geneva: International Labour Office.

Irving, D. (1983), 'Territorial need indicators: a comment', *Journal of Social Policy*, **12**, part 2, pp. 241–5.

Isaacs, B. and Neville, I. (1972), *The Measurement of Need in Old People*, Scottish Health Services Studies, Edinburgh: Scottish Home and Health Department.

Jackman, R. (1982), 'Does central government need to control the total of local government spending?', *Local Government Studies*, **8**, no. 3, June, pp. 75–90.

Jacob, J. (1991), 'Lawyers go to hospital', *Public Law*, Summer, pp. 255–81.

James, C. (1984), *Occupational Pensions: The failure of private welfare*, London: Fabian Society.

Jencks, C. (1971), 'Evidence to the US Senate Select Committee on Equal Opportunity', quoted in J.A. Mecklenberger and R.A. Hostrop (eds.), *Education Vouchers from Theory to Allum Rock*, Harewood, Ill.: ETC Publications.

Jenkin, P. (1980), 'Evidence to the House of Commons Social Services Committee', HC 702, pp. 99–100, London: HMSO.

Johnson, N. (1981), *Voluntary Social Services*, Oxford: Martin Robertson and Basil Blackwell.

Jones, A. and Posnett, S. (1990), 'Giving by covenant in the UK', in *Charity Trends*, 13th edn, Tonbridge: Charities Aid Foundation.

Jones, D.R. and Masterman, S. (1976), 'NHS resources: scales of variation', *British Journal of Preventive and Social Medicine*, **30**.

Jones, G. and Stewart, J. (1983), *The Case for Local Government*, London: Allen & Unwin.

Jones, P.R. (1983), 'Aid to charities', *International Journal of Social Economics*, **10**, no. 2, pp. 3–11.

Jordan, B. (1987), *Rethinking Welfare*, Oxford: Basil Blackwell.

Jowell, R., Witherspoon, S. and Brook, L. (1989), *British Social Attitudes: Special international report*, Aldershot: Gower.

Jowell, R. *et al.* (1983–1991), *British Social Attitudes: 1st to the 8th reports*, Aldershot: Gower and Dartmouth Press.

Judge, K. (1978), *Rationing Social Services*, London: Heinemann.

Judge, K. (1980), (ed.), *Pricing the Social Services*, London: Macmillan.

Judge, K. (1981), 'State pensions and the growth of social welfare expenditure', *Journal of Social Policy*, **10**, part 4, Oct, pp. 503–30.

Judge, K. (1982a), 'The public purchase of social care: British confirmation of American experience', *Policy and Politics*, **10**, no. 4, pp. 397–416.

Judge, K. (1982b), 'The growth and decline of social expenditure', in A. Walker (ed.), *Public Expenditure and Social Policy*, London: Heinemann.

Judge, K. and Hampson, R.H. (1980), 'Political advertising and the growth of social welfare expenditure', *International Journal of Social Economics*, **2**, no. 2, pp. 61–92.

Judge, K. and Matthews, J. (1980), *Charging for Social Care*, London: Allen & Unwin.

Kaldor, N. (1955), *An Expenditure Tax*, London: Allen and Unwin.

Kamerman, S.B. and Kahn, A.J. (1983), *Income Transfers for Families with Children*, Philadelphia: Temple University Press.

Kanter, R.M. (1984), *The Changemasters: Corporate entrepreneurs at work*, London: Allen & Unwin.

Kay, J. (1984), '*Financial Times* Conference on: "*Pensions – Time for a Change*"', *Financial Times*, 14 March 1984.

Kay, J. and King, M. (1989), *The British Tax System*, Oxford: Clarendon Press.

Kelly, A. (1989), 'An end to incrementalism: the impact of expenditure restraint on social services budgets 1979–86', *Journal of Social Policy*, **18**, no. 2, pp. 187–210.

Ketner, P. and Martin, G. (1987), *Purchase of Service Contracting*, New York: Sage.

Kilroy, B. (1978), *Housing Finance: Organic reform?*, London: Labour Economic Finance and Taxation Association.

Kilroy, B. (1982), 'Public expenditure on housing' in A. Walker (ed.), *Public Expenditure and Social Policy*, London: Heinemann.

King, D. (1990), 'Accountability and equity in British local finance: the poll tax', in R.J. Bennett (ed.), *Decentralisation: Local governments and markets*, Oxford: Clarendon Press.

Kings Fund Institute (1988), *Health Finance: Assessing the options*, London: Kings Fund Institute.

Klein, R. (1980), 'The welfare state: a self inflicted crisis', *Political Quarterly*, Jan–March.

Klein, R. (1984), 'Privatisation and the welfare state', *Lloyds Bank Review*, Jan. pp. 12–29.

Klein, R. (1988), *Joint Approaches to Social Policy: Rationality and Practice*, Cambridge: Cambridge University Press.

Klein, R. (1991), *The Politics of the National Health Service*, London: Longman.

Klein, R. and Hall, P. (1974), *Caring for Quality in Caring Services*, London: Centre for Studies in Social Policy.

Kogan, M. and Kogan, D. (1983), *The Attack on Higher Education*, London: Kogan Page.

Kramer, R. (1981), *Voluntary Agencies in the Welfare State*, Berkeley, Calif.: University of California Press.

Kramer, R. and Grossman, B. (1987), 'Contracting for social services: process management and resource dependencies', *Social Service Review*, March pp. 32–55.

Labour Party (1958), *National Superannuation*, London: Labour Party.

Laffont, J–J. (1989), *The Economics of Uncertainty and Information*, London and Cambridge, Mass.: MIT Press.

Laing (1990), *Laing's Review of Private Health Care 1989/90*, London: Laing and Buisson Publications.

Laing, W. (1982), 'Contracting out in the NHS', *Public Money*, Dec., **2**, no. 3, pp. 25–9.

Land, H. (1975), 'Family allowances', in P. Hall, Land, H., Parker, R. and Webb, A. *Change, Choice and Conflict in Social Policy*, London: Heinemann.

Land, H. (1978), 'Who cares for the family?', *Journal of Social Policy*, **7**, part 3, pp. 257–84.

Lansley, S. (1979), *Housing and Public Policy*, London: Croom Helm.

Lansley, S. (1982), *Housing Finance: New policies for Labour*, London: Labour Housing Group.

Layfield Committee (1976), *Local Government Finance*, Cmnd 6453, London: HMSO.

Leather, P. (1983), 'Housing (dis?)investment programmes', *Policy and Politics*, **11**, no. 2, pp. 215–39.

Lee, P. and Raban, C. (1988), *Welfare Theory and Social Policy: Reform or revolution?*, London: Sage.

Lee, T. (1990), *Carving Out the Cash for Schools: LMS and the new ERA for schools*, Bath Social Policy Papers no. 17, Bath: Bath University.

Lee, T. (1992), *Local Management of Schools*, Milton Keynes: Open University Press.

Lees, D.S. (1966), *Economic Consequences of the Professions*, London: Institute of Economic Affairs.

Le Grand, J. (1982), *The Strategy of Equality*, London: Allen & Unwin.

Le Grand, J. (1983), 'Making redistribution work: the social services', in H, Glennerster (ed.), *The Future of the Welfare State*, London: Heinemann.

Le Grand, J. (1989a), 'Markets, welfare and equality', in J. Le Grand and S. Estra *Market Socialism*, Oxford: Clarendon Press.

Le Grand, J. (1989b), 'An International Comparison of Health Inequalities', in J. Fox (ed.), *Health Inequalities in European Countries*, London: Gower.

Le Grand, J. and Robinson, R. (1984a), *The Economics of Social Problems*, 2nd edn, London: Macmillan.

Le Grand, J. and Robinson, R. (1984b), *Privatisation and the Welfare State*, London: Allen and Unwin.

Le Grand, J. and Winter, D. (1987), 'The middle classes and the welfare state under Conservative and Labour governments', *Journal of Social Policy*, **6**, pp. 399–430.

Le Grand, J., Glennerster, H. and Maynard, A. (1991), 'Quasi markets and social policy', *Economic Journal*, **101**, no. 408.

Leibenstein, H. (1966), 'Allocative efficiency versus X efficiency', *American Economic Review*, **56**, pp. 392–415.

Letwin, D. and Redwood, J. (1988), *Britain's Biggest Enterprise*, London: Centre for Policy Studies.

Lewis, J. (1983), *Women's Welfare, Women's Rights*, London: Croom Helm.

Lewis, J. and Meredith, B. (1988), *Daughters Who Care: Daughters caring for mothers at home*, London: Routledge.

Likierman, A. (1988), *Public Expenditure: Who really controls it and how*, Harmondsworth: Penguin.

Lord, R. (1983), 'Value for money in the education service', *Public Money*, **3**, no. 2, pp. 15–22.

Macnicol, J. (1980), *The Movement for Family Allowances 1918–45*, London: Heinemann.

Malpass, P. (1990), *Reshaping Housing Policy: Subsidies, rents and residualisation*, London: Routledge.

Martin, J. and White, A. (1988), *The Financial Circumstances of Disabled Adults Living in Private Households*, London: HMSO.

Maynard, A. (1975), *Experiment with Choice in Education*, London: Institute of Economic Affairs.

Maynard, A. (1978), 'The medical profession and the efficiency and equity of health services', *Social and Economic Administration*, **12**, no. 1, pp. 3–19.

Maynard, A. (1979), 'Pricing insurance and the National Health Service', *Journal of Social Policy*, **8**, part 2, pp. 157–76.

Maynard, A. (1982), 'Private health care sector in Britain', in

G. McLachlan, and A. Maynard, *The Public/Private Mix for Health*, London: Nuffield Provincial Hospitals Trust.

Maynard, A. (1986), 'Performance incentives in general practice', in G. Teeling Smith (ed.), *Health Education and General Practice*, London: Office of Health Economics.

Mays, N. and Bevan, G. (1987), *Resource Allocation in the National Health Service*, Occasional Paper in Social Administration, London: Bedford Square Press.

Mayson, D. (1985), *Revising the Rating System*, London: Adam Smith Institute.

Mayston, D. (1990), 'NHS resourcing: a financial and economic analysis', in A.J. Culyer, A. Maynard and S.A. Posnett (eds.), *Competition in Health Care: Reforming the NHS*, London: Macmillan.

McLachlan, G. and Maynard, A. (1982), *The Public/Private Mix for Health*, London: Nuffield Private Hospitals Trust.

Meacher Report (1983), *The Structure of Personal Income Taxation and Income Support*, House of Commons Treasury and Civil Service Committee, 1982–83, HC 386, London: HMSO.

Meade, J.F. (1978), *The Structure and Reform of Direct Taxation*, London: Allen & Unwin.

Merrett, S. (1979), *State Housing in Britain*, London: Routledge.

Minford, P., Peel, M. and Ashton, P. (1987), *The Housing Morass*, London: Institute of Economic Affairs.

Mishra, R. (1983), *The Welfare State in Crisis*, Brighton: Harvester Press.

Mortimore, P., Sammons, P., Stall, L., Leiris, D. and Ecob, R. (1988), *The Junior School Project: Understanding school effectiveness*, London: ILEA, Research and Statistics Branch.

Moser, Sir Claus (1990), *Presidential Address to the British Association*, London: British Association.

Mueller, D.C. (1979), *Public Choice*, Cambridge: Cambridge University Press.

Mueller, D.C. (1989), *Public Choice II*, Cambridge: Cambridge University Press.

Murray, G.J. (1969), *Voluntary Organisations and Social Welfare*, Edinburgh: Oliver and Boyd.

Musgrave, R.A. (1959), *The Theory of Public Finance*, London and Tokyo: McGraw-Hill.

Musgrave, R.A. (1969), *Fiscal Systems*, New Haven: Yale University Press.

Musgrave, R.A. and Musgrave, P.B. (1989), *Public Finance in Theory and Practice*, London and Tokyo: McGraw-Hill.

National Federation of Housing Associations, *Inquiry into British Housing*, Second report, York: Joseph Rowntree Foundation.

National Institute for Social Work (1982), *Social Workers, Their Role and Tasks*, Barclay Report, London: National Institute for Social Work.
Nevitt, A.A. (1966), *Housing, Taxation and Subsidies*, London: Nelson.
Newton, K. (1976), *Second City Politics*, London: Clarendon Press.
Newton, K. and Sharpe, L.J. (1977), 'Local outputs research', *Policy and Politics*, **5**, no. 3, pp. 61–82.
Newton, K. (1981), *Urban Political Economy*, London: Frances Pinter.
Niskanen, W. (1971), *Bureaucracy and Representative Government*, Chicago: Aldine Atherton.
Nissel, M. and Bonnerjea, L. (1982), *Family Care of Handicapped Elderly: Who pays?*, London: Policy Studies Institute.
Novick, D. (1965) (ed.), *Program Budgeting*, Cambridge, Mass.: Harvard University Press.
Occupational Pensions Board (1981), *Improved Protection for the Occupational Rights and Expectations of Early Leavers*, Cmnd 8721, London: HMSO.
O'Connor, J. (1973), *The Fiscal Crisis of the State*, New York: St Martins Press.
OECD (1976a), *Public Expenditure on Income Maintenance Programmes*, Paris: OECD.
OECD (1976b), *Public Expenditure on Education*, Paris: OECD.
OECD (1977), *Public Expenditure on Health*, Paris: OECD.
OECD (1978), *Public Expenditure Trends*, Paris: OECD.
OECD (1981), *The Welfare State in Crisis*. ed. A.H. Halsey, Paris: OECD.
OECD (1984), 'Social expenditure: erosion or evolution', *OECD Observer*, Jan.
OECD (1987a), *The Control and Management of Government Expenditures*, Paris: OECD.
OECD (1987b) *Financing and Delivering Health Care*, Paris: OECD.
OECD (1988), *Aging Population: Social policy implications*, Paris: OECD.
OECD (1990), *Education in OECD Countries 1987–8*, Paris: OECD.
OECD (1991), *OECD Economic Outlook: Historical Statistics 1960–89*, Paris: OECD.
Offe, C. (1984), *Contradictions of the Welfare State*, London: Hutchinson.
O'Higgins, M. (1980), 'The distributive effects of public expenditure and taxation: an agnostic view of the CSO analysis' in C. Sandford, C. Pond and R. Walker (eds.), *Taxation and Social Policy*, London: Heinemann.
O'Higgins, M. (1983), 'Rolling back the welfare state: rhetoric and reality', in *The Yearbook of Social Policy 1982*, London: Routledge.

Owens, P. and Glennerster, H. (1990), *Nursing in Conflict*, London: Macmillan.

Pahl, J. (1980), 'Patterns of money management within marriage', *Journal of Social Policy*, **9**, part 3, pp. 313–35.

Pahl, J. (1989), *Money and Marriage*, Basingstoke: Macmillan.

Paine, T. (1969), *The Rights of Man*, London: Penguin.

Painter, J. (1991), 'Compulsory competitive tendering in local government: the first round', *Public Administration*, **69**, pp. 191–210.

Papadakis, E. and Taylor-Gooby, P. (1987), *The Private Provision of Public Welfare: State, market and community*, Hemel Hempstead: Harvester Wheatsheaf.

Parker, G. (1990), *With Due Care and Attention: A review of research on informal care*, 2nd edn, London: Family Policy Studies Centre.

Parker, R. (1967), *The Rents of Council Houses*, Occasional Paper in Social Administration no. 22, London: Bell.

Parker, R. (1976), 'Charging for the social services', *Journal of Social Policy*, **5**. p. iv.

Pateman, C. (1973), *Participation and Democratic Theory*, Cambridge: Cambridge University Press.

Pauly, M. (1974), 'Over insurance and public provision of insurance: the roles of moral hazard and adverse selection', *Quarterly Journal of Economics*, **88**, pp. 44–62.

Peacock, A.J. and Wiseman, J. (1967), *The Growth of Public Expenditure in the United Kingdom*, London: Allen & Unwin.

Peacock, A.T., Glennerster, H. and Lavers, R. (1968), *Educational Finance: its sources and uses in the UK*, London and Edinburgh: Oliver and Boyd.

Pechman, J. (1980) (ed.), *What should be taxed: Income or Expenditure?*, Washington, D.C.: Brookings Institution.

Pechman, J. (1985), *Who Paid the Taxes 1966–85*, Washington, D.C.: Brookings Institution.

Pechman, J. and Okner, B. (1974), *Who Bears the Tax Burden?*, Washington, D.C.: Brookings Institution.

Pechman, J. and Timpane, T.M. (1975), *Work Incentives and Income Guarantees*, Washington, D.C.: Brookings Institution.

Piachaud, D. (1982), 'Patterns of income and expenditure within families', *Journal of Social Policy*, **11**, part 4, pp. 464–82.

Pigou, A. C. (1920), *The Economics of Welfare*, London: Macmillan.

Pinker, R. (1971), *Social Theory and Social Policy*, London: Heinemann.

Pirie, M. and Butler, E. (1988), *The Health of Nations*, London: Adam Smith Institute.

Plowden Report (1961), *Control of Public Expenditure*, Cmnd 1432, London: HMSO.

Plowden, W.J.L. (1977), 'Developing a joint approach to social policy', in K. Jones (ed.), *Yearbook of Social Policy*, London: Routledge.
Posnett, J. and Chase, J. (1985), 'Independent Schools in England and Wales', *Charity Statistics*, London: Charities Aid Foundation.
Power, A. (1984), *Local Housing Management: Priority estates project report*, London: Department of the Environment.
Power, A. (1987a), *Property Before People*, London: Allen & Unwin.
Power, A. (1987b), *The PEP Guide to Local Housing Management*, London: HMSO.
Power, A. (1991), *Running to Stand Still, Progress in local management on twenty unpopular housing estates*, London: HMSO.
Power, A. (1992), *Hovels to High Rise*, London: Allen & Unwin.
Pratt, J., Travers, T. and Burgess, T. (1978), *Costs and Control in Further Education*, Windsor: National Foundation for Education Research.
Prest, A. (1966), *Financing University Education*, London: Institute of Economic Affairs.
Prest, A.R. and Barr, N. (1985), *Public Finance in Theory and Practice*, 7th edn, London: Weidenfeld and Nicolson.
Price, R.W.R. (1979), 'Public expenditure, policy and control', *National Institute Economic Review*, Nov., pp. 68–75.
Propper, C. and Maynard, A. (1990), 'Whither the private health care sector?', in A.J. Culyer, A.K. Maynard and J.W. Posnett (eds.), *Competition in Health Care: Reforming the NHS*, London: Macmillan.
Pruger, K. (1973), 'Social policy: unilateral transfer or reciprocal exchange', *Journal of Social Policy*, **2**, part 4, pp. 289–302.
Rainwater, L., Rein, M. and Schwartz J.E. (1986), *Income Packaging in the Welfare State*, Oxford: Clarendon Press.
Rathbone, E. (1924), *The Disinherited Family*, London: Allen & Unwin.
Rathbone, E. (1940), *The Case for Family Allowances*, Harmondsworth: Penguin.
Reddin, M. (1980), 'Taxation and pensions', in C. Sandford, C. Pond and R. Walker, *Taxation and Social Policy*, London: Heinemann.
Rees, P.M. and Thompson, F.P. (1972), 'The relative price effect in public expenditure: its nature and method of calculation', *Statistical News*, no. 18, Aug.
Rhodes, R.A.W. (1979), 'Research into central–local relations: a framework for analysis', *Central–Local Government Relationships*, London: SSRC, appendix 1, pp. 1–45.
Rhodes, R.A.W. (1986), '"Corporate bias" in central–local relations: a case study of the consultative council on local government finance', *Policy and Politics*, **14**, no. 2, pp. 221–45.
Rhys-Williams, Lady (1943), *Something to Look Forward To*, London: MacDonald.

Rimlinger, G. (1971), *Welfare Policy and Industrialisation in Europe, America and Russia*, New York: Wiley.

Rimmer, L. (1982), *The Intra-Family Distribution of Income*, London: Study Commission in the Family.

Rivlin, A. and Wiener, J.M. (1988), *Caring for the Disabled Elderly: Who will pay?*, Washington, D.C.: Brookings Institution.

Robbins Committee (1963), *Higher Education*, Cmnd 2154, London: HMSO.

Robbins, P.K. (1982) (ed.), *A Guaranteed Annual Income: Evidence from a local experiment*, New York: Academic Press.

Robinson, R. (1988), *Efficiency and the NHS: A case for an internal market*, London: Institute of Economic Affairs.

Robinson, R. (1991), 'Health expenditure: recent trends and prospects for the 1990s', *Public Money and Management*, **11**, no. 4, pp. 19–24,

Robson, M.H. and Walford, G. (1989), 'Independent schools and tax policy under Mrs Thatcher', *Journal of Education Policy*, **4**, pp. 149–62.

Robson, W. A. (1954), *Development of Local Government*, London: Allen & Unwin.

Rose-Ackerman, S. (1986), *The Economics of Non-Profit Institutions*, Oxford: Oxford University Press.

Rothschild, M. and Stiglitz, J. (1976), 'Equilibrium and competitive insurance markets: an essay on the economics of imperfect information', *Quarterly Journal of Economics*, **90**, pp. 629–49.

Regional Commission on the Distribution of Income and Wealth (1979), *The Distribution of Wealth in Ten Countries*, Background Paper no.7, London: HMSO.

Royal Commission on the National Health Service (1979), *Report*, Cmnd 7615, London: HMSO.

Rubenstein, P., Munday, R.E. and Rubenstein, M.L. (1979), 'Proprietary social services' in *Social Welfare Forum 1978*, New York: Columbia University Press.

Rutter, M., Maughan, B., Mortimore, P. and Ouston, S. (1979), *15,000 Hours: Secondary schools and their effects on children*, London: Open Books.

Sammons, P. (1991), *The Impact of LMS and Formula Funding on Resource Allocation to Inner London Schools*, London: London School of Economics, Centre for Educational Research.

Savas, E.S. (1977), 'Policy analysis for local government: public v. private refuse collection', *Policy Analysis*, **3**, pp. 44–74.

Savas, E.S. (1982), *Privatising the Public Sector: How to shrink government*, Chatham, N.J.: Chatham House.

Schick, A. (1966), 'The road to PPB: the stages of budget reform', *Public Administration Review*, **26**, no. 4, pp. 243–58.

Schieber, G.S., Poullier, J-P. and Greenwald, M. (1991), 'Health care systems in twenty four countries', *Health Affairs*, **10**, no. 3, Fall, pp. 22–38.

Schlesinger, M., Dorwort, R.A. and Pulice, R.T. (1986), 'Competitive bidding and states' purchase of services', *Journal of Policy Analysis and Management*, **5**, no. 2, pp. 245–63.

Schuller, T. and Walker, A. (1990), *The Time of Our Life: Education, employment and retirement in the third age*, London: Institute for Public Policy Research.

Scott, D. and Wilding, P. (1984), *Beyond Welfare Pluralism*, Manchester: Manchester Council for Voluntary Service and Manchester Social Administration Department.

Seebohm Committee (1968), *Report of the Committee on Local Authority and Allied Personal Social Services*, Cmnd 3703, London: HMSO.

Seldon, A. (1957), *Pensions in a Free Society*, London: Institute of Economic Affairs.

Seldon, A. (1960), *Pensions for Prosperity*, London: Institute for Economic Affairs.

Seldon, A. (1977), *Charge*, London: Temple Smith.

Showler, B. (1982), 'Public expenditure on employment', in A. Walker (ed.), *Public Expenditure and Social Policy*, London: Heinemann.

Schuller, T. (1983), 'Plums, paper bags and pensions', *New Society*, 18 August.

Sinfield, A. (1983), 'The necessity for full employment', in H. Glennerster (ed.), *The Future of the Welfare State*, London: Heinemann.

Slack, K. (1960), *Councils, Committees and Concern for the Old*, Occasional Papers on Social Administration, London: Bell.

Smith, A. (1974), *The Wealth of Nations*, Harmondsworth: Penguin.

Smith, G. (1980), *Social Need*, London: Routledge.

Smith, S. (1988), 'Should United Kingdom local government be financed by a Poll Tax?', *Fiscal Studies*, **9**, no. 1, pp. 18–28.

Smyth, M. and Robins, N. (1989), *The Financial Circumstances of Families with Disabled Children Living in Private Households*, London: HMSO.

Steadman-Jones, G. (1971), *Outcast London*. Oxford: Clarendon Press.

Stevens, R. (1966), *Medical Practice in Modern England*, London: Yale University Press.

Stewart, J.D. (1974), *The Responsive Local Authority*, London: Charles Knight.

Stubblebine, W. (1965), 'Institutional elements in the financing of education', *Southern Economic Journal*, July, pp. 15–34.

Sugarman, S.D. (1980), 'Family choice in education', *Oxford Review of Education*, **6**, no. 1, pp. 31–40.

Sutherland, G. (1973), *Policy-Making in Elementary Education 1870–1895*, Oxford: Oxford University Press.

Taylor-Gooby, P. (1991), 'Attachment to the welfare state', in R. Jowell *et al.*, *British Social Attitudes: 8th report*, Aldershot: Dartmouth Press.

Thain, C. and Wright, M. (1990), 'Coping with difficulty: the Treasury and public expenditure, 1976–89', *Policy and Politics*, **18**, no. 1.

Thane, P. (1982), *The Foundations of the Welfare State*, London: Longman.

Thompson, E.P. (1980), *The Making of the English Working Class*, Harmondsworth: Penguin.

Tiebout, C. (1956), 'A pure theory of local expenditure', *Journal of Political Economy*, **64**, no. 5, pp. 416–24.

Titmuss, R.M. (1950), *Problems of Social Policy*, London: HMSO.

Titmuss, R.M. (1958, 1976), *Essays on the Welfare State*, London: Allen & Unwin.

Titmuss, R.M. (1962), *Income Distribution and Social Change*, London: Allen & Unwin.

Titmuss, R.M. (1968), *Commitment to Welfare*, London: Allen & Unwin.

Titmuss, R.M. (1970), *The Gift Relationship*, London: Allen & Unwin.

Townsend, P. (1962), *The Last Refuge*, London: Routledge.

Townsend, P. (1971), *The Fifth Social Service*, London: Fabian Society.

Townsend, P. and Bosanquet, N. (1972), *Labour and Inequality*, London: Fabian Society.

Travers, T. (1986), *The Politics of Local Government Finance*, London: Allen & Unwin.

Trinder, C. (1990), *Proceedings on Medium Term Prospects for Public Expenditure*, London: Public Finance Foundation.

Tullock, G. (1965), *The Politics of Bureaucracy*, Washington, D.C.: Public Affairs Press.

Tunley, P., Travers, T. and Pratt, J. (1979), *Depriving the Deprived*, London: Kogan Page.

United States Congressional Budget Office (1983), *Tax Expenditures: Current Issues and Five Year Budget Projections, Fiscal Years 1984–88*, Washington, D.C.: CBO.

Uttley, S. (1980), 'Welfare exchange reconsidered', *Journal of Social Policy*, **9**, part 2, pp. 187–205.

van de Ven, W.P.M.M. and van de Vleit, R.C.S.A. (1990), 'How can we prevent cream skimming in a competitive health insurance market?', *Second World Congress on Health Economics*, Zurich.

Walker, A. (1982a) (ed.), *Community Care*, Oxford: Martin Robertson and Basil Blackwell.

Walker, A. (1982b) (ed.), *Public Expenditure and Social Policy*, London: Heinemann.

Walker, A. (1983), 'A caring community', in H. Glennerster (ed.), *The Future of the Welfare State*, London: Heinemann.

Walker, A. (1984), *Social Planning: A strategy for socialist planning*, Oxford: Basil Blackwell.

Walker, R., Lawson, R. and Townsend, P. (1984), *Responses to Poverty: Lessons from Europe*, London: Heinemann.

Warburton, M. (1983), *Housing Finance: The case for reform*, London: Catholic Housing Aid Society.

Washington State Department of Health and Human Services (1979), *Report of Proceedings of a Conference on the Denver and Seattle Income Guarantee Experiment*, Washington State Department of Health and Human Services, Washington State, Olympia.

Webster, C. (1981), 'A social market answer on housing', *New Society*, 12 November.

Webster, C. (1988), *The Health Services Since the War*, Vol. 1, London: HMSO.

Weisbrod, B. (1986), 'Towards a theory of the voluntary non-profit sector in a three sector economy', in S. Rose-Ackerman (ed.), *The Economics of Non-Profit Institutions*, Oxford: Oxford University Press.

West, E.G. (1965), *Education and the State*, London: Institute of Economic Affairs.

West, E.G. (1975), *Education and the Industrial Revolution*, London: Batsford.

Whitehead, C. (1984), 'Privatisation and housing', in J. Le Grand and R. Robinson (eds.), *Privatisation and the Welfare State*, London: Allen & Unwin.

Whiteley, P. (1981), 'Public opinion and the demand for social welfare in Britain', *Journal of Social Policy*, **10**, part 4, pp. 453–75.

Whiteside, N. (1983), 'Private agencies for public purposes', *Journal of Social Policy*, **12**, part 2, pp. 165–93.

Whiteside, N. and Krafchik (1983), 'Interwar health insurance revisited', *Journal of Social Policy*, **12**, part 4, pp. 525–9.

Whittaker, J.K. and Gabarino, J. (1983), *Social Support Networks: Informal helping in the human services*, New York: Aldine.

Wildavsky, A. (1975), *Budgeting: A comparative theory of budgetary processes*, Boston: Little Brown.

Wildavsky, A. (1979), *The Politics of the Budgetary Process*, 3rd edn, Boston: Little Brown.

Wilding, P. (1970), 'Government and housing: a study in the development of housing policy 1906–1939', PhD Thesis, University of Manchester.

Wilding, P. (1972), 'Towards exchequer subsidies for housing 1906–14', *Social and Economic Administration*, **6**, no. 1.

Wilding, P. (1982), *Professional Power and Social Welfare*, London: Routledge.

Wilensky, H.L. (1981), 'Leftism, Catholicism and Democratic Corporatism: the role of political parties in recent welfare state development', in P. Flora and A.J. Heidenheimer, (eds.), *The Development of Welfare States in Europe and America*, London: Transaction Books.

Wilkinson, M. and Wilkinson, R. (1982), 'The withdrawal of mortgage tax relief: a survey and evaluation of the debate', *Policy and Politics*, **10**, no. 1, pp. 43–63.

Willetts, D. and Goldsmith, M. (1988), *Managed Healthcare: A new system for a better NHS*, London: Centre for Policy Studies.

Williamson, O.E. (1975), *Markets and Hierarchies: Analysis and anti-trust implications*, New York: Free Press.

Willis, J.R.M. and Hardwick, P.J.W. (1978), *Tax expenditures in the United Kingdom*, London: Institute of Fiscal Studies and Heinemann.

Wistow, G. (1983), 'Joint finance and community care', *Public Money*, **3**, no. 2, pp. 33–7.

Wistow, G. and Webb, A. (1982), 'The personal social services' in A. Walker (ed.), *Public Expenditure and Social Policy*, London: Heinemann.

Wolfenden Committee (1978), *The Future of Voluntary Organisations*, London: Croom Helm.

Woodhall, M. (1982), *Student Loans: Lessons from recent international experience*, London: Policy Studies Institute.

Woodhall, M. (1989), *Financial Support for Students: Grants, loans or graduate tax?*, London: Kogan Page.

Wright, A., Stewart, S. and Deakin, N. (1984), *Socialism and Decentralisation*, London: Fabian Society.

Wright, M. (1980) (ed.), *Public Spending Decisions: Growth and restraint in the 1970s*, London: Allen & Unwin.

INDEX

accountability, 32, 85, 89, 90–2, 181
adverse selection, 22, 196
agency model, 73
alchohol, drug misuse grants, 193
almoners, 160
amenity beds, 168
Arrow, Kenneth, 16
Audit Commission, 51, 79, 195, 218
Autumn Statement, 61–2, 68–70, 101

Beveridge proposals, 248–50, 262–4
block contracts, 179
blood donating, 144–5
Board schools, 201–2
BUPA, 175
bureaucracy, costs of, 34–5

Cabinet, 51–2, 54, 55, 56, 62, 69, 248, 250
Callaghan, James, 65
capping, rates and poll tax, 82–3, 101, 192
caring, 12, 142–3
cash
  benefits, 11, 65
  kind distinction, 4
  limits, 51–60
  planning, 58–60
central Government, 5, 11, 13
  grants, 7, 13, 169–72, 191–4, 201–3, 205, 211–13, 216–7, 233–5
central–local relations theory, 72–4
Chancellor of Exchequer, 52, 53, 61, 69
charges, 129–40
charity, 9, 19–20, 141–55
chemists' income, 175
child
  benefits, 249–51
  care, 186–7
choice, 35–7, 172–3, 178–82, 191–2, 194–6, 206–7, 210–11, 217–21, 240–4, 262
church schools, 199–201
community care, 172–3
  finance, 191–6
community charge (*see* poll tax)
competition, 22–5, 38–45, 178–82, 194–8, 217–21, 236, 262, 284
  imperfect, 19
contingency reserve, 63
contracts, 34, 44–5, 94
  compliance, 196
  cost-volume, 179
  per case, 179
  personal social services, 194–6
corporate giving, 147–8
CPRS (Central Policy Review Staff), 56, 68
cream skimming, 23, 44–5
cuts, 64–7, 97, 133

dentists' income, 175
District Health Authorities, 43–4
  purchasers, 178–82
drug expenditure, 166

education, Act 1870, 201
  1902, 209
  1918, 202
  1944, 209, 214
  entitlement, 223–4

expenditure, 202–4, 276, 279, 284
fees, 209
finance history, 199–203
Reform Act 1988, 205–6
efficiency, 134–5
allocative, 35–7
productive, 37–8
employers, 9, 256–7, 259–62
equity, 32, 38–9
exit, 36–7, 178–81, 194–5, 219–21, 235–6
externalities, 18

families, 9, 11, 186–7, 191, 197, 219, 273–5
single parent, 12, 254
family
credit, 251
income supplement, 251
fees, 5, 11, 209
Finer Committee 1974, 12
finance
further education, 211–12
provision distinction, 4, 6, 31–5, 199–202, 225
students, 214–5
free-rider problems, 20, 150

Geddes Committee 1922, 202–3
general practitioners
finance, 173–5
fund holding, 172–3, 180–1
giving, 8, 141–55
grants
general, 84, 196–7, 203
percentage, 75, 202–3
specific, 192–3
unit, 75
grant maintained schools, 206

Higher Education Funding Council, 213–14
home helps, 187–8
hospitals, 5, 159–62, 166, 169–73, 175–6, 178–82
finance, 165–6, 169–72, 284
trusts, 43, 179–80
voluntary, 33
households, 8–9, 11
housing
allowances, 240–2
associations, 236–8
corporation, 238
expenditure, 231–3
Finance Act 1972, 228
finance, history, 226–33
future spending, 276
Revenue Account, 233–5
subsidies, 226–8, 233–5, 239–40
transfers, 235–6
House of Commons, 51–3, 57

information failure, 21–5
Inner London Education Authority, 218
abolition, 206
inspection, 80, 190–1, 200, 217
international comparisons
attitudes to taxes, 281–4
education spending 204
health spending 165
overall social spending, 15–6
pensioners, 274
social security spending, 253
taxes, 125–6

Layfield Committee, 73–5, 91–2, 140
local authority
budgeting, 95–8
expenditure, 63–4
housing, 233–4
local government, 11, 13, 72–93
aggregate external finance, AEF, 84
budgets 96–103
capital guide lines, 81–2
management, 98–101
local management of schools, 205–9, 217

Major, John, 67
managerialist tradition, 50
Manpower Services Commission, 152, 215–6
markets, 37–45
education, 217–21
housing, 227–8
inefficient, 138–9
NHS, 172–3, 176–82
personal social service, 194–8
market
economy, 8
failure, 16, 18
for welfare, 270–2
free, 18
quasi, 41–5
Marxists, 25–7, 50, 269
meals-on-wheels, 187

mentally ill, grants, 192–3
mixed economy of welfare, 7, 184–5, 194–8
monopoly
  geographical, 19
moral hazard, 24

National Health Insurance, 163
National Health Service, 5, 8, 39, 133, 141, 159–83
  1990 Act, 41
  administrative costs, 169
  contracts, 179–81
  expenditure, 164–7
  internal market, 178–82
  reform, 176–82
  volunteers, 153
National Insurance
  contributions, 112
  fund, 254–6
non-domestic rate, 84
non-excludability, 17
non-rivalry, 17

occupational
  pension schemes, 252, 259–60
  welfare, 4
old people's homes, 11, 193–4, 197
overseas visitors' health charges, 168
Owner occupier finance, 229–31

PAR (programme analysis and review), 56
PARR (Northern Ireland Health Service allocations formula), 171
partnership model, 72–3
pension schemes, 12, 260–2
personal social services
  expenditure, 189–90
  future spending, 276
  history, 184–9
  private sector, 197–8
Plowden Committee, 54–5, 132
pluralist theory, 47–50
political economy, 25–7
poll tax, 57, 83, 86, 109, 116–7
polytechnic finance, 212–4
population and welfare, 273–5
prescription charges, 167–8, 175
pre-school education, 132
private
  education, 211
  finance, NHS, 177–8
  health care, 175–6
  landlords, 226–9, 238–9
  nursing homes, 7
  pay beds, 7, 168
  pensions, 260–2
  personal social services, 197–8
  provision, 5
  schools, 7, 139
  spending on education, 210–11
  state support, 209–10
privatisation, defined, 7
profit, 5
purchaser–provider split, 179–81, 194–6

quality, 32

RAWP (Resource Allocation Working Party), 171–2
rates, 7, 85–6
  capping, 76, 82–3
  fair, 87
real terms, 60–1
recession spending, 277
redistribution, 11
relative price effect, 277–9
residential accommodation 185–6
  elderly, 198
Revenue Support Grant, 84
ring fencing
  community care, 193
  housing, 233–5

schools, 11
SCRAW (Scottish Health Service resource allocation formula), 171–2
self-help, 154
SERPS (State earings-related pension scheme), 256–7
Smith, Adam, 16
Social Dividend Scheme, 265
social goods, 17
social protection, 16
Social Security
  contributions, 256–7
  expenditure, 252–4
  finance, history, 245–52
  Fowler reforms, 251
  funding, 257–8
  future spending, 275–6
  housing, 231
  residential care, 193–4
social work
  inspectorate, 191

insurance, 247–9
service, 80
Social Services Departments
enabling activity, 194–5
specific grant
community care, 193–4
education, 205, 216–17
mental health, 192–3
Star Chamber, 61
stigma, 19, 129–30
student loans, 215, 222–3

tax, 9, 12, 16, 52, 108–9, 111 (Table 124)
capital, 110–11
capital gains, 111
community charge, 84
council, 7, 85–7, 111
efficiency, 113–21
expenditure, 12, 40–1, 69–70, 112, 258–9
graduate, 223
income, 109
local income, 88
poll, 57, 83, 86, 109, 116–17
property, 111
stamp duty, 111
Technical Instruction Act 1889, 202
tendering, 95
Thatcher, Margaret, 67
third sector, 151–4
Treasury, 9, 13, 52–64
Chief Secretary, 55

ultra vires, 77
unitary government, 32
universality, 32
univerities, 7, 212–6, 220–4
Funding Council, 213
Grants Committee, 213

VAT (value added tax) 112–13, 116, 123, 146, 278
voice, 36–7
volume terms, 57
voluntary agencies, 7, 143–4, 188–9
hospitals, 33, 159–62
vouchers, 5, 9, 40, 219–21

welfare
defined, 3
demand for, 280–4
market, 270–2
mixed economy, 7
occupational, 4
spending, 279–80
supply, 273–80
Wolfenden Committee 1978, 152–4